6.30

The Lancehead Series

Nevada and the West

BOOKS IN THE
LANCEHEAD SERIES

Nevada's Twentieth-Century Mining Boom
TONOPAH, GOLDFIELD, ELY
Russell R. Elliott, 1966

Karnee: A PAIUTE NARRATIVE
Lalla Scott, 1966

Retreat to Nevada
A SOCIALIST COLONY OF WORLD WAR I
Wilbur S. Shepperson, 1966

Nevada Indians Speak
Jack D. Forbes, 1967

Diamondfield Jack
A STUDY IN FRONTIER JUSTICE
David H. Grover, 1968

Silver and Politics in Nevada: 1892–1902
Mary Ellen Glass, 1969

Restless Strangers
NEVADA'S IMMIGRANTS AND THEIR INTERPRETERS
Wilbur S. Shepperson, 1970

Restless
Strangers

Nevada's Immigrants
and Their Interpreters

Restless Strangers

Nevada's Immigrants and Their Interpreters

by Wilbur S. Shepperson

University
of Nevada
Press
Reno, Nevada
1970

This volume in the Lancehead Series
is published with the assistance of a bequest
from the late Dr. Effie Mona Mack.

University of Nevada Press, Reno, Nevada
© 1970 by University of Nevada Press
Library of Congress Catalog Card Number: 78–117219
Designed by Wolfgang Lederer
Printed in the United States of America
ISBN 87417–028–1

To the transplanted,
the sojourners,
and the wanderers,
and to the imaginative
who saw them

Preface

The commanding importance of American immigration has generally been recognized. But the scores of issues related to local settlement and cultural adaptation have not received the attention they merit. Fortunately, in the case of Nevada, the colorful detail to be found in early newspapers and the strangely exciting returns prepared by United States census enumerators offer an attractive entrée into a study of foreign migrants. A survey of immigrant literature, including fiction, memoirs, biography, and short stories, provides a further window through which to observe both the foreign born and the reaction of writers to the foreign born. In short, *Restless Strangers* proposes first to view the immigrant himself, and second to view the immigrant as others have seen him.

Chapter 1 provides a historical and statistical survey of the foreign-born Nevadan as he participated in the social, economic, and political life of the state. Chapter 2 summarizes 522 personal interviews with Nevada's foreign born. Chapter 3 moves to the literary man's view of the immigrant, and particular notice is given to the use, misuse, and nonuse made of the foreign born by early-day writers and journalists. The newspaper portraits and anecdotes discussed in chapter 4, like most news and editorial fare, deal with the world practically and approach every event as a self-contained unit. The newspapers reflect the Nevada immigrant at a basic and chronological level, and they suggest broad trends and yield significant themes. Chapter 5 notes the place of the immigrant in fiction, reminiscence, and other popular literature. Since no collection of novels about Nevada is available and much of the literature is difficult to procure, a brief summary of the most relevant works is included in chapter 5. An ethnographic comparison of the immigrant characters to be found in short stories and the immigrants appearing in biographical history provides chapter 6 with an inexact, but useful, basis from which to draw evaluations.

Clearly, newspaper anecdotes, romanticized memoirs, and the evaluations and interpretations found in literature are highly subjective, but a record of the immigrant as he has been seen in graphic and often moving detail by trained and sensitive observers provides a valuable addition to the more factual historical and statistical evidence. Knowledge of both history and literature, therefore, is central to an understanding of western immigration and the Nevada experience.

Acknowledgments

Parts of chapter 2 have appeared in the *Nevada Historical Society Quarterly* for Summer, 1969, and sections of chapter 4 in the *Pacific Historical Review* for February, 1970. Permission to quote from H. L. Davis's *Honey in the Horn* has been extended by William Morrow and Company, Inc., and the United States Bureau of the Census has allowed the use of data from the enumerators' reports on Nevada for the years 1900, 1910, and 1920. The census records were particularly helpful in pointing up the extent and unique aspects of the foreign-born settlements in the state. A grant from the Desert Research Institute of the University of Nevada significantly assisted in the overall research project.

PREFACE

Many colleagues at the University of Nevada have read all or parts of the manuscript and made critical suggestions on its historical or literary focus. Among those who have been particularly helpful are Robert Armstrong, Walter Van Tilburg Clark, Jerome Edwards, George Herman, James Hulse, Robert Laxalt, and Helen Poulton. A special debt is owed to John Rowe, University of Liverpool, for assistance in developing the immigrant theme and to Russell Elliott, University of Nevada, for guidance in the use of Nevada historical and literary materials.

W. S. S.

April, 1970
Reno, Nevada

Contents

Restless
Strangers

Nevada's Immigrants
and Their Interpreters

The Nevada Setting

Nevada, like much of the early West, was often the object of conscious and boisterous literary exaggeration. The region was commonly described as a howling wilderness where alkali dust and Washoe zephyrs left desolation, where water cost more than whiskey, and where only one death in ten was from natural causes. One writer viewed the area as a "nest of consummate ungodliness," and another saw the state as a "mean ash-dump landscape" which stretched "from nowhere to nowhere, a spot of mange. . . . No portion of the earth is more lacquered with paltry, unimportant, ugliness."[1] On the other hand, authors exploited the fanciful dreams and nervous excitement that spread with each new discovery of gold or silver, and tales were told of newspapers printing an entire edition in ink mixed with gold dust. In 1888, the State Immigration Bureau officially contributed to the overstatement by declaring the climate to be "the most delightful and salubrious in the known world."

> The warmest days of summer are modified by soft south-west winds, laden with the sweet odor of wild flowers and the aroma of the indigenous sage, while the nights are seasons of transcendant loveliness, rendered so by the gentle mountain breezes that waft health and vigor to the sleeper.[2]

But despite the tall tales and the government brochures, it was early recognized that the state's lands and mines required the most assiduous development before they could become productive. And for almost a century, Nevada remained the most sparsely settled state in America, with the most fluctuating and mobile society. A spirit of traditionalism was slow to evolve, and integrated institutions were late in maturing. As the most arid state in the West, agriculture was always limited and it required more than seventy-five years to build a town of thirty thousand people. With only one college, most professional and scholarly personnel were migrants. The area was not regarded as a major contributor to the world of culture or an important marketer of refined ideas. And yet Nevada was not devoid of attractiveness, originality, or cosmopolitanism. The state became a leader in the cause of Populism, free silver, and Socialism, and it pioneered in mining law and federal reclamation. Although always stressing unrestricted individualism and the "American character," it almost immediately became one of the most diverse and colorful immigrant locales in the United States. Within five years after being organized into a territory, Nevada had drawn immigrants from five continents and almost two score countries.

During the nineteenth century, the frontier often expanded westward so rapidly that a well-knit social structure and meaningful traditions and political forms were unable to keep pace. Many western areas were providentially provided with helpful coalescing forces—the old Spanish traditions in New Mexico, the Mormon vortex in Utah, and the geography and economy of northern California all provided certain stabilizing influences for the societies concerned. But Nevada came into existence without an organic structuring of either its institutional or economic order. It became a legal entity without any real ties between community and community or people and government. The terrain was badly broken by mountains and deserts, the area sparsely and unevenly settled and the inhabitants singularly un-

NEVADA

showing principal
towns identified in
Restless Strangers

20°   118°   116°   114°

42°

Mc Dermitt

HUMBOLDT

Cornucopia

Tuscarora

Gold Circle

ELKO

Winnemucca

Dun Glen

Elko   Ft. Halleck

Battle Mountain

Bullion

PERSHING

Unionville

Lewis

Rochester

Hilltop

Ruby Valley

Lovelock

Cortez

LANDER

Mineral Hill

Cherry Creek

Pyramid Lake

Bolivia

EUREKA

WHITE

Newark

CHURCHILL

PINE

rd| Sparks
Reno
Washoe
City

STOREY

Fallon

Wonder

Austin

Eureka

Hamilton

Ely

Virginia City
Gold Hill
Silver City
Dayton

Fairview

Taylor

Carson City

Genoa

LYON

Ione

Minden

Yerington

Grantsville

Gardnerville

Walker Lake

Goldyke

DOUGLAS

Belmont

Hawthorne

La Panta

San Antonio

Tybo

MINERAL

Aurora

Belleville

Reveille

Candelaria

Columbus

NYE

Pioche

38°

Tonopah

ESMERALDA

Caliente

Goldfield

Delamar

Lida

Gold Point

LINCOLN

118°

Rhyolite   Beatty

Bullfrog

Carrara

CLARK

Las Vegas

Lake Mead

NEVADA

Potosi

36°

Boulder City

36°

Goodsprings

116°

114°

Eldorado

Lake Mohave

Searchlight

40°

WASHOE

25   0   25   50   75   100 Miles

stable. At times, much of the state was almost totally depopulated, and the remainder suffered constant exploitation by government, business, and industrial elements that were often neither a part of nor responsible to the local authority. Lawyers, none of whom were educated in Nevada, followed governmental structures and procedures not always suited to local conditions. The large and mixed foreign influx, therefore, found ample room in the loose and unmolded order to move with little hindrance and to exploit as well as to explore. Indeed, the very openness and mobility of Nevada society provided a unique set of circumstances wherein the foreign born are seen in relation to a new and uncertain environment.

Significantly, when Nevada was the most remote and isolated state in America, it attracted a larger per capita foreign-born population than any other state or territory. Although landlocked, it lured Portuguese fishermen from the Azores into the prosperous dairy industry. Although a desert region, Tuscans from the old duchy of Lucca streamed in to become stable ranchers. Swedish-speaking Finns settled in the hot, dry, boom camps of Nye and Esmeralda counties. And soon thereafter, Spanish farmers and fishermen sought the snow-capped mountains of the north for their sheep. Carson City became a home for many Australian-born females at the same time that it was the Chinese center of the state. Koreans who spoke Japanese, Slavs from Croatia and Serbia, and Greeks from Turkey and the Peloponnesus filled the mines and smelters of White Pine County, and Hindus laid rails for the Southern Pacific. In short, a diverse group of human beings helped to build the state and in turn contributed to its unorthodox social development.

In the broad historical sense, the large immigration provided Nevada with certain unique and valuable human features. The area became singularly international in that its people were tied to the conditions of life throughout the world. The famines of China and the conflicts of Europe were felt and reflected in the remote deserts of the West. Furthermore, immigrants more than any other group gave variety, flavor, and motleyness to Nevada life. Regions with more homogeneous and stable populations were denied such an intimate contact with the pluralism of America.

Nevada literature reflected the historical trends. Eighty-five percent of the fiction introduced foreign-born characters, and in approximately one book out of six, immigrants emerged as fundamental to the author's purpose. Obviously, national and regional literary currents also influenced the mood of local writers, but it was more often the singularity of Nevada settlement patterns which produced the human interplay that attracted the interest of a variety of authors, and contributed substance and direction to the literature.

The demographic and economic contributions of the foreign born have been unquestionable. Both the rapid development and the quick exhaustion of the state's two great mining booms—1860–1880 and 1902–1912—were due in considerable measure to the efforts of immigrants. In Nevada, the foreign born often discovered the ore and then supplied the labor and techincal skill to process it. Immigrant enlistees in the United States Army gave the communities military protection, while other Europeans became merchants, artisans, service personnel, and professional men. Foreigners cut the forests and worked the mines; they built, operated, and repaired the transportation system which carried much of the ore and the wealth out of the state. With surprising consistency, they helped make the laws, led the labor unions, printed and edited the newspapers, built the churches and schools, and even supplied the teachers. And to complete the picture, they contributed to the filling of the jails, the brothels, the state prison, and the insane asylum. The foreign born were indispensable to the very existence of Nevada and much of the Far West and were in part responsible for transforming it into a leading economic and political part of the United States.

Most Americans moved West less to escape from the East than to realize greater economic advantages. Most were not bitter, and many considered returning home some day. Many of the foreign born also returned, but their childhood experiences were less directly related to the new western circumstances. Their separation from the past was more complete. For a substantial number of the foreign born, the tie had been cut, and they were free and drifting beings, clinging to little beyond self-preservation. Even the most cohesive and resilient could not always resist the eroding effects of Nevada life. The active and ambitious, the studious and creative, as well as the intemperate and shiftless were all affected. The many immigrants who committed suicide, were found to be insane, or were convicted for crimes of violence attest either to the instability of the foreigner or to the emotional rigors of Nevada or to both.

On the other hand, to categorize the Nevada foreign born as individualistic, transient, fluid, and unresponsive to the needs for stability defies the obvious facts. The natural environment redirected, but it did not reshape them. Rather the state, in part, was reshaped by them. In vague and elusive ways, they clung to the beliefs and the values of their past, and in so doing they often formed oases of thrift and purpose in a notoriously flexible and shifting environment.

In many respects, Europeans integrated into the Nevada life more readily than Americans. The Germans of Carson Valley were an example. On one hand they tended to resist Americanization in that they long maintained the German language and formed German social organizations, but at the same time they cleared the land, dug irrigation canals, and made their valley the most stable and consistently productive community in the state. Although practicing a materialistic philosophy, they were not brutalized, and although cut off from their peasant attachments, they quickly grafted the Old World traditions of tenacity and resilience onto the new Nevada moorings.

There were many clearly distinguishable Italian settlements in the Truckee Meadows and the Dayton area where land-hungry and prudent migrants from Italy secured extensive holdings. The frugal practices of southern Europe were not lost in restless Nevada and within one generation the sons of Italy had become bank presidents, doctors, and leading businessmen. The physically mobile, but culturally homogeneous, Basques also quickly integrated into the Nevada environment; through a singular rigidity of character they preserved many Old World patterns and customs seemingly alien to western America. Although the Basques roamed widely, they were not necessarily of a restless temperament. Their willingness to move never lessened their attachment for home and their perseverance did not detract from their sensitivity.

Clearly, the immigrant role in the overall westward movement has been far from consistent and deserves further study. But to search for what was American and what was foreign in Nevada society becomes pointless. It was all American, often made possible by the brains, the brawn, and the audacity of foreigners. Furthermore, the repeatedly enunciated and generally accepted hypothesis that the foreign born followed in the wake of the American frontiersmen, that they merely filled in as Americans pushed on West, should be restudied. Such an overly simplified pattern did not develop in Nevada and perhaps not in any of the mining and industrial communities of the Far West. Nor does the related supposition that during the nineteenth century the foreign born were inclined to remain in the older settled areas of the East, whereas native Americans moved West, seem to be borne out by the statistics. Not only was Nevada long the leading immigrant state, but between 1870 and 1890, the five leading states or territories with the largest percentage of foreign born were all west of the Mississippi River.

The character and destiny of the western region was still in the process of formation, and conditions allowed and even encouraged the absorption of both people and ideas. Had Frederick Jackson Turner projected a different set of statistics, he might have propounded a thesis suggesting that the West was unique because it had been settled by three times as many foreigners per capita as then occupied the remainder of the United States.

Of course, the mere compilation of lists of foreign-born·Nevadans with a corresponding list of their achievements does not necessarily demonstrate a cultural or social impact upon the state. Filiopietistic groups, as well as historians, have often followed such barren and easily exaggerated practices. While the society of every region in America was made up of many forces and many parts, these cannot be disassembled and the value of any particular part scientifically scrutinized. All cultures are more than the sum of their parts and yet less than the sum of the individuals involved. No doubt many features of immigrant life survived by their being grafted onto the general culture. Nevada's Basque restaurants, Greek bakeries, and Cornish pasties suggest simple Old World customs which blended and accommodated themselves to the new environment. But in a more fundamental sense, it was the infusion of spice and muscle and diversity that made the immigrant historically significant. And it was his response to a volcanic, unstratified, and isolated environment which stimulated much of the literary and journalistic comment. Perhaps the scores of themes set forth by creative

8

writers and the various images left by contemporary newspapers can help reveal the immigrants' impact upon, and reaction to, the rudimentary Nevada society.

[1] William E. Smythe, *The Conquest of Arid America* (New York: The Macmillan Company, 1905), p. 214.

[2] *Tuscarora Times-Review,* February 29, 1888, p. 2 col. 1.

PART ONE

The Immigrants

1
=

Settlement in a Fluid Society

The pace and momentum of early Nevada growth, the later periods of stagnation, and the state's constantly changing character alternately attracted and repulsed the foreign born. The climate, the geography, and the vagaries of nature always powerfully overlaid the human purpose. For some immigrants the wide open spaces and the unstratified town life brought economic success and a personal rejuvenation. But more often the rural isolation and the urban disorder led to bewilderment. As the bustling boom camps shriveled into transient fragments, so did many of their occupants. For half a century the state was caught up in the mineral discoveries, the railway construction booms, and the reclamation projects. Wave after wave of Irish, Cornish, Germans, French-Canadians, Chinese, Greeks, Slavs, Italians, Basques, and Japanese were drawn by the magnetism of opportunity. But the region lacked the necessary prerequisites for economic stability and after becoming an immigrant sponge it was periodically wrung dry. Despite the "boom and bust" cycle, however, the state long remained strangely attractive to the foreign born.

Migratory Patterns

In 1870, only six years after Nevada was admitted to the Union, 44.2 percent of the state's population was foreign-born. On a percentage basis, the new land of sagebrush had already become the largest immigrant state in America; almost 7 percent more of its inhabitants were foreign born than that of second-place California. Only 14 percent of the population of the United States was foreign born in 1870. Furthermore, the Bureau of the Census has estimated that during the following ten years the net foreign migration into Nevada was ten times that of the American-born influx. Although Nevada's population increased by twenty thousand between 1870 and 1880, the census figures suggest that only eight hundred of the new residents were American-born migrants.[1] In 1880, with a foreign-born population of 41.2 percent, Nevada still had 7 percent more foreign-born inhabitants than any other American state. Nevada long maintained its immigrant character and was on a percentage basis one of the top ten foreign-born states in America for more than seventy-five years.

Of the 2,770 men gainfully employed in the mining industry on the Comstock Lode in June, 1880, 816 were Irish born, 640 English born, 544 from other foreign nationalities, and only 770 American born.[2] In addition to the foreign-born white migrants, by 1880, 8.7 percent of the state's total population was from China.[3] By 1900 the Italians, who represented about two tenths of 1 percent of the population of the United States, comprised 3.0 percent of the population of the state of Nevada.[4] Therefore, in 1900, Nevada contained a larger percentage of Italians than any other American state. Indeed, Nevada's percentage of Italian settlers was twice that of any state west of the Mississippi River. By 1910, Nevada had become a major area for Japanese settlement, and along with southern Idaho and southeast Oregon, it had grown into the most significant Basque center in America.

Grantsville, in northwestern Nye County, typified many of Nevada's earlier mining communities. In 1880, 276 of the 502 inhabitants of Grantsville were foreign born; of equal interest, the 276 represented twenty-one regions or nationalities, ranging from New Zealand to Norway, Spain to Slovenia, China to Chile. On the other hand, a quite different foreign-born character was reflected by Ruby Hill in Eureka County. Of the 223 residents of the town in 1900, the fathers of 171 had been born in England, the fathers of 24 were born in Ireland, 12 in Canada, 4 in Scotland and 2 in other foreign countries. Only 10 of the 223 residents of the town had an American-born father. Even a Reno brothel of 1910 could boast of 11 foreign-born girls out of a total of 19; the prostitutes had come from nine different countries including England, France, Italy, Spain, Ireland, Russia, Belgium, Canada, and Japan.[5]

Another feature of Nevada immigrant society can be seen by noting the residents along the Prince Mine Road which ran from the town of Pioche to the camp of Highland, about six miles to the southwest. On June 19, 1880, Highland had a total population of sixteen people representing twelve different countries. With one Dane, one Swede, one Italian, one French-Canadian, one Portuguese, one Norwegian, one Chilean, one American, two Mexicans, two Frenchmen, and three Irishmen, there was obviously little indigenous American society with which to integrate, and the men were required to work out as best they could their own social adjustments. No doubt all responded first to the physical environment and later absorbed bits of the customs and language of the others. The Americanization that took place in Highland in 1880 was little more than the meeting and mingling of transients on a common ground.[6]

Forty years later, in 1920, the camp of Highland had disappeared, but fifty-four persons still lived in cabins along the Prince Mine Road. The ten Americans were mainly wives and children, and of the remaining forty-four persons, nine were Mexicans, nine Italians, five Bulgarians, three Irishmen, three Greeks, three Spaniards, two Swedes, two Austrians, one was Russian, one Pole, one Dane, one Englishman, one Frenchman, one Montenegrin, one Scot, and one Uruguayan. The figures suggest that the original Highland settlers did not remain and that their children did not form the backbone of a stable society in the original or in adjoining communities. It is obvious that the inhabitants of Nevada's four hundred ghost towns moved away, but it is sometimes less obvious that many of the inhabitants of the more stable communities remained for less than a generation. Thus, Nevada became something of a perpetual immigrant frontier. Perhaps life in a city ghetto would have been socially preferable in that it could have provided cohesiveness, a kind of permanence, and a recognized base upon which immigrants and their children could have built.[7]

The impact of the foreign born on the society and community life of any region depends on many factors: the circumstances surrounding the migration, the sophistication and urbanization of the receiving society, and the age, occupation, sex, stability, and education of the foreign settlers. Most Nevada immigrants lacked the time, the opportunity, and the inclination to impress their customs on the state in the way the New Mexico Spanish, the Louisiana French, the Pennsylvania Germans, the Boston Irish, or the San Francisco Chinese did. Many forces operated against the establishment of immigrant folk culture in Nevada. Only rarely did a single nationality colonize a particular town or community; consequently, the ethnic effect of the alien tended to be diffused rather than concentrated. The imbalance of the sexes in Nevada—ranging from 288 foreign-born white males per 100 foreign-born white females in 1880, to 331 per 100 in 1910—limited the number of family units and detracted from the immigrants' social and cultural influence.[8] Many male migrants lived for the day when they could flee to more hospitable surroundings to enjoy the fruits of their Nevada success. Even during the prosperous decade of the seventies, a very small percentage of the supposedly stable Germans remained in the state for as long as ten years. In the largely agricultural and commercial counties of Douglas, Lyon, and Washoe, less than 15 percent of the 339 German-born immigrants who appeared in the census lists of 1870 were still in the state in 1880. In the mining and industrial counties of Storey, Lander, and Esmeralda, only 7 percent of the 940 Germans remained throughout the decade.[9]

Even the large number of ethnic and cultural organizations, which came into existence for the specific purpose of serving the immigrants, often failed to perpetuate the foreign-born spirit which they were designed to sustain. The Nevada mobility was so great that new societies sprang into existence without reference to the old. As late as 1905, a body of Reno Germans naïvely suggested that they were organizing the first German society in the state. They seemed totally unaware of the three German newspapers that had once been published in western Nevada and the German organizations that had existed in at least nine different Nevada communities, including Reno. In the last third of the twentieth century, Basque, French, German, Danish, Italian, Portuguese, Mexican, Slavic, Greek, Japanese, and other ancestral organizations continue to flourish. Most of the fraternities, however, have not maintained any real contact with their antecedents, and few of their members have any significant knowledge of the history and settlement of their people within the state. The reasons for this strange phenomenon seem obvious: the social and psychological element of national origin has not been sufficient to hold most groups together. Nevada immigrants have not wished to merge their individuality into a particular ethnic identity. National origin, common speech and religion, and even distinct racial characteristics have failed to provide a major focus or a common orientation. In short, it has been the American penchant for clubs and organizations, rather than deep-seated foreign ties, which has led to the formation of most of the immigrant societies.

Nevada attracted an abnormally large and peculiarly diverse group of foreigners. Most of the immigrants were not genuinely remarkable men; most would not have drawn the attention of either the novelist or the historian under normal circumstances. Most of the foreign born were oriented toward immediate and narrowly materialistic ends. They often dissipated their energy and talents without leaving a very clear imprint of their heritage on the land. But Nevada desperately needed leadership and participation in its social, economic, and political life, and it provided thousands of both creative and nondescript immigrants with a unique opportunity to mold and stamp a character upon the emerging society.

Social Organization

As the largest community in Nevada throughout most of the nineteenth century, the Comstock most vividly reflects the social activities and organizations growing out of the foreign influx. Particularly in the earlier decades, the immigrant groups were almost uniformly seen as worthy and desirable additions to Virginia City life. A newspaper report of a Turnverein Ball held on August 6, 1876, typifies the public reaction. The *Territorial Enterprise* of Virginia City courteously gave the article a German title, "Bahn Frei."

> The Germans know how to enjoy life much better than we do. They are educated in all parts which go to make up the physical, intellectual and moral being. They be-

lieve in a sound mind, a sound body and in the development of social nature as well. They mingle in their everyday life the beautiful with the useful and, instead of one member of the household withdrawing to meet others of the same class likewise withdrawn, the whole family go together, participate together and thus grow to a fulness of capacity to which all exclusiveness are and must ever be strangers. And so it was at the ball given by the Turn-Verein at their new hall Sunday evening. It was attended by men, women, and children, and all participated to the fullest extent in the enjoyments which were there in abundance.[10]

Even the songs, banners, and flags honoring the Fatherland were declared to be in good taste: "the man who can forget the land of his nativity may easily forsake that of his adoption."

An idea of the extent of organized foreign-born activity can be gained from a look at Virginia City's social calendar during the year 1875. New Year's morning dawned on the Comstock with the Germans still singing and dancing at Athletic Hall, and with the French and Italians joining together to sing each other's songs at Gregorie's Saloon in the heart of town at Union and C streets. Later in the week, the sixteen-piece Cornish Orchestra and the English Choral Society greeted the New Year more reverently at the Methodist Church. The Swiss also helped to usher in 1875 with their minstrel show, and late in January the British Benevolent Association held the first of its semiannual elections.

The first part of February was taken up with preparations for the Chinese New Year; the feasts, parades, and fireworks supplied by the Chinese generally resulted in a temporary reduction of Caucasian hostility toward the Orientals. The semiannual ball of the Italian Benevolent Society was held in mid-February, and on Washington's Birthday the Emmet Guard, largest of the Irish military companies, presented its annual parade. March, of course, was also an Irish month. By 1875, the long-standing feud involving the Emmet Guard, the Sweeny Guard, the Ancient Order of Hibernians, the Irish-American Band, the Fenian Society, and the Sarsfield Guard of Gold Hill had ended in a compromise. They alternated in leading parades and presiding at the Saint Patrick's Day Ball.

With the coming of spring, the usual round of prizefights, wrestling matches, and footraces began. James Tickell, James Rodda, James Trevillian, and Jack Skewers, all of Cornwall, were the leading pugilists in 1875. Skewers, who had saved the lives of twelve people in a mining accident in his homeland, was unusually popular with the saloon crowd. "The Stump of Norwich" who had fought in England and Australia before arriving in Nevada, Irish Sullivan (actually born in Bishopsgate, London), Sparks of Sydney, Patsy Hogan, and Dublin Pete helped to balance the scales against the Cornishmen. Perhaps the most exciting match of 1875 was the fifty-two-round bout between the Cornishman Bing Williams and the Englishman James Chatham; neither side was completely happy with the decisions made by the French referee. Alf Williams and Joe Williams, both Cornishmen, were the leading wrestlers, and an Australian became the Comstock footrace champion for 1875.

By May, the Turnverein's fortnightly Sunday evening socials were in full swing with special festivals being held at Von Bokkelen's Beer Gardens. By the mid seventies, the German May picnic had been expanded to include both Sunday and Monday —some of the participants had found it difficult to walk the two miles from the German Brewery in Six-Mile Canyon back to Virginia City by Monday morning. During 1875, German Catholics, German Lutherans, the French, and the French-Canadians all worshipped on the Comstock in their native language. And the death of locally prominent Germans commonly resulted in a military cortege in which former German soldiers marched in their uniforms of Prussian blue.

On May 5, a Mexican "jollification" celebrated the victory over the French at Puebla thirteen years earlier, and on May 29, a second Mexican program marked the anniversary of Maximilian's being made a prisoner. In 1875, the British cancelled their annual dinner on Queen Victoria's Birthday. But in late May, the Welsh organized a socioreligious order under the leadership of the Rev. Thomas Moses, a local justice of the peace. A reporter for the *Territorial Enterprise* was so moved after listening to a Welsh religious service which he could not understand that he declared Welsh "a universal language felt and understood alike by all." After attending a further service in June, the reporter explained, "The Welsh are a sturdy race when uncorrupted, and the movement on foot will, if successful, do much toward keeping them to their native faith and purity." [11] On June 6, the Italian Club celebrated the anniversary of the adoption of the Italian constitution. Italian and German flags were intertwined for the full length of North C Street, and the Italians staged several dinners emphasizing their recently achieved national unity.

The extent of the foreign activity was emphasized by a page in the *Territorial Enterprise* of June 8, 1875. Page 3 carried reports of a German gymnastic competition, a German band concert, a ball and Turnverein fest, a shooting prize given by the Emmet Guard, a road accident involving several Germans, a review of the "The Flower Girl of Paris" given at the opera house, a Chinese shooting affray, a Welsh language sermon in the Miners' Union Hall, and a gathering to celebrate the adoption of the Italian constitution. Announcements told of the receipt of uniforms for the Irish-American band, the forthcoming Emmet Guard picnic, and a Cornish wrestling match.[12]

The Fourth of July invariably produced a series of diversified celebrations, which often ended in violence. In 1875, there were the usual individual catastrophes: a German woman tried to commit suicide, a Mexican had his leg blown off, and a Frenchman claimed that a Cornishman cheated when he carried dirt in his hand while climbing the greased pole. James Orndorff, an inventive Frenchman, provided great excitement by sending kittens and firecrackers up in his balloon. He, along with his two brothers, dazzled the people of the Comstock with balloon ascensions of the Montgolfier type, with velocipede riding, with expert billiard shooting, and with the promotion of prize fighting. The Orndorff brothers ran various saloons in Virginia City, but their chief interest was the gaily arranged bar at the International Hotel. The display of orange and banana trees with the fruit ripening on the branches and of botanical plants with colorful tropical foliage made the International Saloon justly famous.

In August, a veritable barrage of social activities was staged by the foreign born. After remembering Robert Burns's birthday in January and holding a social on the anniversary of Sir Walter Scott's birth in August, the Scottish societies held their "Gathering of the Clans," which was concluded with the Caledonian picnic. Four hundred dollars was given in prizes for the best performers of Scottish games. During the late summer and autumn, the Scottish Bagpipe Band under the direction of Professor Cara gave regularly scheduled public concerts; Professor Varney's German Band played fortnightly; one of the town's three Irish bands played weekly; the band of the Odd Fellows' lodge, composed mainly of Cornishmen, offered several performances; and groups of strolling players drifted through the city. It was not uncommon for a single production at the opera house to offer songs in English, French, German, Spanish, and Italian.

A series of women's walking matches staged by young Europeans apparently did not detract from the services held by John Treyman, the free-thought preacher from Australia, or the messages on spiritualism given by the Reverend T. H. McGrath of Ireland. But the Reverend J. O'Connor drew larger crowds when he argued that Adam and Eve, as well as Middle Eastern civilizations, had sprung from Irish soil. On August 14, 1875, the Episcopal Bishop, O. W. Whitaker, dedicated a church in Chinatown for its Christian pastor, the Reverend Ah For. Ah For, who had once conducted a Presbyterian service in Carson City, had been assisted by Caucasians in the construction of the Comstock chapel, and until the building burned in March, 1876, Orientals and Caucasians mingled together at Ah For's Sunday sermons. In September and October, the Miners' Union Hall was converted into a "Polish Synagogue" for Rosh Hashanah and Yom Kippur, and throughout the autumn, B'nai Brith actively solicited funds for humanitarian purposes.

On September 16, the Mexicans of Virginia City celebrated their 1810 independence with a marching band, a parade, and a ball, but more exciting was the morning, noontime, and evening firing of a cannon. The Chileans made a desperate effort not to be overshadowed when they followed with their independence celebration on September 18. Also during September, the Canadian Relief Society met to study the problems of unemployment, and the British Association opened a reading room. In their sedate fashion, the British offered scholarly and scientific papers on such subjects as the molecular structure of steel and the effects of heat on precious metals.

At least twenty different foreign groups or societies were functioning during the autumn of 1875, but none received as much attention as the Hop Sing and Sam Sing companies, which embarked on a tong war in December. Oriental warriors were imported from California, and the chaos continued until March, 1876. Although the Christmas season inspired many social events, the former residents of the Isle of Man most fittingly brought the activities of 1875 to a close. On December 31, the Manxmen met with an Irish preacher, T. H. McGrath, in prayerful service; at the stroke of twelve, McGrath blessed their newly born babies so that they might be the first persons in the United States "christened to American citizenship" on the one hundredth anniversary of the founding of the republic.[13]

At times, Comstock journalists attempted to transform insignificant news items into epics and many overemphasized the town's interest in social and colorful pursuits; nevertheless, the activities of Virginia City's foreign born were extensive and humanly meaningful. In Nevada, as throughout the West, those immigrants who arrived early in the community's development were not thought to be of a new, or different, or lower class. The ambitious found social escalation almost automatic, and despite a lack of experience or background, the merchant, brewer, or dairyman often became one of the community's elite within half a decade. Most of the immigrant societies therefore, were directed by leading citizens and most were accepted as pleasant and purposeful adjuncts to Comstock life. Each year saw the arrival of new immigrants who reconstituted and enriched the societies' foreign flavor.

Economic Success

Most of Nevada's immigrants were caught up in a materialistic philosophy and a clamor for rapid advancement. In general, they were men of action and ambition or they would not have sought out Nevada in the first place. Therefore, the state's rather primitive social environment, indifference to culture, and general isolation neither disturbed nor hindered them in their drive to obtain possessions. Indeed, the immigrant was often better equipped to compete and more willing to accept hardships in the race for material rewards than were the native-born Americans.

Merle Curti has produced the best detailed and empirical study of the foreign born, vis-à-vis the American born, in their economic adaptation to a frontier environment. In *The Making of an American Community,* Professor Curti demonstrated that after twenty years in the community, the non-English-speaking nationalities of Trempealeau County, Wisconsin, owned more land per family than the native-born farmers.[14] In the nineteenth-century Nevada towns, the foreign born apparently became economic equals of the American born somewhat more rapidly than in the agricultural districts studied by Professor Curti.

A limited survey of the 1870 census seems to indicate that about a decade was required in Nevada for the average immigrant to become as wealthy as the average American. A study of ownership of property, both real and personal, in the towns of Belmont, Washoe City, and Winnemucca suggests a trend. The mining camp of Belmont had been founded in 1865 and became significant when it was designated the seat of Nye County in 1867. In August, 1870, the town's 88 white adult foreign-born persons (17 were women) owned property worth an average of $264 each, and the 166 white American born (47 were women), $688 each. Twenty-four percent of the foreign born and 27 percent of the American born held some property. But most striking, 9 Germans in Belmont held over half of all the wealth claimed by the foreign born.[15]

When the 1870 census was taken, the agricultural and trading center of Washoe City had been a viable community for some eight or nine years. The permanent population of the small county-seat town totaled 125 foreign-born and 206 American-born adults. Slightly over a third of each group were females.[16] The 125 foreign born held property worth an average of $314 each, whereas the 206 Americans were worth $341 per person. Although the average wealth of the Americans was slightly greater, 33 percent of the foreign born and only 20 percent of the Americans were listed as property holders. And reflecting the same trend as found in Belmont, 10 Germans held more than 40 percent of the wealth claimed by the foreign born.[17]

In 1870, Winnemucca had been an active settlement for approximately a decade, but during the later sixties the village expanded rapidly when it became a prosperous commercial center on the Central Pacific Railroad. The average wealth of the 94 white adult foreign born (17 were females) was an impressive $785, while the average for the 101 white adult American born (19 were females) was only $321. Furthermore, 31 percent of all the foreign born held property, whereas only 19 percent of the Americans were credited with any real or personal possessions. And following the trend found in Washoe City and Belmont, 10 Germans held 62 percent of the foreign-born wealth.[18]

Clearly, random surveys of three small Nevada communities in 1870 do not provide sufficient data for the formulation of either an immigrant or an economic hypothesis, but the study does allow for a few tentative conclusions. Within ten years after a Nevada town was founded, immigrants were somewhat more likely than Americans to have economic stability. A larger percentage held at least *some* property and the individual holdings of the foreign born were generally greater than those of the American born. Furthermore, a few Germans in each community overshadowed all other national groups in the amassing of wealth.[19]

A broader, more subjective analysis suggests three major economic categories into which the foreign born can be grouped: itinerant laborers, lesser proprietors, and prosperous businessmen. First, there were the bands of itinerant foreign laborers who seldom possessed any tangible wealth and who worked in a constantly shifting environment. The enumerators' reports for the United States census graphically isolate the French-Canadians who cut the forests, the Chinese who laid the rails, the Irish and Cornish who dug much of the ore, the Italians and Swiss who burned charcoal, the French and Spanish Basques who herded sheep, and the Slavs and Greeks who smeltered copper ore. A few from each of these bands of workmen saved their wages, bought land or a small business, and became permanent residents. But in time most drifted on to the next available manual labor.

A second group of the foreign born was composed of the artisans, small proprietors, and marginal landholders. This element almost instinctively began to save, accumulate, and grow roots in a way unfamiliar to most Americans. In the periods of rapid expansion in the sixties and seventies and again after the turn of the century, small merchandising businesses were to a surprising degree taken over by European proprietors. A study of the shop owners on North C Street in Virginia City in 1880 rather vividly points up the pattern.

At the heart of Virginia City, at C and Union streets, stood the six-story International Hotel. It was truly international. On June 17, 1880, the resident staff of twenty persons was drawn from eight different nationalities. The manager was Austrian and his wife, the hostess, was Swiss. The two desk clerks were German, the carpenter was a Canadian, the cook a Frenchman, the assistant cook Chinese, and the baker a Frenchman. Of the four waiters, two were Irish, one was German, and one was American. The chambermaid was Irish; and of six servants, four were Chinese, one was Irish, and one was American. The steward was an American.[20]

Moving north from the hotel, there was a total of thirty-five businesses fronting on C Street within the first long block. Of the thirty-five shops or businesses, six were operated by American-born proprietors, six by Germans, four by Irishmen, four by Austrians, four by Italians, three by Frenchmen, two by Canadians, two by Swiss, one by a Scot, and one by a Portuguese. In addition, there was a storeroom for one English peddler and two Austrian hucksters. The Germans ran two butcher shops, a candy store, a photograph gallery, and two grocery stores. The Austrians (mainly Slavs) ran saloons and grocery stores, the Italians were mainly shoemakers and saddlers, the Canadians and French operated restaurants, saloons, and a bakery, one Swiss was a watchmaker, the other a locksmith, and the Portuguese was a barber.[21] A cursory check of hotels throughout Nevada suggests that the foreign staff of the International Hotel was rather typical of the rooming houses of the state and that North C Street was fairly representative of Main Street, Nevada, nineteenth century.

In the early twentieth century the pattern changed little. For example, the new boomtown of Tonopah was serviced mainly by foreign businesses in the decade before World War I. Immigrants like David Rosenthal, F. H. Lutjen, Isadore Sura, James LaMarque, John Guisti, Parpo Del Levis, Charles Miller, Gatens Barelia, Christopher Serzstick, and many others constituted the competition for the surprisingly small number of American-born proprietors. A rough calculation from the 1910 census suggests that a fourth of the businesses which served the city's four thousand people were operated by persons born in Slavic or Latin regions of Europe and another fourth came from Germanic districts.

A relatively small percentage of Nevada's total migrants settled on the land. However, over the decades many of the more tenacious farmers, ranchers, and herders were European. A survey of one sparsely inhabited valley in central Nevada suggests that in 1895 about half of the adult white settlers were foreign born. Smoky Valley, extending south from Austin for over fifty miles, typifies a dozen marginal agricultural communities in central and eastern Nevada. By 1895 some nineteen Caucasian families had arrived in the isolated district and were engaged in dry farming and stock raising. The adults in eight of the families were American born, in eight foreign born, and in three families one member was foreign born. The immigrants had been drawn from five countries of northern Europe and from Canada.[22]

By the turn of the century, many small remote communities reflected an even greater national diversity. In 1900 some 43 of the 119 people trying to farm the barren Bartlett Creek district of northwest Nevada were immigrants from thirteen different countries. The largest foreign contingents were from Germany, Portugual, and France.[23] During the following two decades a score of livestock precincts scattered across northern Nevada became predominantly Basque. Ragged Top and Linton Wells in Pershing County, Dewey and Salt Marsh in Washoe County, King's River and Kennedy in Humboldt County, and Byron and White Rock in Elko County were typical of the settlements which reflected the Basque influence. But Nevada's larger agricultural areas also absorbed a heavy immigrant influx. By 1910 the fertile Lovelock district had become one of the more prosperous and varied foreign communities in the state. Almost 40 percent of the district's 1,600 people were foreign born; they had been drawn from twenty-four different countries.[24]

A third category of the Nevada foreign born comprised the small group of prosperous ranchers, mine operators, and successful businessmen who rose with surprising rapidity to form the state's financial plutocracy. Comparatively little literary notice has been given to the early-day immigrant ranchers who became landed padrones. The German H. F. Dangberg, the Dane Henry Anderson, the Scot John Taylor, and the Basque Pedro Altube were significant community figures in that they encouraged the migration of, and at the same time provided employment for, their fellow countrymen. Immigrants like James Fair, John Mackay, John "January" Jones, Adolph Sutro, and others who became famous as mining promoters, industrialists, and speculators will be noted in a later chapter. They typify the "rags to riches" success story and have attracted considerable literary and historical attention.

Although Nevada's most prosperous foreign business element was German, a few of the French, some of the south Slavs and eastern European Jews, and a scattering from other nationalities also attained success quickly. Most were among the first settlers in the community: through the careful buying of merchandise, wise investment in town lots, or limited speculation in good land, they rose to become local capitalists. The amassing of property led to elective office and to the building of relatively stable Nevada families. The ambitious who arrived early did not have to push anyone above them into a higher class; rather, they almost automatically formed the upper class. Their manners, their religion, and even their political views were not shaped by an elite, but rather by what they considered their immediate needs. Physical wealth seemed to be the surest way to comfort and position. The most successful of the foreign born readily comprehended and actively supported the idea that materialism was the key to frontier success.

The Melatovich Association of Virginia City typified the foreign merchant families. The Melatovich grocery store at 93 North C Street and a nearby saloon had, in 1870, been providing the community with foreign delicacies for almost a decade. In addition to Scotch, English, and Irish whisky, Jamaica rum, and French brandy, the Melatoviches specialized in "French and Italian wines, truffles, Italian mushrooms, roasted chestnuts, Italian, English, Holland, Swiss and California cheese, Dutch sardines and herrings, Russian caviar, Pagoliano syrup," and dozens of other foreign items to please the most discriminating epicure.[25] During the summer of 1869, Vincent Melatovich decided to retire to the sunny Adriatic, but Andrew, along with other relatives, continued to direct the Comstock businesses, including the first and apparently the largest winery every operated in Nevada.

During the same period, Michael Cohen of Prussia and later of England developed an extensive dry goods firm in eastern Nevada. Although Cohen's first business was opened at Virginia City in 1860, he quickly moved east, and over the following forty years built stores at Eureka, Hamilton, Pioche, Ward, Taylor, Ely, and Delamar. The Reinhart company extending across northern Nevada survived even longer and for several decades was the largest merchandising establishment in the state. The Reinhart family, Simon, Benjamin, Eli, Moses, Edward, Amson, and young Simon, were all from the small community of Oberlustadt, Germany. With additional interests in bank and trust companies, water and light companies, land and livestock companies, freight lines, wool industries, and lumber yards, the Reinharts were for almost two generations one of the major economic forces in Nevada.[26]

The Melatoviches of western Nevada, Michael Cohen of eastern Nevada, and the Reinharts of northern Nevada were in some ways surpassed as businessmen by Solomon Summerfield and George Davidovich of southern Nevada. The Russian-born Summerfield operated a chain of stores from Sutro, near the Carson River, south to Hawthorne and Tonopah. The diversified interests of George Davidovich included not only the largest mercantile house in Sodaville and Tonopah, but also mining claims and construction firms. He was also general advisor on, and sometimes importer of, Slavic labor for southern Nevada's mines and railroads.

In an economic sense, the various immigrant nationalities were surprisingly well balanced between rural and urban pursuits and between the worker and the employer classes. And while later immigrant arrivals tended to gravitate toward the occupations already opened up by their countrymen, members of all nationalities (with the possible exception of the Orientals) became landowners, shopkeepers, and capitalists. Of course, a statistical analysis or evaluation based on the occupation of, or property held by, various racial or national groups suggests little beyond the facts presented. Statistics do not prove the absence of prejudice or social conflict, and sometimes groups became economically prosperous in spite of, or perhaps because of, discrimination. Nevertheless, the reasonably happy economic balance enjoyed by Nevada's many nationalities must be borne in mind when evaluating the accounts of distrust and intolerance presented in later chapters.

In one area of economic activity, foreigners and their American friends demonstrated phenomenal naïveté. Immigrant leaders and local business interests often became wildly visionary and unrealistic in their plans to form immigrant agricultural colonies. Although substantial sums of money were spent on several of the projects, these colonies provide a catalogue of economic and personal misadventure. The 1892 move to settle a thousand Danes along the Walker River,[27] the 1898 eastern European Jewish colony in Smith Valley,[28] the 1907 program by Father T. W. Horgan to locate a thousand Irish in the Carson Sink,[29] the 1907 proposal by four hundred Polish families to settle near Fort Halleck,[30] the 1911 plan by a hundred Italians to establish vineyards at Unionville,[31] the 1915 attempt by a party of German-Russians to farm in Elko County,[32] and the half-dozen plans between 1912 and 1916 to locate Russians, Finns, and Estonians on the lands of the Nevada-California-Oregon Railway were typical of the short lived or stillborn ventures of the era. A proposed South African Boer colony in northern Nevada, a Hindu colony in Churchill County, Japanese colonies in the Ruby Valley, at Fallon, and at Las Vegas, a Siberian Baptist colony in Washoe County, a Danish colony in the Carson Valley, a Norwegian colony on the lower Carson River, and a Greek colony near Reno further suggest the extent of the colonizing mania during the years preceding World War I.

For the foreign born of Nevada, the economic picture was obviously mixed. Opportunities were always greater near the edge of settlement where conditions were fluid and expansion more or less assured. Enterprising immigrants boldly capitalized on the uncertainties and became land owners and industrialists as well as merchants, artisans, and service personnel in the new communities. If the settlement prospered, they and their children rose in the social structure; if it collapsed, they moved on to try again. Few of the immigrants who came specifically to cut timber, burn charcoal, or lay rails, and almost none of those who joined planned agricultural communities, became permanent residents. In short, the urban shopkeeper more often than the lonely prospector, the individualist more often than the cooperator, the persistent European realist more often than the dauntless Yankee frontiersman enjoyed economic success in Nevada.

Political and Professional Activity

Although great migrations have always influenced the social and economic patterns of a receiving society, they have not uniformly played a major role in the official and professional life of the host country. But in Nevada the immigrant quickly became an active participant on the political scene. Indeed, there are instances where the foreign born voted and were even elevated to official position only to learn years later that they had not taken the necessary steps to become citizens.[33] From 1870 until after the turn of the century, always one and often two of Nevada's three Congressional posts were filled by men who were foreign born. Also before 1900, three of the state's governors were immigrants and a fourth had been reared in Canada. There were foreign-born delegates at both of the Nevada constitutional conventions and the superintendent of printing as well as his chief assistants were often Europeans.

Unfortunately, most of the Biennial Homographic Charts which document the background of all major officials in Nevada government have been destroyed. However, an examination of the extant charts points up the many public positions filled by the foreign born. For example, of the twenty state senators in the legislature of 1891, eight were foreign born, and of the forty assemblymen, sixteen were foreign born. They were mainly merchants, miners, and hotel keepers; there was one banker, one lawyer, and one blacksmith. Twenty-three were Republicans and one was a member of the Democratic party. Out of a total of ten assemblymen and three senators elected from Storey County (the Comstock), all of the senators and six of the assemblymen were immigrants. The average age of the foreign-born legislators was some four years greater than that of their American-born colleagues, and they were somewhat more likely to be single men.[34] Other available homographic charts suggest that the representation of the foreign born in the 1891 legislature was more or less typical for Nevada in the nineteenth century. Thus there is little doubt that a significant body of Nevada's immigrants rose as rapidly and became as politically influential as their American-born neighbors.

A formative and expanding region offers obvious opportunities for persons trained in many different professions. As a town or campsite developed, there was a need for engineers, surveyors, lawyers, doctors, preachers, newspapermen, and even a few schoolmasters. Dozens of third-rate professional men achieved a kind of status, and sometimes wealth, in a land where few questions were asked and no examination required. For decades Europeans dominated the photography industry in the state, and with the coming of the railroads, Britons and Canadians occupied most of the technical posts such as telegraphers, switchmen, and locomotive engineers. Immigrants became music teachers, dancing instructors, fencing masters, and foreign-language professors to the almost complete exclusion of Americans. And at peak periods in the nineteenth century, about 20 percent of all of Nevada's school teachers were foreign born.

Nevada drew a surprisingly large number of foreign-born physicians. For example, as the scattered communities of 1860 began to take shape, three of the five doctors in the territory were from Europe. John Milhouse, a Frenchman, was military surgeon at Fort Churchill; A. Hep, a German of Silver City and Dayton, ministered to the needs of the settlers along the Carson River; and George Atcheson, a Scot, functioned on the Comstock. Over the following ten years, the French became an important element in Virginia City's medical corps. On May 4, 1868, the Belgian-born, but Paris-schooled, Dr. Van Der Mursch, died just as he was preparing to return to Paris to visit his wife and family after an absence of eighteen years.[35] At about the same time, Dr. L. Lasvignes, also trained in Paris, became so depressed with living alone in America that he committed suicide.[36]

But Dr. Lefevre and Dr. Charles Desch, also of Paris, seem to have maintained their Gallic buoyancy. Lefevre, who specialized in female illnesses, supplemented his income by importing "genuine" French perfumes for his clients, while Desch became known as one of the leading philosophers and natural wits of the city. In September, 1871, he created considerable bewilderment when he painted a jackass with a red rose in its mouth on his office window overlooking Union and D streets. The riddle was finally deciphered when a newspaperman read Lucius Apuleius' second-century book *Metamorphoses* or the *Golden Ass*. The work told of a man turned into a jackass and forced to wander over the earth in search of a red rose, which, when found, would allow the man to reassume his original form. Dr. Desch claimed to have the rose of knowledge which would turn the jackasses of the Comstock into healthy men if they would but frequent his office.[37]

Reno always attracted a large number of foreign-born and often foreign-trained physicians. In 1870, when the village was but two years old, two doctors from the small German state of Hanover had already arrived, and forty years later when the town had grown to ten thousand people, there were at least twelve foreign-born doctors, as well as many foreign-born dentists, practicing in the city. Three of the medical doctors were French, two Canadian, two Italian, two German, one English, one Russian, and one Swiss.[38] The foreign-born physician played a role in almost all of Nevada's major communities and has often

36

been the only practitioner in many of the more isolated regions. In the late 1860s, Newark Valley's Dr. Henry Key of France traveled over hundreds of miles to minister to the needs of people in White Pine and Eureka counties. The only two doctors in the Belleville-Columbus-Candelaria district of Esmeralda County during the early eighties were a French-Canadian and an Englishman, and the only physician in Rawhide in the years before World War I was Alexander McFirth McMaster, a Scottish-Canadian. For more than twenty-five years, a New Zealander, followed by a Welshman, served the scattered communities of northwest Humboldt County. In 1880, one of Eureka's leading doctors was from Poland and another from Russia. By 1910, the state's first foreign-born female physician was practicing at Goldfield, and by 1920, physicians who had been born in Peru, Armenia, Austria, Bermuda, South Africa, and other distant lands were practicing in Nevada. Equally as significant, many of the nineteenth-century doctors and some of the later ones (at least four of the twelve who were in Reno in 1910) were foreign trained.

Foreign clergymen long predominated in Nevada churches. For over two generations, Irish-trained priests, mainly from All Hallows Seminary, Dublin, flowed into northern California and Nevada. Indeed, the Irish influence was so extensive that all but one of the priests, and most of the assistant priests, to serve the Virginia City parish from its official organization in 1862 until its absorption into the Carson parish in the 1930s were born in Ireland. But Protestants as well as Catholics came from Ireland. Of the seven clergymen who ministered to the seven thousand persons in Virginia City in 1870, all were from Ireland, and of the four in nearby Gold Hill, two were from Ireland, one was from Scotland, and one was an American. Furthermore, of the eight sisters in the Virginia City convent in 1870, six were from

Ireland, one was from Australia, and one was an American. As late as 1910, three of Virginia City's four clergymen were foreign born.

An impressive number of Methodist preachers from England made their way to Nevada before World War I. John Thompson, Thomas Leak, and James Whitaker of Yorkshire, J. L. Trefren of Cornwall, George Wharton James of Lincolnshire, S. W. Altbone of London, John M. Dixon of Wales, and a dozen other Englishmen like David Wingford, John Collins, William R. Jenney, William Rule, and Colen Anderson provided the leadership for the Methodist Church in Nevada. The Episcopal Church enjoyed a similar infusion from Canada and England. Many of the Episcopal preacher-missionaries returned to their homeland after serving an apprenticeship on the frontier. Not atypical was an article which appeared in the *Reese River Reveille* of August 6, 1900, in which the community was informed of the marriage in Reigate, England, of their former pastor, the Reverend William Hamilton Stewart.[39] John Brown traveled directly from Scotland to organize one of the first Presbyterian churches in Nevada,[40] and other foreigners like Richard Waddell and James Woods led the early Presbyterian missions. At least a score of immigrant spiritualists, preachers, priests, and rabbis from non-English-speaking areas like Holland, Belgium, Norway, Denmark, Germany, Poland, Greece, Brazil, India, Italy, China, Peru, France, the West Indies, and the East Indies have played a role in the history of religious activity in Nevada.

Both the newspapers and the literature of Nevada greatly profited from the relatively large number of immigrant journalists and foreign-born travelers who were attracted to the state. The Irishman J. Ross Browne, in his witty and humorous *A Peep at Washoe,* was apparently the first to observe the rush of foreigners over the Sierra. In the half century following Browne's exposition, at least a score of immigrant writers contributed to the enrichment of Nevada journalistic literature. The Englishman George Dawson, the Australian D. E. McCarthy, and the Prussian A. Zehandelar all used the foreign born to enliven their stories of the Comstock. The Englishman John Booth and the two Frenchmen Andrew Casamayou and Andrew Maute followed a similar pattern as joint and separate proprietors of some half-dozen central and western Nevada newspapers. The Scotsman Arthur B. McEwen moved from the Comstock to Reno to San Francisco and finally to chief of editorial writers for the Hearst organization in New York City.

Patrick Mulcahy of Australia was the founder and longtime publisher of the *Sparks Tribune,* and William Sutherland of Quebec organized the first typographical union in the state and worked for over fifty years as a Nevada compositor. The French-Canadians T. E Picotte, editor of the *Lyon County Times,* and Alfred Chartz, writer for the Carson City *Morning Appeal,* along with the Englishman R. R. Parkinson, editor of *The Daily Nevada Tribune,* and the Scot William Webster, longtime owner and editorial writer for the *Nevada State Journal,* further typify the foreign-born newspapermen of western Nevada. J. F. Hahnlen was proprietor of the short-lived German language *Nevada Pionier* and later of the *Deutsche Union,* both of Virginia City, and H. M. Bien founded the *Staats Zeitung* to promote his candidacy for the Nevada assembly.

After the turn of the century, M. Paggi published the *Corriere Di Nevada* in Sparks and F. Moracci published the *Italian-French Colony* in Reno. Between 1915 and 1944, John Granata used the widely popular *Bollettino Del Nevada* to counsel and lecture the Italian community of Nevada and northern California. The presence of a German editor, Theodore F. Potlhoff of Goldfield, and an English editor, James Morris of Tonopah, along with German and French-Canadian cartoonists, points up the foreign influence in early twentieth-century southern Nevada. In addition, many of the foreign-language newspapers of San Francisco like the *Courrier Français des Etats-Unis* enjoyed an extensive circulation east of the Sierra. The German language edition of the *American Agriculturist,* and *The European Mail* of London, the *Cornish Telegraph* of Penzance, and a Serbian paper of Belgrade found a large number of subscribers in Nevada.[41]

The Italian businessman Lambert Molinelli authored an 1879 study of Eureka, and at about the same time, an Alsatian brewer, Jacob Klein, published *Founders of Carson City*. The numerous works by the Italian-born Reno attorney Anthony Turano have enjoyed a wide reception. A book-length memoir by the Swede Axel P. Johnson and short stories by the Cypriot Paul Ralli evaluate the lives of immigrants. Nevada has produced few collections of immigrant letters, but those written by H. F. Dangberg of Carson Valley to relatives in Germany before Nevada became a state are particularly valuable. They portray the dangers and hardships faced by a European settler on the edge of the frontier. The some half-dozen accounts penned by Heinrich Bruhn of the Unionville and Rye Patch area to relatives in Denmark point up the reactions of the mobile and uncommitted miner of the seventies.[42] Dozens of letters from Nevada were printed in the *Cornish Telegraph* of Penzance and the *West Briton* of Truro; and several Slavic letters were written to the *Borax Miner* of Columbus by former Nevadans who had returned to the Adriatic.

The professional and official positions held by the foreign born in the city of Hamilton typify the immigrant activity in one of Nevada's major towns. In June, 1870, Hamilton boasted a population of 3,913 people, almost half of whom had come from thirty-five different foreign countries. The mining superintendent for the largest company in the area was Austrian, a topographical engineer was Danish, and an architectural engineer Nova Scotian. One of the city's lawyers was from New Brunswick and another from Ireland. Hamins Herrick, the best known physician in town, was born and educated in the Netherlands, while Dominick Monteverde, the Catholic priest, was from Italy. German teachnicians generally operated the smelting furnaces, but a majority of their foremen were from England. Of eight practicing musicians in town, one was American, one was from Argentina, and six were from Germany. However, most of the city's 234 Germans, along with the 7 Russians and 7 Poles, were engaged in various forms of merchandising. Most public offices were held by the American born; however, several of the town's 480 Irish were on the police force, David Stribens of Malta was deputy county treasurer, and the keeper of the county records was an Englishman. Women from around the world participated in the oldest profession: China, Costa Rica, Chile, Peru, Mexico, the West Indies, New Granada, Ireland, France, and the German states supplied girls, many of whom were only sixteen or seventeen years of age. The main toll road into Hamilton was kept by a South African. And the *Daily Inland Empire,* like newspapers in other communities, was mainly an immigrant enterprise. James Ayres of Scotland was editor and publisher, while his printing and technical staff were Irishmen.[43]

Nevada's immigrants were always more than a silent minority, an ill-trained peasantry, or an intellectual mediocrity. They were among the social, economic, and political leaders of the state. Scores of the foreign born were able to find a personal meaning in Nevada and to translate their inheritance into a new perspective. They helped to make history and to create a legend.

Clearly their success was related to their heritage as well as to their environment. They applied both old and new values to the land and they gave significance and purpose to an age.

But in assessing a great migration, failures as well as successes must be noted. Many foreigners were repulsed by Nevada's sinister deserts, extravagant behavior, and general desolation. They deliberately refused to adopt the tempo or accept the values of Nevada's shifting society. In addition, many emotionally unstable persons were doomed to failure. Their fate is also part of the immigrant story.

[1] *Historical Statistics of the United States, Colonial Times to 1957* (Washington, D.C.: U.S. Bureau of Census, 1960), pp. 45–46. In addition to the seven-to-one net increase of foreign-born white over native-born white, there was also a net increase of 2,300 foreign orientals in the decade 1870–80. Thus the over-all foreign-born migration into the state was over ten times greater than the total American-born influx.

[2] Eliot Lord, *Comstock Mining and Miners* (Berkeley: Howell-North, 1959; a reprint of the 1883 edition), pp. 383–86.

[3] William Petersen and Lionel S. Lewis, *Nevada's Changing Population* (Reno: Bureau of Business and Economic Research, University of Nevada, 1965), p. 49.

[4] Eliot Lord and others, *The Italians in America* (New York: B. F. Buck and Company, 1905), p. 5.

[5] Enumerator's Report, Census of 1900, Eureka County, Nevada; and Census of 1910, Washoe County, Nevada.

[6] Enumerator's Report, Census of 1880, Lincoln County, Nevada.

[7] Enumerator's Report, Census of 1920, Lincoln County, Nevada.

[8] Petersen and Lewis, *Nevada's Changing Population*, p. 25.

[9] Mary Ellen Glass, "The Deutschen of Douglas: The German Foundations of Douglas County, Nevada, 1856–1930" (Master's thesis, University of Nevada, 1965), p. 49.

[10] *Territorial Enterprise*, August 8, 1876, p. 3, col. 3.

[11] *Territorial Enterprise*, June 15, 1875, p. 3, col. 3.

[12] *Territorial Enterprise*, June 8, 1875, p. 3, col. 3.

[13] *Territorial Enterprise*, January 2, 1876, p. 3, col. 2.

[14] Merle Curti, *The Making of An American Community* (Stanford: Stanford University Press, 1959), pp. 61 ff. and 154 ff.

[15] Enumerator's Report, Census of 1870, Nye County, Nevada.

[16] In addition to the 125 permanent foreign-born adult residents, there were 55 single French-Canadian, Italian, Swiss, and French wood cutters and charcoal burners who held no property and were employed in the hills several miles from town.

[17] Enumerator's Report, Census of 1870, Washoe County, Nevada.

[18] Enumerator's Report, Census of 1870, Humboldt County, Nevada.

[19] The German economic dominance in Douglas County has been sketched in a thesis by Mary Ellen Glass. During the 1880s when the Germans accounted for about 8 percent of the county's population they paid for over half of the advertising in the local *Genoa Weekly Courier* and owned more than one third of the pieces of property listed by the county assessor. By the early twentieth century, when German immigrants totaled about 12 percent of the county's population, they owned more than half of the pieces of property in the county. Glass, "The Deutschen of Douglas," pp. 70–71.

[20] Enumerator's Report, Census of 1880, Storey County, Nevada.

[21] Ibid.

[22] Interview with Myrtle Myles and Louise Dron, December 27, 1963. Both Mrs. Myles and Mrs. Dron were early residents of Smoky Valley.

[23] Enumerator's Report, Census of 1900, Humboldt County, Nevada.

[24] Enumerator's Report, Census of 1910, Humboldt County, Nevada.

[25] *Territorial Enterprise,* April 29, 1868, p. 3, col. 1.

[26] Sam P. Davis, *The History of Nevada* (Reno: The Elms Publishing Company, 1913). See volume II biographical entries for Michael Cohen and Eli Rinehart.

[27] *Morning Appeal,* January 24, 1892, p. 2, col. 1.

[28] See some twelve articles in the *Yerington Rustler, Reno Weekly Gazette, Gardnerville Record,* and *Mornnig Appeal* between October 1897 and October 1898.

[29] *The Carson Weekly,* November 4, 1907, p. 4, col. 3.

[30] *The Carson City News,* October 27, 1907, p. 1, col. 5.

[31] *The Humboldt Star,* March 29, 1911, p. 1, col. 3.

[32] *Morning Appeal,* January 22, 1915, p. 4, col. 2.

[33] *Morning Appeal,* November 9, 1879, p. 3, col. 2.

[34] One copy of all the presently available homographic charts is pre-

served in the Special Collections department of the University of Nevada Library, Reno.

[35] *Territorial Enterprise,* May 5, 1868, p. 3, col. 2.

[36] *Territorial Enterprise,* February 12, 1873, p. 3, col. 2.

[37] *Territorial Enterprise,* September 15, 1871, p. 3, col. 1.

[38] Enumerator's Report, Census of 1910, Washoe County, Nevada.

[39] *Reese River Reveille,* April 6, 1900, p. 3, col. 5.

[40] Myron Angel, ed., *History of Nevada* (Oakland: Thompson and West, 1881), pp. 193 and 216.

[41] *Tuscarora Times-Review,* July 25, 1887, p. 3, col. 3; and *Nevada State Journal,* February 10, 1876, p. 3, col. 2.

[42] The Dangberg letters are in the possession of Miss Grace Dangberg, Minden, Nevada. Waldemar Westergaard, *Denmark and Slesuig* (London: Oxford University Press, 1946), p. 119 ff.

[43] Enumerator's Report, Census of 1870, White Pine County, Nevada.

2

Immigrant Response to Nevada Life

Seldom have students of history had the opportunity to evaluate their work by questioning key participants in the events. Fortunately, part of the immigration to Nevada has been sufficiently recent to allow for personal interviews, and many of the first-person accounts have proven to be particularly cogent and revealing. Over a period of some four years during the mid-1960s, the writer talked with several hundred of Nevada's immigrants. Although all of those contacted contributed to a better human understanding of the foreign born and their problems, a set of rather well-defined criteria was eventually established, and statistics were compiled to help make the interviews more meaningful and objective.

There were approximately 1,500 immigrants eligible for interview under the guidelines, and 522 of these were questioned. The broad requirements of the survey were that the interviewee had migrated to Nevada as an adult (fifteen years of age or over) and that he had settled in Nevada before World War II. To eliminate misleading duplication, only one member of each family was included, and none of the interviewees' brothers or sisters also living in Nevada were counted. Every county and all foreign nationalities in the state were canvassed in approximately the same manner and with the same persistence. A complete canvass was relatively easy to make in small towns and rural areas, but

National or Cultural Background of Interviewees

Argentinean ...1	Czecho-	Norwegian 6
Armenian 1	slovakian ...1	Polish 1
Australian 1	Chinese 4	Portuguese ...22
Austrian 3	Danish 22	Russian 4
Basque	Dutch 5	Spanish 3
(French) ...26	Finnish 4	Swiss (French) 1
Basque	French 8	Swiss
(Spanish) ..63	German 44	(German) ..5
Belgian 1	Greek 28	Swiss (Italian) 10
Brazilian 1	Irish 16	Swedish 9
British 18	Italian 152	Turkish (Greek
Canadian	Japanese 6	speaking) ...5
(English) ...1	Latvian 1	Yugoslavian ..30
Canadian	Lithuanian 3	
(French) ...4	Mexican 12	

Residence of Immigrants at Time of Interview

NEVADA COUNTIES

Churchill 28	Humboldt 23	Ormsby 14
Clark 31	Lander 10	Pershing 26
Douglas 20	Lincoln 10	Storey 8
Elko 35	Lyon 28	Washoe 165
Esmeralda 5	Mineral 13	White Pine ...78
Eureka 15	Nye 13	

even in the cities Nevada's limited population, particularly before World War II, greatly facilitated the search.[1] In brief, the 522 persons represented something more than a random sample or a selected cross section of Nevada immigrant life. The interviews provided solid historical documentation and at the same time enlivened and humanized the census figures.[2]

The interviewees ranged from forty-four to ninety-nine years of age; the average migrant was retired and sixty-seven years old. They arrived in Nevada between 1884 and 1941, but over 50 percent had settled in the state before America entered World War I. Thirty-five percent of the interviewees were women and 94 percent were, or had been, married.

Approval, Criticism, and Mobility

Nevada became a magnet for immigrants after the discovery of the Comstock Lode in 1859. Over the following decades, the state experienced its first great population boom. Five of the immigrants interviewed arrived in Nevada during the eighties—at the end of the Comstock era. Sixteen (3 percent) settled in the state before the turn of the century. The second great rush occurred between 1902 and World War I; 57 percent of those questioned arrived during the first two decades of the twentieth century. A trickle of German and Russian refugees [3] and a larger number of Basque sheepherders, Danish dairymen, Portuguese farmers, and Italian laborers settled in Nevada during the 1920s and 1930s. The migration, therefore, spanned three-quarters of a century and the migrants offered personal observations on every major era of Nevada history with the exception of its territorial days and the early phase of the Comstock excitement.

Presumably, the lengthy residence within the state had allowed the foreign born to adjust to the environment and become favorably disposed toward western ideas and institutions. Those who disliked the area had been given several decades in which to leave. Thus, to justify their original decision to settle in the West and to explain their current status in life, it seemed rea-

47

sonable to expect older and established migrants to be rather sympathetic toward and uncritical observers of Nevada. A minority were vague, repetitive, and uncritical, but a majority were thoughtful, original, and highly independent in their thinking. Although cut off from their original roots, the foreign born had developed new connections, new beliefs, and new sources of strength. Their style was straightforward, their comments were revealing.

In general, the immigrants had not been well educated before their arrival in the state. Only twenty-seven (including ten priests) had the equivalent of a high school education. At the time of interview, twelve migrants could neither read nor write any language, four were unable to sign their names, and four spoke almost no English.[4] The majority were aware of, and in a sense were humbled by, their academic deficiencies. At the same time, most were conscious of their strengths. They understood their past. They knew loneliness and deprivation; they knew themselves. Most were not reluctant to say what they thought. Rather than trying to please by tacit agreement, many had developed a pleasant and dignified bluntness. Most were refreshingly forthright in their attitudes toward the Old World, toward Nevada, toward religion, and toward death. They were willing and often anxious to be of assistance. In the course of meeting over a thousand immigrants only nine persons pointedly refused to discuss their experiences and only two were insulting and threatening. Indeed, while conducting the interviews the author looked at dozens of well-tilled vegetable and flower gardens, received numerous gifts of tomatoes, corn, cucumbers, zucchini, apples, pears, roses, salami, and fish, and consumed much red wine and Turkish coffee.

A substantial majority of the men questioned (339, or 65 percent of the total were men) projected a positive reaction to Nevada. They emphasized the rough and masculine nature of the country, the opportunities to hunt and fish, the pleasant climate, and the lack of controls. A typical comment was that of an Italian who had worked as a school janitor for over forty years. "The day I arrived in Nevada I felt like an eagle. I have felt that way ever since." [5] Most men denied ever having been lonesome or homesick. An eighty-year-old native of Genoa who arrived in Ely at the turn of the century declared that he was so happy to get away from his family, from the church, and from poverty that he had never once doubted the wisdom of his decision. A seventy-four-year-old Tuscan who settled in Sparks responded, "To Hell with Italy. Life was miserable. It's not picturesque to see a woman with bare feet trudging up a steep dry mountain with a shock of hay on her back."

Perhaps thirty men justified their migration, but were more circumspect about both Nevada and themselves. An elderly Spanish Basque, who had only occasionally left Humboldt County during his forty years in America, explained, "I came because everyone seemed to be coming, and all young people want to go someplace." A Dutchman reflected the same ambivalence when he declared, "I don't know why I came to Austin. Some people are always looking, and I am one of them." Almost half of the men interviewed admitted that upon leaving their homeland they did not plan to settle permanently in the West. The reaction of an eighty-five-year-old Cornishman was typical. In his first letter home after arrival in Nevada, he emphasized that "under no circumstances will I remain in this state for more than five years." He had not been out of the state for more than two days at any one time since 1906.

A thoughtful and sensitive minority of some fifteen men readily admitted that they suffered from deep melancholia while in Nevada. The young Irish priest Daniel Murphy arrived at the Virginia City depot at dusk on February 1, 1907. "I saw buildings hanging on the side of a hill; they were in need of paint and repairs. It was cold, bleak, and depressing. I thought I had come to the end of the world." In 1930 a young Swiss farmer with an Austrian wife arranged by mail to be employed at a ranch near the isolated settlement of Hiko. "As we traveled by auto from Las Vegas we saw dead animals and sensed the forlorn desolation. When we arrived we found the place wretched, the end of the trail. There was no electricity; water was scooped from a ditch; and it was forty miles to a barber shop. I had been told in Switzerland that America was fifty years ahead of Europe and I found it fifty years behind." A French Basque who at nineteen arrived in Elko County to herd sheep confessed, "Of course I was homesick. If I had had the money I would have returned. Every evening as it got dark I started to cry. I didn't even have a tent until I had made enough money to buy one. I had borrowed money in France to come and would have borrowed more to return if it had been possible. I went to town twice in eight and one-half years. Yes, I saved money, but I was a damn fool to live that way. No, it cannot have been worth the sacrifice."

Many of the 183 women interviewed stressed an emotional apprehension upon arrival in Nevada. Only one said that she was confident and at ease as she traveled to the West, and only a minority agreed with the elderly Portuguese lady who reflected the traditional optimistic view of America. In 1922 she had settled on a remote sheep ranch near Battle Mountain. Ten years of her childhood had been spent in Brazil, but she had lived most of her young adult life in Lisbon. "People tell me that Lisbon must have been a beautiful city. I say, yes, it was if you were wealthy. But then the rich live well everywhere. The intelligent dominate everywhere. A few people succeed everywhere. But the poor, the uneducated, and the common people are a part of the dominant life here in Nevada. I am an American because I quickly understood and became a part of America. It is for the common people."

The Portuguese lady was an exception. Many women were depressed rather than impressed by the openness, the freedom, and the individuality of Nevada. More realistic and family-oriented than the men, they generally craved the personal association and social protection of an older and more stable environment. The better-educated women sensed the opportunity to build a new life and they appreciated the natural beauty of the country. But for most immigrant women, years passed before they learned to tolerate what they could not change.

Most women migrated reluctantly and their distress became particularly pronounced when they were forced to settle in an isolated community. In 1923 a London-born lady who had been converted to Mormonism arrived in McGill. She wrote home to England, "If we had gone one mile further into the wilderness, we would have dropped off the earth." She became despondent, tried to starve herself to death, and feigned tuberculosis so that she would be sent to a city for treatment. After over forty years in America she still "hated and despised" most aspects of western life. A seventy-year-old woman who had not seen her native Argentina for fifty years prayed nightly that she might be allowed to return home to die. And a woman who had been in Nevada for thirty-five years cried throughout much of the interview when she began to recall her "once happy life" in Italy. Soon after the turn of the century, a Swedish girl was drawn to the desolate camp of Blue Eagle (located halfway between Tonopah and Ely) to become a schoolteacher. Sixty years later she contended that "sagebrush, drunken Indians, and overwork" were the chief commodities of Nevada. A reflective Italian lady seemed to summarize the views of scores of Nevada immigrant women when she explained, "If we had not left Torino in 1922 we would have been better off socially, religiously, and probably financially."

Despite the lingering unhappiness of many of the immigrant women, the West proved to be an area where they were in great demand. A remarkably high percentage of Nevada's immigrants quickly formed family units. Indeed, all of the 183 women and all but 32 of the 339 men questioned (ten were Catholic priests) were or had been married. Seven had had as many as three spouses, and at least two score had been married twice.[6]

Of the 522 persons, 44 were married before their arrival in America, 272 married a person of the same nationality after arrival in the United States,[7] 30 traveled home to be married and quickly returned to Nevada, and 5 were married by proxy. In short, 351 of the 522 immigrants selected a spouse of their own nationality and/or culture, 117 selected an American-born spouse,[8] and 22 persons married someone from another foreign background. Rather surprisingly, numerically small foreign elements tended to marry within their national group as often as large immigrant groups. For example, there were few Czechs, Poles, Latvians, Finns, or Belgians in Nevada, and yet every interviewee from those foreign countries had a spouse of the same nationality.[9]

Immigrant marriage patterns were directly related to the foreign settlement patterns. Nevada was geographically isolated and demographically mobile; nevertheless, a close association developed between particular European communities and specific Nevada communities. One immigrant family tended to draw others. Almost two-thirds of the Italian farmers in the Yerington and Fallon areas came from the small Tuscan duchy of

Lucca. Redruth, St. Austel, Bodmin, and other Cornish towns provided Nevada with so many immigrants during the sixties and seventies that the newspapers in Cornwall spoke of the prosperity of Austin, Pioche, and Gold Hill as though they were in a neighboring valley. Many Dalmatians and Montenegrins of the Columbus and Candelaria area enjoyed an equally close contact with the ancient Adriatic port of Cattaro. Sixty percent of the state's Portuguese came from two small islands in the Azores. The agrarian Germans and Danes of Carson Valley were responsible for the migration of scores of young people from Hanover, Westphalia, and Schleswig-Holstein. Newly arrived girls generally were greeted by prospective bridegrooms anxious to renew memories of home. Of the 272 interviewees who married a person of the same nationality after their arrival in America, at least 57 of the men had known their future wives or wives' families in the Old World.

Even in remote Nevada many immigrants maintained a close connection with their parent country. For example, 278 of the 522 persons interviewed migrated directly to the state.[10] Of the interviewees in the fertile valleys of Douglas, Lyon, and Churchill counties, 86 percent had left their homeland for a Nevada farm. The 72 persons were almost equally divided among Germans, Danes, Basques, Portuguese, and Italians.[11] Conversely, a majority of the migrants in the newer urban centers had migrated to America and then drifted into Nevada: 87 percent of the immigrants questioned in Clark County (Las Vegas) had not known of Nevada before they left their homeland.

The close links between the Old World and the New World allowed immigrants to move back and forth with surprising ease. At least 39 of the 522 interviewees deserted Nevada to return to their native countries and then, after a stay of a year or more, made their way back to the West. Some 5 of the interviewees had returned home as many as five times before finally deciding to settle permanently in the state. In addition to the 39 who returned for an extended period and the 30 who returned to be married, at least 110 additional interviewees had visited friends and relatives in their native countries.[12]

Not only were many immigrants long uncertain as to whether they would remain in America, but almost one-fourth of the interviewees indicated that at least one of their brothers or sisters had become involved in the movements to and from America. In only 168 instances was the migrant questioned the only member from his family who had traveled to the United States.

Perhaps too much emphasis has been placed on the idea of two worlds; clearly, ties were not always completely severed. The Italians in particular sought to blend the old with the new. For example, the fathers of six of the Italians interviewed in the Dayton area (and seven others in Reno) had once lived in Nevada. They had returned to Italy, married, and reared a family. As the sons grew up they, in turn, migrated to Nevada. Such immigrants arrived already half-Americanized. Particularly in the twentieth century, thousands of Europeans have been able to maintain their connections at home and at the same time nurture a new life abroad.

Many immigrants came from mobile families. In eighteen cases a majority of the interviewees' brothers and sisters had migrated to another foreign country. Some of the Italians, Basques, and Portuguese had relatives in South America and Mexico, and several of the Germans, British, and Irish had family members in Canada and Australia. In addition, the parents and grandparents of migrants had sometimes moved from the Pyrenees to England, from Sweden to Denmark, Italy to France, Germany to England, or Austria to Switzerland. For a significant number of the foreigners in Nevada, migration was a family tradition.

Materialism, Discrimination, and Americanization

For practically all of the interviewees, the overwhelming objective had been to find employment. Work became their great design. Work was mentioned over and over again as though it had a purifying quality. Work, economic realism, and material success, along with frugality, ownership of property, and persistence, were considered the cardinal virtues. They formed the immigrant code. Few of the foreign born had any difficulty in accepting the competitive society or the American brand of materialism. Their willing hands readily fitted them into the traditional pattern of frontier life. The immigrants would tolerate few parasites. At the same time, they were more reluctant to desert a stagnant community or a dying town than were American-born pioneers. The foreign born of Nevada were slow to react when economic collapse loomed on the horizon. The Cornish lingered behind at Austin and Unionville, the Italians at Eureka and Dayton, the Irish at Virginia City and Gold Hill, and the Chinese at a score of declining mining camps.

Perhaps 80 percent of the persons interviewed had acquired economic or professional respectability. There were some fifty doctors, lawyers, professors, priests, preachers, artists, administrators, influential ranchers, and prominent businessmen. Over two hundred immigrants had become farmers, shopkeepers, foremen, and artisans. In addition, a number gained rewards of a more elusive, but no doubt more meaningful, kind. The Greek parents whose sons had progressed from athletics to become high-ranking military officers and the Basque parents whose sons became lawyers, a writer, and a governor of Nevada achieved the age-old, yet ever new, immigrant dream. The Armenian who migrated to the United States, then to France, to Egypt, back to France, and finally to the American West was equally proud of the athletic and professional success which his sons had earned. The fact that he had worked in a lumber mill, a battery factory, a railroad yard, a machine shop, a barber shop, and a dozen other jobs merely added to his confidence and security.

There were many human success stories. An eighteen-year-old Italian youth left his farm home near Rome in 1903. He traveled to Canada and became an agricultural laborer for a year, but returned to Italy in 1905. Again becoming dissatisfied, he worked on land and at sea and drifted to Turkey, Egypt, Palestine, India, Ceylon, Australia, China, Hawaii, and finally to California. While preparing to move to Alaska, a friend told him of the mines at Tonopah and in 1910 he arrived in Nevada. He had grown wheat in Quebec, traded silk in Smyrna, sold garden produce in Beirut, raised cattle in New Zealand, stripped sugarcane in the East Indies, and worked in a score of countries; nevertheless, he was fascinated with the human potpourri and natural panorama of central Nevada. For the next fifty years, he worked at odd jobs and grew fruit and vegetables on the desert. Many such immigrants found purpose and meaning by ignoring the social and materialistic pressures of the community. Such men were generally stubborn but receptive; they were often eccentric but realistic; they traveled their own road to a personal contentment.

On the other hand, not all immigrants were successful in Nevada. One interview was conducted in a dilapidated bus which had been converted into a house for four persons. Another elderly interviewee literally had no home other than a crude protection built between three huge rocks. His drinking water was stored in a rusty fifty-gallon gasoline barrel, and a kerosene lantern was used for light. A Portuguese who had left the mellow island of Flores in the Azores forty-three years earlier watched the wind and dust whip against the door of his rural home and remarked, "You need a good sense of humor to farm in Nevada." An eighty-one-year-old Irishman lived in a small yellow railroad shack between Wadsworth and Lovelock. His pension check was signed over to the proprietor of a small store who supplied his basic grocery needs. During his almost sixty years in Nevada, the lonely son of Galway had worked in every county in the state. He had finally grown old, and with neither a wife, nor relatives, nor close friends, he was quietly awaiting death in the railroad cabin. After patiently answering the interviewer's questions he explained, "This is the first time in my sixty years in America that anyone has shown the slightest interest in who or what I am." Most immigrants were neither rebels, nor heroes, nor martyrs, but many were subjected to the greatest of all indignities: they were ignored.

Almost 80 percent of the interviewees emphasized that they had experienced no prejudice or discrimination in Nevada. The expression, "I have always been treated right," was repeated with slight variations by scores of immigrants. Several persons were sufficiently relaxed to turn the question into a joke. A Norwegian lady explained that she had endured only one instance of unfriendliness; she had once been mistaken for a Swede. A French-Canadian who was referred to as "Froggy" insisted that he had never eaten frog legs, and a Scot claimed to have experienced "nervous frustrations" caused by hearing a local bagpipe band. A Dane who had been kicked by a cow declared that he had suffered personal harassment.

All of the twenty-two Danish interviewees expressed satisfaction with their treatment in America. The response of a sixty-seven-year-old cafe operator was typical. "Never, never, never have I experienced problems because I am foreign born. America has treated us royally." Two national groups expressed the belief that as foreigners they had enjoyed a distinct advantage in the state. Several French-born persons suggested that the cordial relationship maintained between the United States and France, along with their French accent, had assisted them in securing favorable economic and social positions. The Irish projected a similar affirmative outlook. One immigrant declared that it would be "a dark day indeed" when an Irish accent was frowned upon in America. A small number of Italians and Basques also believed that, in their search for employment, they had received special consideration. A few of the older interviewees explained that before World War I, persons who spoke only English were seldom employed in certain rural Nevada communities.

Despite the humor, the flippancy, and the favorable comment, some immigrants spoke seriously of real or imagined injustices, and members of certain nationalities were particularly sensitive about their foreign background. Some of the Basque, Italian, Portuguese, Greek, Slav, and Swiss migrants were critical of their treatment in Nevada. In the case of Basques, the complaint was mainly of a social nature. Parents cited incidents when their children were labled "Bascos." After the interviewer was invited through an unusually pleasant and well-kept home, a retired rancher pointedly asked, "Would you call us dirty Bascos?" Occasionally, members of other southern European nationalities spoke of social discrimination, but they were more often concerned with economic hardships. An elderly Portuguese woman declared: "Our problem was not whether we were accepted or not, our problem was trying to survive." An Italian mine worker contended, "We got the dirtiest jobs, we were paid the lowest wages, and we had to prove ourselves. But in the process of proving ourselves we worked twice as hard and thereby became a threat to union men." Several Croats and Serbs admitted that they were "sidewinders." When "treated worse than Negroes," they "dropped off" and looked for other employment. A Greek resented being forced to remove his hat when applying for work on the railroad. He eventually changed his name, kept on his hat, and got a better job.

Ironically, the foreign born were often intolerant of other immigrants. An Italian-Swiss farmer who settled in Carson Valley in 1920 asserted, "Yes, I faced real discrimination in Carson Valley. I had to prove myself not once, but many times. I was treated worse than Negroes in the South, not by American families, but by immigrants and the sons of the immigrants. German landowners and the English and Scots were the most unpleasant. A schoolteacher even told my children that the Germans and British made the best citizens." A well-educated German-Swiss sensed a different kind of bias among his fellow migrants. At any hint of criticism of American life or culture, his European friends would retort, "If you don't like it, take a boat."

Although fewer than a hundred persons recalled any examples of prejudice or bigotry, verbal indignities were not uncommon. The terms Hun, Dago, dirty Basco, black Portugee, dumb Bohunk, and stupid Greek were indelibly burned into the consciousness of a few of the newcomers. Of course, some foreigners were overly sensitive, some were neurotic, and some were unprepared for life in Nevada. A seventy-seven-year-old Austrian who arrived in the United States in 1907 proclaimed his loyalty to Emperor Franz Josef throughout both world wars and surrounded himself with Viennese mementos. He haughtily refused to become a citizen of the United States and vocally supported all things Germanic. Obviously, he experienced serious antagonism and was never accepted by the community.

Nevada's Japanese faced material and psychological repression during World War II. Although not placed in relocation centers, they were forbidden to leave the state, sometimes denied admission to the high school graduation of their children, and often economically plundered. Nevertheless, twenty years later, the Japanese registered little bitterness and stoically described the war as an "unfortunate catastrophe."

Many German immigrants found the war even more humiliating than did the Japanese. Traditionally, few groups had been accepted more completely than the Germans and none had blended more quickly into Nevada life. Although they had fought vigorously for their foreign-language press and had established many national societies in the state, their loyalty and Americanism had never been questioned. Suddenly, in World War I and again in World War II, these proud and sometimes arrogant people found themselves the object of attack. Almost 70 percent of the forty-four Germans interviewed believed that the action of both public and private groups created an atmosphere in which they were reduced to second-class citizens. Some interviewees dismissed the anti-German frenzy as the product of hysterical and deranged minds, but most Germans could not forgive a society which questioned their honesty and restricted their actions. In many instances neither the Germans nor the nativists acted or reacted wisely, and while time has healed the wounds, it has not fully repaired the emotional injury.

Although numerous interviewees noted examples of prejudice, only a few persons, mainly from the mining communities of central and eastern Nevada, had experienced major racial tension or violence. Some of Nevada's immigrants were affected by the antiforeign tide which swept across America in the decade before World War I, but almost none of the newcomers were discriminated against during the anti-immigrant hysteria of the

1920s. Most of the instances of conflict were of a personal and individual nature. Most immigrants within the state were active, politic, and realistic, and most quickly rose above petty animosities. Only the wars left scars which could not be expunged.

Perhaps the comments of the 522 interviewees allow for several broad generalizations about both the foreign born and the Nevada scene.[13] Several trends seem obvious. Most Nevada immigrants were not average or typical of their native communities. They did not represent a cross section of any foreign society; rather, they were persons who, for one reason or another, did not fit into their home environment. They were drawn to America and the West because of specific opportunities and certain urges and as a consequence they abandoned the balance which their traditional society had provided. They convinced themselves that the one or two advantages to be obtained in Nevada would overshadow the loss which they would sustain through emigration. Therefore, they were intense if somewhat narrow, energetic if somewhat single-minded; they were not typical of the rich cultures from which they came.

On the one hand, most of Nevada's immigrants did not wish to transfer the Old World to the New, or reproduce in the West the customs they had left behind. When exposed to new forces and new pressures, their national traditions were quickly blurred and their native temperament reshaped. Yet, on the other hand, most of the immigrants were robust spirits intent on retaining an independence of mind as they were Americanized. Most were genuinely proud of their background and unashamed of their immigrant status. Seldom were their customs and attitudes totally erased.

Obviously, most broad generalization must be qualified and circumscribed. For example, a few of the foreign born with wide European experiences had tenaciously held to their old ideas and culture; they seemed fearful of becoming homogenized. Others with a similar background had enthusiastically adopted the new ways of living and thinking. But even the most Americanized immigrants were sometimes the least receptive to American practices. Some quite sophisticated and well-integrated French, German, and British migrants were keenly critical of Nevada society. Equally paradoxical was the immigrants' attitude toward their own cultural organizations. They tended to become active in their local festivals only after many years in the state. The Basques were typical of the trend. More than any other ethnic group they had retained their colorful traditions, but they seem to have accomplished it less through direction than by accident. As they encouraged their own Americanization, they simultaneously reawakened an old romantic association with the past.

Of course, each immigrant group projected its peculiar character and talents. The Italians were the most likely to have had a father who had once lived in America and to have relatives in another foreign country. The Basques were the most likely to have traveled directly to Nevada, to have married someone of the same nationality, and to have remained loyal to their religion. The Irish and Swedes were most likely to have drifted into the state. None of the Swedish or Irish men interviewed joined relatives or friends in Nevada. The Yugoslavs were the most likely to have changed or discarded their religious faith. The Greeks were the most loyal or emotionally attached to their homeland. At least seven of the Greek men interviewed had returned at one time to their native country to join the army. The Chinese and the Mexicans were the most likely to have failed to become citizens and the most disinclined to engage in political or social comment.[14] The Germans were the most likely to have rebelled against their family and rather blindly set out for

America;[15] they most often professed atheism and were the most critical of their treatment in Nevada.

A few immigrants became traditionalists in that they clung to memories and ideas from the past. Since they had been able to bring little with them to America, they soon came to reaffirm the value of their old religious, moral, or social beliefs. But the majority of immigrants, while maintaining their basic religious philosophy, readily agreed that Nevada life had forced a change in their religious practices and even in their spiritual outlook. In the vast distances of the West, the authority of the bishops shriveled. Many of the older immigrants had blended their religion with humanism. They professed a faith, but were confused and a little critical of the religiosity and church attendance of their American-born children and grandchildren. Thirty-seven persons stressed their nonbelief in any established religion and nine were antireligious. Ten men declared that they left the Old World, in part, to escape from the "nonsense of the church." A German summarized the attitude of several immigrants when he explained, "I don't believe in God or the Devil, in Heaven or Hell. I believe in evolution, nature, and common sense. There was no beginning and there is no end. I dislike bigots, the church, and self-appointed patriots."[16]

Two-thirds of the interviewees had become members of the Republican party, but almost all viewed Nevada as a great equalizer. Arrival in the state had been their first step on the road up as well as a move toward greater personal independence. As strangers without credentials, they had been allowed to engage in the race for wealth and position. And although not always pleased with the results, relatively few migrants argued that they had not been allowed to compete.

The number of occupations open to immigrants in Nevada was always limited. Upon their first arrival in the state, almost none had surplus capital with which to speculate nor did the majority have sufficient funds to invest in ranches, or mines, or forests, or businesses. At least four hundred of the interviewees had been reared in a rural or village environment, and many started their career in Nevada by engaging in some form of agriculture. Nevada became famous for its mines, its railroads, and later for its tourist industry, and many immigrants dug ore, laid rails, or became service personnel. Some of the foreign born converted dilapidated shops into lucrative businesses and others helped to transform boom towns into industrial centers. However, the largest single number of interviewees were first drawn to the state by friends and relatives who offered them jobs working on the land.[17] It was the foreign born more often than the American born who turned arid hills into profitable sheepwalks, scrub cedars into valuable charcoal, and wasteland into rich farmlands.

Although Nevada's immigrants practiced a vigorous brand of materialism, most circumvented moral rigidity and the straight-laced codes of the early twentieth century; most clung to the belief that life was given to be enjoyed. The foreign born helped to make a physically vast region into a rather colorful and intimate state; they offset Nevada's political provincialism with a personal cosmopolitanism. They did not undertake to expose social wrongs, and they were not personally outraged by the injustice of the age. They engaged in little psychological penetration; they were objective and materialistic rather than contemplative and visionary. They were a paradox. Their lives were usually dull and flat and linear and yet they were warm and sympathetic and they filled Nevada with contrast.

[1] There were 11,011 foreign-born persons in Nevada in 1940. Some had not migrated as adults; many died or left the state before the mid-1960s;

In 1867, at eighteen years of age,
William Frederick Zadow (left) emigrated
from Czarnikau in Pozen to Eureka, Nevada.
He quickly opened a butcher shop which
he operated until the first World War.
The Italian Philip Paroni (second from
right) also ran a butcher shop in Eureka.
Picture taken in 1880. (Courtesy
of Nevada Historical Society)

Reno, looking north up Virginia Street from
the Truckee River, about 1870. Note the
"liquors, wine, and fruit depot" of Andrew Milatovich.
Milatovich, an immigrant from Dalmatia, owned one
of the most cosmopolitan stores in Virginia City
and in 1868 opened one of the first stores in Reno.
The Reno store was operated by M. Radovich and
Z. Chicovich, also from Dalmatia.
(Courtesy of Nevada Historical Society)

In 1866, as a lad of sixteen, Angelo Ferretto traveled
from Genoa, Italy, across Europe to England where he
embarked for Panama. After walking across the Isthmus
he sailed for San Francisco, then hiked over the Sierra
to Virginia City. In Nevada he was employed loading
camels and cutting timber but eventually bought
land at Huffakers, south of Reno, and developed an
extensive freighting business. The picture shows
one of Ferretto's outfits in Virginia City
in 1887. (Courtesy of Nevada Historical Society)

Lucky Boy, located seven miles southwest of
Hawthorne, was typical of the short-lived
mining towns of early twentieth-century Nevada.
The camp was founded in early 1909; this
photograph was taken later the same year. By 1910,
twenty-four different national groups were represented among the community's 274 inhabitants.
Harry Cantor, born in Mexico of Serbian parents,
and Amelia Murphy, a Syrian with an Irish
husband, ran restaurants. The barber was a
German, the self-proclaimed doctor-nurse
a French-Canadian, and probably the town's
first prospector was a native of Gibraltar.
(Courtesy of Nevada Historical Society)

In 1880, 59 percent of the 7,086 people in
Eureka County were foreign born. Some 12 percent
of the county's population was from Italy.
The twenty-eight-year-old Swiss-Italian
Louis Monaco had become one of eastern Nevada's
leading photographers and social critics. He
played a leading role in the "Italian Wars" of 1879.
This is from a stereopticon of Eureka taken by
Monaco at the time of the conflict in 1879.
(Courtesy of Nevada Historical Society)

The photograph shows the central and southern
part of Virginia City in 1869. In the immediate
foreground is Van Bokkelen's Park, the site of many
German picnics. In the right foreground is the famous
Chinese garden which supplied the city with its finest
vegetables. (Courtesy of Bancroft Library, Berkeley)

The new International Hotel on the west side
of C Street in Virginia City was completed
in 1876. Both the hotel and the businesses
along C Street were operated almost exclusively
by immigrants. Picture taken in 1877.
(Courtesy of Bancroft Library, Berkeley)

No 9680.

CURLING & Co
ASSAYERS
VIRGINIA CITY N.

1630.70. OZS.

SILVER 962 FINE

GOLD 032.5 FINE

SILVER $ 2028.26.

GOLD $ 1095.50.

TOTAL $ 3123.76.

FÜR

DIE VERWUNDETEN UND HINTER-
BLIEBENEN DER GEFALLENEN
IM DEUTSCH-FRANZÖSISCHEN
KRIEGE 1870 VOM STAAT

NEVADA.

GERMANY, BATTLING FOR UNITY
AND CIVILIZATION, COMMANDS
THE SYMPATHY OF REPUBLICAN
AMERICA. WE MAY NOT DRAW
THE SWORD, BUT WOULD HELP
TO STANCH YOUR WOUNDS.

VIRGINIA. NEVADA.

A gold and silver bar worth $3123.76 and measuring 20″ by 8″ by 3½″ was forged for the Germans of western Nevada and sent to Berlin in late 1870. The brick was to be used "for the wounded and the widows and the orphans of the fallen" in the Franco-Prussian War. (Courtesy of Doten Diaries, University of Nevada, Reno) most were married to another immigrant and were ineligible for interview; and several had foreign-born brothers or sisters in the state who were also ineligible for interview. Therefore, only an estimated 1,500 persons were available for special study under the restrictive guidelines.

[2] During the eight years since the first interviews were conducted, many of the subjects have died. On July 1, 1963, the author was scheduled to talk with an elderly Russian immigrant. Upon arrival at his home the house and street seemed peculiarly quiet, and the writer learned that most of the small community was attending the old gentleman's funeral. Numerous similar instances of death or mental decay suggested that the last of the foreign-born frontiersmen were rapidly passing.

[3] Other nationalities also supplied refugees. For example, in 1866 a Danish child was carried from his home in Holstein as the Prussian military entered the village. His parents refused to live under German rule, and in 1884 the young man made his way to Nevada and became a stage driver between Bodie and Carson City. When interviewed in 1963 he had been a resident of Nevada for 79 years.

[4] Two of the four non-English speakers were Basque women who had been in Nevada for over forty years.

[5] Approximately one-third of the interviewees requested that their names not be used, and approximately one-fourth asked that their comments not be associated with them or their community. Therefore, notes will not be used to identify specific quotes.

[6] To eliminate confusion only the first marriage is used in the statistics.

[7] The 272 marriages were between persons of similar cultural and linguistic backgrounds. For example, ethnically related peoples such as Spanish Basques and French Basques, Italian-Swiss and Italians, English and Irish, Orthodox Turks and Greeks are considered to be of one nationality.

[8] The Germans, British, and Scandinavians were the most likely to select an American-born spouse.

[9] Approximately half of the 114 husbands and wives who were American born were from homes in which one or both parents were of the same nationality as the foreign-born spouse.

[10] Only two immigrants had been in the United States for over twenty years before arriving in Nevada.

[11] Of the 28 Basques interviewed in Elko County, 25 had migrated directly to Nevada to engage in some form of agriculture.

[12] Mexicans and Canadians were only slightly more likely to return to their homeland for a visit than Europeans or Asiatics. Only 4 of 12 Mexicans interviewed had recrossed the border.

[13] George W. Pierson of Yale University has advanced several hypotheses and pointed to many human characteristics which help to explain the historic movement in America. Perhaps Professor Pierson's most concise discussion of movement and mobility is found in Franklin D. Scott, ed., *World Migration in Modern Times* (Englewood Cliffs, N.J.: Prentice-Hall, Inc., 1968), p. 51 ff.

[14] Only 62 of the 522 interviewees had not become American citizens. Many of the Orientals had been denied citizenship by statute and some of the Mexicans had entered the country illegally. They had tended to avoid any complications with immigration officials.

[15] A young Polish-German boy made his way to the port of Danzig in 1907. There were ships in the harbor preparing to sail for Australia, South America, and the United States. He asked for passage on the ship scheduled to sail first and rather by chance arrived in America.

[16] Of the 522 interviewees, 312 were Roman Catholic, 101 Protestant, 44 Orthodox, 6 Mormon, 4 Buddhist, 2 Hebrew, 37 nonbelievers, and 9 antireligious.

[17] Five interviewees proudly declared that they earned their livelihood during the twenties as bootleggers, a girl was attracted by the opportunity to become a maid at the Governor's Mansion, one man was confined in the penitentiary soon after his arrival, and others were engaged as band directors, sculptors, and artists. But the most common occupation for the newly arrived foreign born was that of sheepherder, ranch hand, dairyman, section hand, or mine laborer.

PART *Two*

The Immigrants' Interpreters

3

Early Journalists and Novelists

In clarifying and interpreting immigrant life, novelists, biographers, and journalists have sometimes caught the forces of human emotion and the habits of a people's mind more tellingly than the empirically oriented interviewer or historian. Literature, newspapers, and adventure stories have helped to fill out the immigrant scene. Often the romantic notions which played their part in the migratory movement became more meaningful when fictionalized. At any rate, the immigrant has emerged as a valid subject for fiction and biography. Of course literature has not always elevated and clarified; sometimes it has diminished a subject (note the many trite and stereotyped westerns). But while the various Nevada writers have not always uncovered hidden secrets, they have often noted common foreign-born themes.

Scores of Nevada journalists transformed nondescript and otherwise insignificant news items into local color. They recognized that their isolated communities had only limited reading matter and that almost anything would be welcomed by their subscribers. Most editors competed with the town grapevine and at the same time gave extensive coverage to state, national, and international affairs. Entertaining vignettes from magazines and other papers as well as descriptive and historical essays filled several columns in most local papers. But above all, work on a western journal gave room for individuality, and the lack of feature services called for originality. Each community's newsmen learned to weave a diverse assortment of miscellaneous bits into humorous, engaging, and boisterous stories, and thus many western journalists became novelists.

For over fifty years, journalists and newspapermen tended to fill Nevada's literary vacuum. Throughout many of the narratives ran the usual strand of frontier hyperbole and audacious exaggeration. The more talented writers often mixed metaphors, misquoted the scriptures, contorted English grammar, scorned eastern elegance, and delighted in western wit and wisdom. Many were more intent on reflecting than correcting the group mores. They were pragmatic, yet they were inspired as much by man's failure as by his success. They were romantic, yet they emphasized the drab and the debilitating. Their stories were often selective, interpretive, and image making. Nevadans are no doubt what they are today partly because the early writers fashioned an image for the state. Traditions do not exist in themselves. If a literature grows out of a society it also transforms a society, and critics like J. Ross Browne, Dan De Quille, and Mark Twain revealed traits about their milieu which helped to create and transform as well as to delineate and explain Nevada life.

Three Pathfinders

One of the first writers to capitalize on the Nevada theme was the widely traveled and versatile journalist J. Ross Browne. Browne's father had been editor of the *Dublin Comet,* but a continuing opposition to British policies resulted in the paper's suppression and the editor's serving a short term in prison. He eventually sailed with his family for America in 1833. Young Browne helped at a sawmill in Indiana, operated a ferry out of Louisville, Kentucky, worked on a flatboat on the Ohio and Mississippi rivers, became a correspondent for newspapers, enrolled in a medical college, and served as a stenographic reporter in Congress. After trying a dozen different occupations, he signed on as a merchant seaman with a Portugese crew which traveled to the Indian Ocean. Browne left the ship at Zanzibar, lived among the Arabs, sailed with a whaling and fishing fleet, became a writer for *Harper's Magazine,* held confidential appointments with the government, and hastened to California during the gold rush of 1849. He was employed as a stenographer for the California Constitutional Convention, traveled to Europe as a journalist for several magazines, moved on to the Holy Land, returned to California to become a rancher, accepted a government appointment to work with the Indians, and in March and April of 1860 he participated in the rush to the Comstock.

"A Peep at Washoe" was a humorous account of Browne's first trip to Nevada. The essay originally appeared in *Harper's Monthly Magazine* in December, 1860, and in January and February, 1861. It was fortunate that a man of Browne's broad experience and marked ability was in the vanguard of the group of journalists and writers who for the next twenty years publicized and interpreted life on the Comstock. He not only knew how and what to write, he also knew how to develop the merest reality into an exciting adventure. The genial Irishman had observed and recorded the peculiarities of mankind in the Azores, Madagascar, Peru, Syria, Algeria, Iceland, Spain, and Russia. In 1853 he had published *Yusef—A Crusade in the East,* in which the grand tour was satirized and a literary approach laid for Mark Twain's *Innocents Abroad*. In "A Peep at Washoe" he satirized the grand rush to the Comstock and provided a forerunner for *Roughing It*.

As Browne moved east through the Sierra in March, 1860, he noted that

> an almost continuous string of Washoeites stretched 'like a giant snake dragging its slow length along' as far as the eye could reach. In the course of this day's tramp, we passed parties of every description and color: Irishmen wheeling their blankets, provisions, and mining implements on wheel-barrows; American, French, and German foot-passengers leading heavily-laden horses, or carrying their packs on their backs, and their picks and shovels slung across their shoulders; Mexicans, driving long trains of pack-mules, and swearing fearfully, as usual, to keep them in order . . . in short, every imaginable class, and every possible species of industry was represented in this moving pageant.[1]

While making little attempt to analyze his fellow travelers carefully, Browne, like Mark Twain a few years later, had a quick eye for character and an unfailing good humor. He smilingly repeated the typical clichés and attitudes of the day. On one occasion he cautioned all "freeborn Americans . . . unless you were born in Ireland, which is so much the better, or in Germany, which is better still," not to persist in their headlong rush to Nevada.[2] And he used a German Jewish rogue, who stole his socks on the way to Virginia City and his boots on the return to California, to exemplify the personal hazards associated with the trip to Washoe. Browne's Spanish-speaking vaqueros, German stage stationmasters, and European organ-grinders provide the narrative with zest, variety, and a rapid tempo, and at the same time they identify the immigrants and give them both a farcical and a human simplicity.

In the same year that Browne wrote "A Peep at Washoe," a less experienced and sophisticated, but equally sensitive, reporter trekked over the Sierra from California. William Wright (Dan De Quille) had been born in Ohio of Quaker stock and had moved with his parents to Iowa in 1847. Ten years later, when twenty-eight years of age, he joined the ranks of the California miners. Arriving on the Comstock during the spring of 1860, De Quille built a stone hut in Gold Canyon near Devils Gate, collected lizards, toads, and scorpions for pets, and within two years had sent forty-four articles to the leading journal of the West, the *Golden Era* of San Francisco. During the spring and summer of 1861, he traveled about Nevada and composed a series of tales known as "Washoe Rambles." They first appeared in the *Golden Era* between July and December, 1861. Although De Quille has generally been known for *History of the Big Bonanza* (1876) and *A History of the Comstock Silver Lode & Mines* (1889), "Washoe Rambles" was superior to either of the later works in literary technique. De Quille, like Browne, has been given credit for establishing the style followed in *Roughing It*.

Many of the stories incorporated into "Washoe Rambles" were not original. Literate and alert travelers like De Quille often seized upon local tales and became the middlemen in creating the frontier hero, in capitalizing on the eccentric backwoodsmen, or in poking fun at the unwary newcomer. De Quille's most pointed immigrant story involved the occupants of a stagecoach who attempted to cross the mountains during the winter of 1860 and were caught in a Sierra snow blizzard. All of the stranded travelers cooperated in the emergency except a German merchant, "a grumbling thief of a Jew," who drank his own whiskey, seized more than his portion of the food, and refused to do his share of the work. Eventually the Americans decided to correct the injustice. With a typical frontier cunning they sharpened their bowie knives and spoke in quiet tones of the coming feast. The "lubberly Teuton" was almost instantly frightened into the performance of a multiplicity of tasks. In making himself indispensable to the group, he gathered the wood and cooked the food and even agreed to search for José, a Spaniard in the party who had become lost in the storm. When José was found nearly frozen to death it was the German's whiskey which helped to revive him.[3]

De Quille used the Jewish peddler as a foil with which to flatter the American reader and interject the meaning of comradeship and frontier democracy. There was an unwritten, but well-understood, code which drew men together in times of danger: all were to forsake personal ambition and coalesce to combat the common enemy. Since the time of Captain John Smith, frontiersmen had sensed nature's indifference to their needs; therefore, cooperation for survival had become instinctive for Americans, whereas uninitiated and egotistical foreigners had to be taught the necessity of mutual dependence.

The incongruity of the term "Teutonic Jew" was not readily apparent to De Quille's nineteenth-century readers. Both Browne and De Quille built stories around the arrival of German Jews, and later novelists like the popular William MacLeod Raine returned to the theme in the twentieth century.[4] The subject was a logical one for De Quille and his imitators since many of the leading merchants and itinerant peddlers of Nevada were German Jews, and much of the small-town wealth was in their hands. While the federal census does not list religious preference, many nineteenth-century Nevada census takers entered the term Yiddish or Hebrew in the column requesting native language spoken. Indeed, German Jews seem to have been partly responsible for the impressive financial dominance enjoyed by the Germans in early day Nevada.

Most of the estimated 250,000 Jews in the United States in 1880 were from Germany. They were scattered throughout the country, but many had gravitated to German communities in the Middle West and Far West. While in Europe, the Jews had absorbed German culture and borrowed heavily from Christian customs; they had a limited feeling for religious unity and organized relatively few Jewish societies. They considered themselves thoroughly Germanized, but like most Europeans quickly substituted the American system for their ethnic background. Tradition could not compete with the open society, and the more clannish Eastern European Jews later referred to them as "capitalistic oppressors." The clash of interests could be seen on the Comstock in 1875 when the few Polish and Russian Jews organized a synagogue while the much larger body of German Jews generally refused to participate.

De Quille suggested that the "Teutonic Jews," after a few simple object lessons, quickly assimilated into the frontier culture. There were obvious rewards for identification with the new society. Within a generation many of the immigrants were numbered among Nevada's oldest and most distinguished families. In the absence of discrimination, many rose to positions of public prominence and often simultaneously became Episcopalian. Although the Nevada novelists saw the Jews as requiring orientation, no ethnic group in Nevada adapted more readily, more completely, and more successfully.

Dan De Quille also made forays into the field of western and immigrant drama. As the first Nevadan to write theatrical literature, he early linked the foreign born with the state's boom-camp environment. In this, he was capitalizing on the successes enjoyed by the Nova Scotian James Stark. After a tour throughout Europe and Australia, Stark introduced the comedy *Irish Immigrants* on the Comstock in 1861. Other plays dealing with immigrants quickly followed, and De Quille, seizing upon the idea, emerged with the comedy *The Wheelers of Washoe: or Taking in a Stranger from the Bay* in March, 1862. The play created Dennis O'Flaherty, "a fine Hibernian lad," who protected and wooed a local "Yankee gal of the right stripe." At least a dozen Irish comedies were staged in Virginia City during the early sixties and an even larger number of foreign artists arrived to provide theatrical talent. During the late sixties and throughout the seventies, the Nevada mining towns followed the lead of eastern cities by staging scores of immigrant oriented plays.[5]

In 1861 when Orion Clemens was appointed Territorial Secretary for Nevada he selected his younger brother Samuel (Mark Twain) as his private secretary. Arriving in Nevada during the summer, Sam was immediately fascinated by the "perpetual circus parade." After enjoying a short excursion to Lake Tahoe, he joined the rush to the Humboldt in December of 1861, but failed to find either fame or fortune at Unionville. Upon returning to Carson City, he learned of the rich strikes in Esmeralda County and within a few weeks traveled south to the Aurora district. Again he was unsuccessful. Consequently, in September, 1862, some fifteen months after his arrival in Nevada, Sam accepted a post as reporter (temporarily vacated by De Quille) on the Virginia City *Territorial Enterprise*. He remained on the *Enterprise* after De Quille returned, but in May, 1864, left for San Francisco.

The younger Clemens did not particularly stress the foreign-born complexion of Virginia City. However, his most famous Nevada article, the hoax of October 28, 1863, introduced an important immigrant feature in a story about a madman who massacred his wife and seven of his nine children near Nicholas Ambrosia's stage station on the Carson River. Both Browne and De Quille had used Ambrosia in their writing, and as the result of Clemens's "Dutch Nick's Affair," the station became a significant frontier landmark in both fact and fiction. For a hundred years, Nevada's journalists and novelists have embellished and dramatized the Dutch Nick theme.[6]

In 1869 Mark Twain published the immediately popular *Innocents Abroad*. His success with burlesque and the amusement aroused by his parody on Old World culture led him to follow a similar approach when he fictionalized his western experiences. *Roughing It* (1872) was the zestful but formless account of the author's travels to Nevada, California, and Hawaii. The best anecdotes and most exuberant tales were drawn from the Nevada years.

The book made numerous references to the foreign born of territorial days. There were the Chinese whom the young Missourian hoped to employ to do his swearing for him; the "Irish Brigade" who had accompanied Governor Nye from New York; the German baker of Aurora who had fits; the Irish landlady at Carson City who was amusingly characterized as French; the Irish girl who secured favors from Mormons with the aid of a butcher knife; the Virginia City telegraph boy who substituted impressive names from the Berlin city directory for those of local Germans; and the Swede who sang the maudlin song about "sister and brother" and a child "in the grave with its mother."

Three of the stories in *Roughing It* carried a distinct foreign-born theme. On the return to Carson City from the Humboldt in early 1862, Mark traveled with two associates. The aggressive and overconfident Prussian, Allendorff, consistently selected the wrong trail, overturned the canoe on the Carson River, lost the supplies, and finally led his two fatigued companions into a blinding snow storm. And when the small party became convinced that it was to die of cold and exposure, the Prussian emerged as a frightened and uncertain man. But while the German's actions were aggravating and often preposterous, Twain refrained from ridicule or caricature and even emphasized that the foreigner's confusion or fear was no greater than that of the other members of the trio. Mark Twain cleverly selected and identified certain of the foreign types drawn to the frontier. He used their extreme behavior for amusing and occasionally dramatic effect. But despite annoying foreign characteristics, he suggested that a man's place of origin had little to do with his true character.

In a second major notice of Nevada's foreign born, Twain recaptured the raillery and pungency of *Innocents Abroad*. He argued that since a community could best be understood by the type of person it honored with a stylish funeral, the burial of Buck Fanshaw fairly revealed the progress and sophistication of Virginia City. Buck was a mature all-around citizen. He had killed a man, lived with a mistress, held a post with the fire department, and operated a saloon. When delirious with typhoid fever, he had taken arsenic, shot himself, cut his throat, and jumped out of a fourth story window; therefore, at the inquest the authorities determined that he had died "by the visitation of God." But most significant, he had preserved order in the town by licking "four Greasers in eleven minutes," by driving some stone-throwing "Micks" away from the Methodist Sunday School, and by taking as his motto in life "No Irish Need Apply." Buck used the phrase repeatedly in connection with his public and private business enterprises; therefore, after the funeral service was finished and the last prayer had been offered up for his soul, a pall-bearer and mourner responded "in a low voice, but with feeling, 'Amen. No Irish Need Apply.' " [7]

78

One chapter of *Roughing It* was devoted exclusively to Nevada's Chinese and to their peculiarly harsh treatment at the hands of white men. The Orientals were portrayed as a quiet people who, when treated "no worse than dogs," remained placid and cooperative. But they were daily scorned and insulted by the community and occasionally they were beaten and stoned to death in broad daylight without arousing a single protest. Twain sarcastically emphasized that "ours is the land of the free," and then suggested that westerners were peculiarly conscious of their freedom since they refused to extend it to the Orientals. Voting, testifying in court, and educating their children were denied to the non-Caucasians.[8] The tongue-in-cheek exaggeration and the subtle wit characterizing most of *Roughing It* was temporarily set aside while Twain offered a serious lecture on the disgraceful handling of Oriental aliens. He categorized the anti-Chinese leaders as scum and the policemen and politicians who carried out their wishes as "the dust-licking pimps and slaves of the scum."[9] In the Chinese chapter Twain moved beyond both satire and irony and dealt directly with the sham and the tragedy of the frontier. He saw the savage and cruel capability of man— so deftly handled later in *The Adventures of Huckleberry Finn*.

Mark Twain arrived on the Comstock at a moment that permitted the spontaneous exploitation of the society's temperament. He was able to create an individual style with unmistakable elements of novelty. He worked hard, enjoyed good luck, and became a master artist. He used humor to reflect the popular and the ridiculous and he employed the immigrant as both a colorful embellishment and a human motif in his writing. Even the peculiarities, acts of folly, and annoying practices of the foreign born were amusingly reviewed and brushed aside, and he remained patient and pleasant in exposing the hypocrisy, the religious bigotry, and the snobbery of various American types. But while Mark Twain made a joke of the violence and despair to be found in Nevada's mining camps, he also pointed to the dark side and the gloomy aspects of western life. And finally, native attitudes toward the Oriental tended to fortify his pessimistic evaluation of mankind.

Although not specifically immigrant novelists, Browne, De Quille, and Twain all blended the foreign born into the Nevada phenomenon. As astute chroniclers of the picturesque, they developed a folk tradition into a popular literature, and as reporters of the exuberant frontier, they used the immigrant to develop a vein of humor and ridicule which was highly profitable. Unfortunately, neither the provocative attitude toward western life nor the sensitivity to the foreign born was maintained by some of their nineteenth-century successors.

Literary Contrasts

John Franklyn Swift and Charles C. Goodwin were typical of the authors who stubbornly ignored or blindly overlooked Nevada's foreign born. Swift's work *Robert Greathouse* emphasized a kind of "know-nothing attitude" whereby the writer neither identified himself with nor considered the social complexities of Virginia City life. Over a period of several years, Swift made his way from a Missouri farm to a major San Francisco business firm. As a successful produce merchant, he turned in 1852 to the study of law, became a diplomat and friend of Lincoln, traveled widely in Europe, wrote articles, authored a book about his experiences in the Middle East, joined the advocates of Chinese exclusion, and led the anti-Catholic forces as a candidate for governor of California. He consistently refused to believe that the arrival of poverty-stricken Catholics, Jews, and Orientals should in any way change the Anglo-Saxon features of American or Western life. Before becoming minister to Japan, Swift spent considerable time in Nevada and in 1878 published his lengthy novel *Robert Greathouse,* based on his observations of Comstock society. Despite the scores of characters and an involved discussion of American institutions, women's rights, miners' unions, religion, and politics, Swift failed to develop a single immigrant character and seemed strangely unaware that 73 percent of the male work force of Virginia City was foreign born.

Seldom has human reaction been less objective and human judgment more defective than in the romanticized memoirs and reminiscences of Charles C. Goodwin's *As I Remember Them* (1913). Although Goodwin was a leading Nevada journalist and a longtime editor of the *Territorial Enterprise,* his work, much like Swift's *Robert Greathouse,* was the product of emotional assumptions. Both refused to see the immigrant tide which had rolled across the Comstock. Goodwin explained that the 250,000 men who arrived in the Sierra with the first discovery of gold "were all more or less home boys and the best of them had a full quota of provincialism." Over the years most of the migrants had come as miners, "and who were these miners? They were as a rule just American boys and young men." Indeed, the key to an understanding of the early California and Nevada camp life, said Goodwin, was to remember that "the mothers they [the boys] kissed when they left home were American mothers, and as the differences among American mothers are the differences of environment it did not require long for their sons to recognize that fact." [10]

After discussing the major contributions of leading Nevadans like Senator John P. Jones, General P. E. Connor, promoter Adolph Sutro, speculator James G. Fair, and mining magnate John W. Mackay, Goodwin suggested that such strong men established an orderly society "with Anglo-Saxon directness."[11] Goodwin overlooked the fact that none of the five men had been born in either England or America.

Fortunately, Goodwin's fiction reflects fewer easy generalizations, and a less self-conscious patriotism. The novels, more than the reminiscences, provide a device for better understanding the community, its traditions, and its foreign born. For example, in the novel *The Comstock Club,* published in 1891, the immigrant influence in Virginia City was given considerable, albeit inadvertent, notice. The account revolved around seven men who formed a club, rented a house, hired a Chinese cook named Yap Sing, and lived pleasantly while they continued their employment in the mines. After dinner the men often exchanged stories and gossip and expressed their opinions on the issues of the day. The club had been formed to escape the rigors of Irish rooming houses, and many of the tales revolved around local Irish characters ranging from washerwomen to millionaires. Although the Irish were seen as peculiar people, they were at the same time accepted as equals; indeed, one of the seven members of the club, Barney Corrigan, was Irish born.

When Corrigan died, he was deeply mourned by his associates, who delivered impressive eulogies and sent their condolences to his Irish relatives. Yap Sing benefited from a similar double standard. While the Chinese were degraded and declared to be "animals of fixed colors,"[12] and responsible for unemployment, prostitution, and crime, Yap Sing emerged as a great prize because of his superb qualities as a housekeeper and cook. Jews, while occasionally described as greedy and demanding, were not marked for disfavor by the club members. And the "poor Italian, with organ and monkey, dreams while turning his organ's crank, that this year or next, or sometime, he will be able to procure a little home, have a garden of his own, and that his children will

grow up—sanctified by citizenship—defenders of our flag." [13]
The Comstock Club not only mirrored Goodwin's subconscious
opinions, but also reflected a typical view of the foreigner. Any
white man who became a citizen, ceased to speak with a troublesome accent, and accepted American standards of appearance,
employment, and outlook was accepted into the Comstock community.

Goodwin's memoirs stressed the hearty American character of
the western miners, yet his novels provided a revealing antidote
for his history. Indeed, his second work of fiction was built
around an immigrant theme. *The Wedge of Gold* (1893) followed the life and loves of John Browning, an honest Devon-
shire lad who made his way to Virginia City and to quick, but
well-deserved, wealth as a miner. Later Browning returned to
England, and with a rich Comstock friend, Jim Sedgwick, he
settled down to a pleasant, if somewhat spectacular, way of life.
But the unsuspecting Browning was quickly cheated out of his
property, and Sedgwick drifted to South Africa and further success as a mine operator. Frenchmen, Portuguese, and other foreigners are drawn into the plot which was set in Virginia City,
London, and South Africa. In the grand Victorian manner,
Sedgwick masterminded the recovery of Browning's fortune,
both men were happily married, and the hard-earned Nevada
bullion at long last supplied the heroes with an opportunity for
gracious English living.

Goodwin and Swift typified a peculiarly provincial school of
Comstock writers. They seemed to pledge themselves to provide
only the kind of literature guaranteed to hurt no feelings, to reveal no weakness, and to shock no sensibilities. Goodwin's uncritical *As I Remember Them* suggested a narrowly parochial
sentiment and insisted upon an overly simplified basis for western life. In the reminiscences he ignored human difference and

83

subtlety and he discounted the cosmopolitanism brought to the community by the foreign born. But his novels implied that all right-thinking and industrious migrants who welcomed adversity could enjoy high adventure and achieve success on the Comstock.

Henry Mighels and Sam Davis were newspapermen who frequently indulged in journalistic feuding. However, their book-length works were the product of a humane common *Brush Leaves,* published a few days after his death in 1879, rep- sense overlaid with a disarming poignancy. Mighels's *Sage* resented the compilation of his best writings while he served as editor of the Carson City *Morning Appeal.* As an intelligent and sensitive man, Mighels refused to be stampeded into the anti-Chinese crusade of the late seventies; and because of his sane pronouncements, he lost the bid for lieutenant governor in 1878.

On election day, the rival *Daily Nevada Tribune,* operated by the English-born Parkinson family, declared that Mighels had "not only caused to be printed but a thousand times said on the streets of Carson City, that a Chinaman was as good as any other foreign son of a _____." In an obvious attempt to divert the European vote from Mighels, the *Tribune* declared that the nominee for lieutenant governor had once written, "Let us bless God that an emigration has set in from the Orient to offset the pampered barbarism from the insufficiently persecuted precincts of Ireland and Cornwall. . . . Speed the day, say we, when a citizen of Chinese birth shall be endowed with as much power of self-protection as the naturalized citizen of European parentage or the citizen of native birth." [14] The Parkinsons were successful and Mighels was the only Republican candidate for major state office to be defeated in 1878.

The articles comprising *Sage Brush Leaves* represent a meandering, philosophical, and fictionalized approach to both traditional and contemporary problems. Mighels suggested, for instance, that the language of the Bostonian and that of the Chinese might appear as different as "the braying of an ass and the singing of a meadow lark," yet "the native of the Celestial Empire thinks of turnips and bread and boots and rice and bathing and bedding and dying just as clearly as your Boston man." [15] In a wry jab at his anti-Oriental readers, he proposed that they stop stoning Chinamen during the few weeks before Christmas so as to make sure that Santa Claus would come; and in another witty account, he excoriated a drunken "Mongol" for taking the liberty of copying the manners of "his brandydrinking betters." [16]

Sam Davis, also a longtime editor of the *Morning Appeal,* was even more in the tradition of western humorists than his predecessor Henry Mighels. Although an active politician and major Nevada historian, Davis has been remembered best in literary circles for his famous short story *The First Piano in Camp* (1919). The work originally appeared in the *Virginia Chronicle* and was almost immediately republished in scores of newspapers and journals throughout the United States and Europe.

In a small mining community near the isolated town of Pioche, Nevada, a large wooden box was hauled into camp one day. The crate was at first thought to be the coffin of a murdered man, but upon closer investigation it was found to contain a piano. The bored and lonesome miners agreed to set it up in a nearby saloon where there was a fiddler and "a greasy Mexican" who played a discordant guitar.[17] Soon the entire camp became engaged in a frenzied, but futile, search to find a piano player.

Finally, on Christmas Eve, when most of the men of the camp were gathered at the saloon, an old and haggard Englishman drifted in out of the night. After being given his supper by the proprietor, the old man fell to telling stories and reminiscing about the old country—"the heather of the Scottish hills, the White Cliffs of Britain." [18] And at the same time, he flexed his fingers and began to play the piano. As he played he seemed to regain a long lost mastery of the keyboard and with it he gained complete mastery of the emotions of his sentimental listeners. The old man performed new songs and old songs, Christmas songs and sad songs, and when he had finished, all the miners, filled with memories of home, filed out of the saloon and down the dark road to their cabins. The men had scarcely left when the piano player suddenly became ill and, apparently in great pain, requested the saloonkeeper to hurry to the cabin of an Englishman by the name of Driscoll. The sick man explained that Driscoll was his brother whom he had once wronged and whom he had not seen since they were separated in England years earlier. The saloonkeeper rushed out not thinking to lock the cash drawer in which much of the camp's wealth was stored. Upon his return with Driscoll, both the piano player and $10,000 had disappeared into the falling snow of Christmas morning.

Sam Davis's prose was economical, supple, and precise, and he deftly caught the melancholy of those isolated in Nevada's mining camps. The brother from the Old Country, the musically proficient Englishman, and the family left behind were equally realistic ingredients. Davis had the power to render enormous that which was regarded as miniscule, and he knew that a good story should disturb and not reassure. But at the same time the pathos and the romantic morality of *The First Piano in Camp* was reminiscent of the tall tale, the audacity, and the sentimentality of the West. Davis, perhaps more effectively than any pre-World War I newspapermen who turned novelist, blended the immigrant into the western character and transformed the foreign nondescript into a participant in Nevada life.

Not only did journalists sometimes become novelists, but the spirit of a particular newspaper was sometimes woven into a book. Oscar Lewis's 1955 compilation of stories from early issues of the *Reese River Reveille* typifies the ribald and spirited nature of many Nevada papers and provides a sampling of the *Reveille*'s approach to the foreign born.[19] When both Austin and the *Reveille* were but a few months old an editorial set forth the international flavor of the community.[20]

Every day at Main and Cedar streets in the center of Austin there gathered "the buyers and sellers of feet, auctioneers, bummers, prospectors, fruit vendors, men of leisure, bull drivers, millionaires, paupers, and every species of bipeds" from "every portion of the world." There was the "brawny, burly Englishman whose fat capon lined paunch" told of "tables loaded down with roast beef and 'alf and 'alf in days gone by." Frenchmen gesticulated over "the fair damsels and wine-clad hills of La Belle France," the delicious flavor of a traditional dish, and the merits of a mineral claim. "Gloomy looking, sallow complexioned, moon-eyed Celestials" silently elbowed their way through the crowd. There was the "little, sharp nosed Jew in deep meditation, calculating the gains to be made on his stock of clothing," and a German who expounded "upon the good qualities of his stock of tobacco, cigars, picks, coffee pots, and bacon." Apple vendors and shoemakers, cooks and blacksmiths, dancing masters and carpenters formed a mixed crowd of Teutons and Slavs, Anglo-Saxons and Latins, Celts and Orientals.

Some of the *Reveille* reporters collected colorful immigrants and other interesting people as if they were connoisseurs; they gave them cameo appearances in irreverent articles which were often as vivid and intimate as diaries. In *The Town That Died Laughing,* Lewis often capitalized on the *Reveille*'s flair for immigrant drama. A prizefight between an Englishman and an

Irishman conducted in the streets of Austin by winter moonlight reflected the town's progress in "muscular Christianity"; the profuse swearing in three languages by a Chinaman who worked in a German barbershop portrayed the linguistic and cultural facility of the citizenry; and a "red-headed Arabian" camel tender and driver from south Ireland pointed up the great versatility of the Celtic race. The *Reveille* brand of the tall tale was used to fill newspaper columns on dull days, and while it seldom offered an evaluation of the complex feelings and passions of the foreign born, it did, nevertheless, emphasize the variety, the tragedy, and the humor to be found among the immigrants.

An English scholar has suggested that the raucous style used by the best Nevada journalists was reminiscent of a Chaucer and that the shooting scrapes and mayhem provided topics and characters worthy of a Hogarth or a Rowlandson.[21] Humorists like Mark Twain used burlesque, disdain, and outrage to describe the immigrant drama, while humanists like Henry Mighels joked, pled, and scolded in an effort to acquaint society with the immigrant needs. Most of the journalist-novelists saw the foreign-born influx as a unique but not peculiar, as an important but not paramount, as a vital but not remarkable, feature of the times. In general they allowed the immigrants to blend naturally and honestly into the myths and the realities of Nevada life. Perhaps no greater tribute could have been paid to the thousands of foreign born who were entering the state.

[1] J. Ross Browne, *A Peep at Washoe and Washoe Revisited* (Balboa Island, California: Paisano Press, 1959), pp. 29–30.

[2] *Ibid.,* p. 102.

[3] Dan De Quille, *Washoe Rambles* (Los Angeles: Dawson's Book Shop, 1963), see chapter 9.

[4] In Raine's *Bonanza: A Story of the Gold Trail* (1921) a German Jewish peddler was frightened off the stagecoach at Carson City by a

clever Yankee who expounded on the danger from Indian raids. The Yankee wanted the German's seat on the stage to Virginia City.

[5] Margaret G. Watson, *Silver Theatre: Amusements of Nevada's Mining Frontier* (Glendale, California: The Arthur H. Clark Company, 1964), pp. 76–81.

[6] While never put into direct literary focus or completely developed as a character, Dutch Nick and his saloon became a permanent feature and a symbol of western Nevada life. He presented the balance between an acceptance of the new West and the retention of old ways. He encouraged gaiety and the enjoyment of life, yet remained an industrious and prudent German. He signified perseverance and stability in a land of constant change. He never learned to write and he clung to German habits, yet he was elected to public office. References to Dutch Nick are difficult to take seriously, yet it is through such half-legendary figures that the frontier has often been best delineated. At the very least, the Dutch Nick theme demonstrates that the Nevada environment did not recast all immigrants into a common mold.

[7] Mark Twain, *Roughing It* (Hartford: American Publishing Co., 1872), p. 338.

[8] *Ibid.,* p. 391.   [9] *Ibid.,* p. 397.

[10] Charles C. Goodwin, *As I Remember Them* (Salt Lake City: Commercial Club, 1913), p. 26.

[11] *Ibid.,* p. 119.

[12] Charles C. Goodwin, *The Comstock Club* (Salt Lake City: Tribune Job Printing Company, 1891), p. 196.

[13] *Ibid.*

[14] *The Daily Nevada Tribune,* November 5, 1878, p. 2, col. 1, and p. 3, col. 1.

[15] Henry R. Mighels, *Sage Brush Leaves* (San Francisco: Edward Bosqui and Company, 1879), p. 14.

[16] Philip Mighels, the son of Henry, was also a journalist and author. He moved from Carson City to San Francisco, to New York, and later to London. Two of Mighels's five novels touched on Nevada, and *The Furnace of Gold* (1909) was built around the foreign born. But Mighels's characters seem to have been sketched in Hyde Park or Central Park; they project little of his childhood association with Nevada.

[17] Sam Davis, *The First Piano in Camp* (New York: Harper and Brothers Publishers, 1919), p. 19.

[18] *Ibid.,* p. 27.

[19] Oscar Lewis, *The Town That Died Laughing* (Boston: Little, Brown and Company, 1955).

[20] *Reese River Reveille,* November 7, 1863, p. 3, col. 1.

[21] John Rowe, "Western Mining Frontiers" (a manuscript to be published by the University of Liverpool Press).

4
==

Newspaper Themes

An early American adage declared that once printer's ink got on a boy's shirt it seldom could be washed out in less than three generations. Clearly there was a great fascination for printing and particularly for newspapers on the frontier. Ray Billington has shown that in 1840 in the West there was one newspaper publisher for each 12,000 people. Nebraska supported over a hundred papers when only a decade old, and by the mid-1850s San Francisco produced more newspapers than London.[1] By 1870 at least thirty-eight papers had been founded in Nevada, but only eighteen, or one for every 2,500 people, were still being published. Most of the early editors were self-educated drifters who followed the flow of population. They demonstrated a remarkable trust in the power of the press and a mystic faith in their own convictions. With fearless zest they dragged their presses to the ragged mining camps and often single-handedly provided the only cultural or literary force in the area. Exuberant and quarrelsome, the journalists had talent; their interest in community affairs commonly overshadowed that of other professional men. They were an influential group who reflected their environment and yet they possessed little sense of attachment to any particular paper, particular place, or particular social class. Most journalists wrote editorial, promotional, and literary columns and quickly found that the public expected all to be spiced with wit and humor.

Although today only about twenty Nevada communities issue a newspaper, over the past century some 120 districts have provided the state with nearly 450 news periodicals. Six of the papers were foreign-language publications. From the era of Mark Twain to the generation of Henry Mighels and from Henry Sinclair Drago to Octavus Roy Cohen and Robert Laxalt, many of the leading cultivators of the immigrant theme have been, at least in part, journalists.

Nevada journalism was of its time and was inevitably transient. Yet there were many ways for a newspaper to listen to the emotions of the society, countless things to listen for, and different methods of relating and recounting what was heard. The journalist who listened wisely and who cared could sense the ambitions and the joy, the misery and the dread of his community. No doubt Mark Twain, Alf Doten, and many other early Nevada reporters remained popular because they felt deeply about the future of their society. Despite the fact that they chronicled sweeping changes and lived among a people with a buoyant hope, no newspaperman wrote of utopianism. Beneath the conflicting overstatement and popular exaggeration, they saw the true hardships and noted the frequency of failure. They saw the barren land, the transient life, and the lure for quick gain.

Often neither the documentary nor literary value of the papers was great; however, the candor, inventiveness, and flavor employed in delineating people and situations provided Nevada journalism with an unusual human dimension. With records poorly kept and with little thought given to literature, if the newspapers had not assumed the role of priest, prophet, historian, and critic, much that is now prized would have been lost.

Literature and history, like culture in general, depends for survival on the continuing criticism of contemporaries, and in Nevada, often only the journalists bothered to comment. Numerous immigrant overtones emerge from the day-to-day news stories and the vividness of personal reporting. Six of the more readily apparent topics or thematic devices used by the newspapers were humor and fakery, color and off-color, initiative and enterprise, distrust and discrimination, rivalry and conflict, and loneliness and despair.

Humor and Fakery

Every age has created its comforting illusions and tragic comedy. The ability to laugh when chronicling doubt and reporting disaster characterized the Comstock era. Much of the humor was cruel rather than compassionate, indulgent rather than pleasant. The lengthy and frequent articles which reported the hand-to-hand and verbal combat between Jews and Chinese were thought hilarious. Grotesque insults were exchanged, and "the heathen" regularly enlarged on the Jew's responsibility for the death of Jesus Christ.[2] In the same vein the papers thought it highly amusing when a "Dublin drifter" shot off the ear of a "careless Cornishman" and when a "London rough" repeatedly terrorized the "Cantonese coolies." A formal dinner held by the Saint George's Society was reported as an "English gunpowder tea"; a minor Slavic disagreement became a "brutal fight by the Slavonian beef dissectors"; and some newly arrived Italians were declared to be "land lovers" because they carried so "much of it on them."

An equally bizarre approach to pleasure grew out of injury, desperation, or defeat. A *Territorial Enterprise* article entitled "A Zampillaerostationist" explained how a German had fallen fifteen feet and suggested that if he had "gone farther," he would have "done worse." More notice was given to the Prussian who suffered repeated financial failures and at last, finding himself ill and without work, attempted suicide by shooting himself in the mouth. The ball lodged in the back part of the immigrant's throat, which prompted the reporter to conclude that if he lived through the experience, he would "probably be troubled with a very sore throat for some time to come." [3]

Over the decades the leading papers of the state developed the tall-tale into something of a trademark and almost uniformly used the foreign born to punctuate its effectiveness. There was the Irishman who won seven hundred dollars gambling in Virginia City and on his way home to Gold Hill was stopped by three footpads intent on robbing him. With great composure, the Irishman explained that they were the fourth band of thieves to attack him since he left the gambling hall and that he had long since been relieved of his winnings. "Jolly Irish McGinnis," the Virginia City jailer of the mid-sixties, supposedly left the door unlocked so that scoundrels could escape back to California and thus save the "good people of Nevada" both time and money.

Some stories seem to have been born out of confusion, rather than design. For example, during the great prison break of September 17, 1871, in which twenty-nine convicts escaped, the papers emphasized the bravery of an inmate known as "Gallant Frenchy." The Frenchman was supposed to have saved the life of the warden's six-year-old daughter, the life of a visiting lady, and finally that of a prison officer; Frenchy then had to face the hostility of his fellow convicts, who tried to kill him for his gallantry. The Frenchman was never named, and it is somewhat disappointing to learn that there was no Frenchman in or associated with the prison at the time of the escape. An equally innocent joke was the suggestion that a willow tree in Riverside

Park in Reno had grown from a slip cut from a bough which shaded Napoleon's Parisian tomb. With nationalistic fervor, local Frenchmen flocked to the park with knives and carved so extensively on several willows that the *Nevada State Journal* declared that many trees "have suffered, and many have been badly disfigured." [4]

One of the more commonplace types of frontier amusement was the hoax. This often savage humor was popularized in Nevada by Mark Twain's story of October, 1863, in which he reported the massacre at Dutch Nick's on the Carson River. Less than two months after the Dutch Nick story shocked the West, Philip Lynch of the *Gold Hill Daily News* presented his version of a "terrible infanticide." The story, appearing the day after Christmas, told of an unwed German mother killing her infant and of the legal action that was being planned against her. Lynch quickly lost his nerve, however, and admitted that the article was a hoax based on the Mark Twain pattern. [5]

One of the more successful and sensational deceptions was engineered by the *Reese River Reveille* in the spring of 1878. On March 30, the paper reported that two English-educated Hindus had walked into Nevada from the Bodie district. The foreigners had visited and worked at Columbus, Ione, and other towns and were on their way to Austin when one of them, Pietro Las-Como, became so completely exhausted that he died at a ranch house in the Reese River Valley. His companion, Ramel Acknoor, walked on to Austin and asked the mayor for permission to cremate his friend so that the ashes might be sent back to Calcutta. After long deliberation, the mayor approved the burning and appointed a committee to observe the ceremonies and evaluate the merits and demerits of the custom, since the city fathers might wish to adopt a similar means of disposing of the local dead. The following morning half the town rushed to

Birchim's Ranch on the Reese River to observe the cremation, and the other half expressed their indignation that the practice of Christian burial was being questioned by the officials. On April 1, 1878, the editor replied to the citizens' queries with the comment "April Fool."

Another use made of the hoax revolved around the acquisition of foreign wealth or the inheritance of an English title. The story of an unimpressive immigrant becoming the pride of the community when he fell heir to lands and a title in the Old World was a standard American tale. During the sixties and seventies the Comstock rags-to-English-riches version became a regular feature of newspaper reporting. The Jack Sheppard case was not unique. In May, 1873, the *Territorial Enterprise* explained that Sheppard, a hard-working member of the ropes gang at the Imperial Mine, had inherited $1,500,000 and had left for England. Since neither Sheppard nor his associates read the papers, it was several days before they learned of the fantasy.

When the drifter Frank McDru explained that he had acquired four million dollars and planned to desert Sparks for a home in London, a newspaper reporter noted McDru's love of the West and sensed "a hidden thread that all the wealth in the world could not break." McDru agreed, and declared that it was not the money that drew him towards England, but the possibility of "going back to my folks." [6] Presumably the Canadian George Shea was equally happy to return home when, after languishing in a Winnemucca jail, he suddenly found that he had received a large benefaction, whereupon he became a local hero and was released from custody. [7]

A slightly different emphasis was suggested by a *Morning Appeal* headline of 1879. The caption read "The Son of a Noble English House in Carson and Begging for a Meal on the Street." [8] The Englishman had drifted from wealth and aristocracy in London to rank and power in the British army to a sheep ranch and alcoholism in Australia to a small farm and desperate poverty in Nevada. The story was implemented with much biographical detail and high praise for the noble Englishman. But out of deference to the gentleman's pride, the reporter had not printed the tale until after the immigrant had left town. The spring of 1879 was apparently a good season for aristocrats in Carson City since less than two months later the same reporter sighted a man with a full, thick, black beard waiting in the railroad station. After careful questioning the foreigner admitted to the alert newsman that he was a Russian army officer and nobleman and had participated in the 1866 plot to murder Alexander II. After escaping from a Siberian prison and making his way across much of Asia and Europe, he at last had found freedom in Nevada.[9] The Russian, like the Englishman, was seen only by the nimble reporter. When it became necessary to improvise to fill newspaper columns, the nobleman's flight to the West long remained a preferred tale.

Well aware of the excitement generated by wealth or aristocrats, even the more responsible newspapers were inclined to exaggerate the presence of either. Many a poor, but quick-witted, immigrant lad elevated himself to wealth and prominence in Nevada. Typical was the case of Jacob Greahk, a thirty-three-year-old Austrian, who worked with a Virginia and Truckee Railroad section gang. When Greahk became ill and explained that he would surely die, he asked that a lawyer be sent to draw up his will. The attorney could not keep a secret, and within hours the newspapers repeated rumors that the foreigner had twelve thousand dollars in cash, plus valuable stocks and other securities. The next day Greahk was invited to move from his room near the railroad tracks into one of the better homes of Gold Hill, and although his illness vanished, he continued to enjoy the finer features of town life. After living on credit for some weeks, he disappeared and left his debts behind.

A Mr. Lazard used a less subtle approach. He arrived in Winnemucca in May, 1881, rented a small building, and advertised himself in the local papers as a "practical watchmaker, jeweler, assayer, lapidary, repairer of astronomical, mathematical, nautical, and surveying instruments, music teacher, piano tuner, etc., etc." [10] After assuring the local populace that he was fluent in Greek, Latin, Turkish, Arabic, and other European and Asiatic languages, he founded a local orchestra and feverishly collected jewelry, watches, instruments, and other valuable items that needed repair. After two months in town, Lazard left Winnemucca at night, was apprehended and forced to return the stolen property, and then freed to practice his art on another unsuspecting community.

Nevadans were unquestionably interested, amused, and impressed by the foreign born who commanded special favors and elicited special attention. The newspapers reveal a constant procession of bogus aristocrats like Count Mitkiewicz of Poland. Mitkiewicz charmed Virginia City society during the first part of 1872, while he was searching for a rich heiress to marry. Later in the year, he found and married a wealthy lady in Rochester, New York, only a few days before he was exposed as a charlatan. Not all would-be aristocrats were as lucky. On February 8, 1873, the *Gold Hill Daily News* revealed that Albert Sobieski, a Polish nobleman, had died penniless in the county hospital. Before his death Sobieski had explained to a local bartender that although he was heir to great estates, he had chosen exile rather than the trammels of Europe and had spent his life wandering throughout the world. The reporter remembered the Pole as intelligent, cultivated, a master of languages, a brilliant conversationalist, and a good athlete. He was often seen waiting at the

Virginia City post office for money that was to have been dispatched from Europe. But the funds did not arrive and Sobieski sat up in saloons because he could no longer pay for lodgings. Whether nobleman or peasant, he finally died, a public charge, at the county hospital.

The presence of European nobility was dramatically portrayed by an article in the *Eureka Daily Sentinel* of March 11, 1875. Captioned "A Russian Count . . . Slinging Hash in an Eureka Restaurant," the editorial recounted the life history of Alexander Von Huhn, a waiter at the Lafayette cafe. According to the story, Von Huhn's father was a scion of the House of Hapsburg, and his mother, a Russian countess, could trace her lineage directly to Peter the Great. The youth grew up in a mansion on the Neva River, entered the royal army, became an escort for Czar Alexander II and a companion for the monarch's son. Unfortunately, while at court, he fell in love with a lady betrothed to another officer. Challenged to a duel, he married the lady and straightway left the candlelight of the church to defend his honor. After killing the fellow officer, he sought asylum in western Europe, but was pursued throughout the continent. Even in America, Von Huhn did not feel completely safe until he arrived at Eureka, Nevada, where he at last found contentment. The Count had failed to say goodby to his mother and young bride, however, and could never write them for fear his letters might be traced to the Far West. The reporter found the new waiter fluent in French, German, Italian, Spanish, and Russian, but he spoke little English. His "careworn face, his strange demeanor, and unobtrusive ways" had awakened curiosity throughout the town. He had shown pluck, and although an aristocrat, was "not too proud to bend the knee to circumstances and seek a living in an honest way."[11] The article was so floridly overwritten and so patently false that the editor was either indulging in a modified type of the Dutch Nick hoax or else attempting to attract customers for the Lafayette restaurant.

Many early Nevada journalists and editors brought to their work an intellectual vividness, a rich framework of ideas, a perspective that was at one and the same time tragic, apocalyptic, comic, and anecdotal. Such journalists applied the imaginative resources of fiction to their daily commentaries. Somewhat freed from the necessity of noting only hard facts, their reporting often became creative. They were not orthodox journalists who probed only for realism; rather they embraced the fictional element and tried to produce their impression of society. Clearly, their emphasis on manners, on attitudes, and on jocular fantasy did not always provide a penetrating insight into the lives of the foreign born. However, most reporters were serious despite a surface humor, and most found that immigrants animated their stories.

Color and Off-Color

Another thread running through Nevada newspapers and frequently employed by novelists can perhaps best be described as immigrant color. Certain foreigners were sometimes viewed as bizarre or perhaps even bewitching characters who could provide an opportunity for mixing myth with reality and interjecting fiction into history. Nevada editors filled their columns with stories about Chinese Mary, Russian Pete, Sauerkraut Schell, and literally hundreds of other colorful foreigners. Typical was the case of William Herhily, better known by his sobriquet, The Emigrant.

Herhily was a railroad worker who had saved a few dollars and started home to Ireland. He became intoxicated while traveling near Battle Mountain, and during a fight, cut the throat of a fellow Irishman. While being transported to the jail at Austin, he almost succeeded in igniting the powder which was to be used for a Fourth of July celebration. After his stay in the Lander County jail had provoked criticism by taxpayers, and after an attempt to turn him over to the Storey County authorities had failed, Herhily was finally escorted to the California border and told not to return to the state. The confused foreigner found the injunction impossible to honor, since Nevada had to be crossed on his way to Ireland. Therefore, Herhily again drifted into the state and the farce of apprehension and release was reenacted. California authorities finally escorted the persistent Irishman to Sacramento where they agreed to investigate his sanity.[12]

Russian Pete, actually a thirty-six-year-old Finn, was more of a true desperado than the confused and mentally-deranged Herhily. After robbing and killing throughout the Sierra, Pete finally took refuge in a mine tunnel at Virginia City. The sheriff promptly dammed the mouth of the shaft, hoping that in time the ruffian would be either drowned or forced to surrender. After hours of confusion and the killing of another man, Pete quenched the excitement and carnival-like atmosphere at the mouth of the tunnel by committing suicide.[13]

The early Nevada press was crowded with cases like those of The Emigrant and Russian Pete. The West in general, and Nevada in particular, became a land where hundreds of immigrants chose violence and a raw, corrosive, senseless life in their confused and misdirected search for respect, or attention, or success. The Wild Irishman of Austin enjoyed the notoriety of driving over people with his wagon. Irish Tim and the Irish Man-eater became famous because of an ability to fight with their teeth. Irish Mike was so well known for his wife beating that both the state and national governments considered laws for the protection of wives. Dublin Pete had a tendency to kill his opponents in fist fights, while Irish Riley, Irish Charley, French Charley, Chinese Charley, and French Lefevre were among western Nevada's more pugnacious drunks and brawlers. Indeed, "crazy French Lefevre" once tried to kill the warden of the state prison and on numerous occasions, while incarcerated, attacked the guards. Irish Tom became known as the "father of the Nevada state prison" and Chinese Chow eventually earned the appellation "dean of the state prison." Few Nevada immigrants were given as much attention either before or after death as Frenchy Navarre of Beowawe. Frenchy fractured many skulls during his lifetime, but some weeks after burial, his body was exhumed to see if his skull had been fractured by a murderer or if he had died of natural causes during a playful scuffle.

In many instances, foreign-born females also led active lives. English Waller, the "Pioneer Mountain Actress," sang "The 'orn of the 'unter is 'eard on the 'ill" to thousands of miners before her death in 1899. When Mrs. Waller first brought her English songs to the Sierra Nevada, she faced stiff competition from a hurdy house operated by German Schultz. In 1868 Schultz staged Nevada's first "prostitutes ball," at which there was food, dancing, and fun for all. In the same year, English Ida, who worked at a competitive brothel known as Bow Windows, was making a name for herself and for her house; Ida died of morphine and opium after only four short years on the Comstock. Also in 1868, English Gussie became famous when she so effectively disposed of her infant child that its body was never found. And at the same time, in a neighboring house, Irish Mary killed Galway Farry while both were drunk. Irish Mary and a colleague, Madam Irish, became notorious as the most vulgar and degenerate of the Comstock women.

Bow Windows was the scene of violence in 1871 when "The German Muscle Woman" used a whip on a propsective Irish client because he tended to support the French in the Franco-

Prussian War. Dutch Mary became outraged a few weeks later when members of the vigilance committee, known as the 601, broke into her room, seized a customer, and later executed him on Geiger grade. She lodged a complaint with authorities on the grounds of improper entry. Bow Windows added further color to Virginia City later in 1871 when Blanche de Maude earned the sobriquet "Suicide Frenchy" because two attempts at suicide were foiled by the prompt arrival of a doctor. Perhaps Scottish Laura, who died of an overdose of laudanum, and English Nell, who died of morphine, were fortunate; they both succumbed before a physician could arrive.

English Georgia's brothel, known as the Brick House and located a few doors north of Bow Windows on D Street, also suffered from a series of fights and suicides. On May Day, 1868, a client hit Spanish Mary on the head with a rock and almost killed her. Two weeks later a group of Irish prostitutes became involved in what was commonly known as the Kilkenny fight. In late 1868 and in early 1869, acute problems of competition developed at Bow Windows and the Brick House when several of the musical group known as the Swiss Bell Ringers (actually an English female troupe from Lancashire) remained in Virginia City to practice their second profession.

Of course other towns vied with Virginia City as entertainment centers, and girls from many countries competed as dance hall performers. Gustave Chevel, a French-Canadian restaurant owner of Eureka, became famous for his importation of foreign women, and August Jesse of Carson City brought over many girls from his old home in Germany. Jesse insisted that the German females would "raise the tone of dance houses in Carson." [14] Many women sought opportunity in Nevada. It was claimed that at least 150 unmarried females flocked into the Glenbrook area of Lake Tahoe during the summer of 1879 for the purpose of enticing some of the hundreds of French-Canadian woodcutters into marriage.

But in many ways, the piquancy, drama, and action surrounding the life of Chinese Mary surpassed that of any other hurdy dancer in the state, including that of the well-known Julia Bulette. After being responsible for several fights and one killing in Carson City, Mary, in May, 1875, was abducted by members of a rival tong and transported to Wellington. On the way, she repeatedly tried to escape, and upon arrival at Wellington she jumped into the Walker River in an attempt at suicide. The Chinese captors eventually decided to remove her to Genoa, but since they were afraid of an opposing tong, they employed two white men at five dollars each plus costs to carry out the assignment. A Chinese man accompanied the white men in an effort to assure prompt delivery. Outside Wellington, one of the men maneuvered his partner and the Chinese out of the wagon and then drove off with the valuable cargo. He traded Mary to a Chinese at Aurora for $220 and a silver watch and chain. The new owner promptly married his prize. But Mary's path of chaos continued on south, and by 1876 she had provoked several Chinese riots and at least one shooting in Esmeralda County. On one occasion, at Columbus, nine men claimed her simultaneously. All were arrested.[15]

Obviously not all immigrant color was associated with crime, violence, or debauchery. Angelo Cardela received favorable publicity when he became known as the "Reno Hercules," the strongest man in the world,[16] and Frenchy (Charles) Venini was widely heralded as the great Nevada racehorse trainer. Eureka's tattooed Greek, George Costentenus, was billed as the most decorated man in the world, and most persons conceded that Dutch Sal was the most boisterous man in the world even though he and a mulatto mistress kept a lonely stage station.

"The counterfeit Pole of Humboldt" had no wish to become famous or share in the picturesque immigrant traditions. In early June, 1879, Frank Schollata was arrested in Winnemucca for counterfeiting half dollars. The authorities seized the plaster of Paris molds, lead, babbit metal, antimony, ladles, and other equipment. But while being transported to Carson City, Schollata jumped off the train near Lovelock and for over a week eluded a sheriff's posse of nearly a hundred white men and a band of Indian scouts. Eventually captured on the Oregon border, Schollata was taken to Carson City and brought to trial in November, 1879. To the dismay of the federal officers, the Pole was acquitted by a jury who seemed to agree with the defense attorney's arguments that Winnemucca needed a mint, that Nevada needed more coins, and that no one had proved that Schollata planned to use the newly minted money illegally.[17]

"Chicken Thief Charley of Yorkshire" also elicited the public sympathy which so frequently abetted the rogue. Of the ten men in jail at Virginia City on April 20, 1871, nine were foreign born and six were accused of stealing chickens.[18] It was not Charley's first offense. Indeed, he had been caught on previous occasions and in one instance cut off the ear of the man who apprehended him. Finally, in September, 1871, many of the good people of the Comstock, including at least one clergyman, became concerned with the case and often visited the culprit while he was in jail. Since Charley claimed that the chickens were stolen to get money to return to his beloved England, it seemed unfair to the preacher that he should be detained in jail. One prayer soliciting God's help in the matter asked that Charley might "become blind to the attractions of such plump pullets as may stray across his path, and deaf to the crowing of the cock. Send him in the way to find honest employment, and when he has secured sufficient gold return him to his own place in Yorkshire, in England." [19]

Many reporters deliberately emphasized the immigrant as a unique source of color in their otherwise drab communities. An article modestly entitled "Cosmopolitan" from the *Eureka Sentinel* suggested the zest with which some journalists reported on the foreign born.

> For variety of nationalities, we believe that Eureka is entitled to the palm. We were particularly impressed with this fact yesterday, by noticing a group standing in front of a saloon on North Main Street. There was a native of Madagascar, an East Indian, a Spaniard, an Italian, a Chilean, and a man born on the Island of Tahiti. In close proximity was a group of Shoshones playing cards, and a Chinaman watching the game. English, French, Scotch, Irish, Slavonians, and Negroes passed during the time that our attention was attracted, and a member of the group referred to gave us the item in regard to the nativity of those first mentioned. Americans were sadly in the minority, and but few were to be seen. There are representatives from almost every race on the globe residing on the Base Ridge, and we doubt if another town in the United States can show such a cosmopolitan community. [20]

The *Tonopah Bonanza* was less friendly in viewing the inrush to Caliente in 1903. In "It's a Hot Town" the reporter noted,

> The Irishmen [are found] in every kind of a position from running a saloon to spading out a ditch. The natives of southern Europe are here in force. Italians, Greeks, Austrians and Syrians all speaking their own jargons, and

boarding themselves and saving their money. They evidently want to save their pile and go back, which is better for the country than to have them stay, for they are evidently too ignorant to make good citizens.[21]

Other newsmen fancied themselves ethnic analysts. A Carson City reporter declared that when intoxicated "a Frenchman wants to dance, a Geman wants to sing, a Spaniard to gamble, an Englishman to eat, an Italian to boast, a Russian to be affectionate, [and] an Irishman to fight." [22]

But in the final analysis, it was immigrant cutthroats and foreigners engaged in vice and crime who provided material for the most striking sketches. Patsy Dwyer left Nevada with his "sainted Irish mother" after killing his third man; "The British Blondes" became famous more for prostitution than for their musical performances; Killer Neroni, while in a Nevada jail, declared himself eligible for membership in the Black Hand because he had murdered twelve victims; Jew Mike, the German tailor, took turns at shooting up Eureka, Pioche, and other eastern Nevada towns; and Irish Tom, after a long residence in Mexico, became conspicuous for his misdeeds in Aurora and Austin but died a trusted police officer in Hamilton. The Buenos Aires Kid, the Teuton, the Big Swede, the Duke of Bedford, Killer Lopez, Cockney Tim, Butcher-knife John the Serb, Jackass Dutch Billy, Christian Dutch Sinner, Tall George the Slovenian, Greek Louckas the "King of the Prostitutes," and Dutch Voss the "Daniel Boone of Nevada Brewing," further suggest the almost inexhaustible list of foreigners who turned Nevada into a surrealist landscape of variegated shade and tone.

Clearly, Nevada was a land of externals; it was a disordered land, raw and fascinating. But as migrants from many cultures moved into the state, the colorful customs of the Old World blended with the colorful customs of the new West. For over a century the embellishments of the journalists filtered through onto the pages of history and literature. The newspapers helped to mold and to stereotype the age. The most sensitive novelists and historians used journalistic color with skill and restraint, but others tended to discolor rather than vivify, to chronicle rather than illuminate. Nevertheless, virtually all Nevada commentaries, if not all of Nevada society, have been touched by the richness of the journalistic color and by the vast and varied parade, assembled from the entire human race, which swept through the state.

Initiative and Enterprise

Nevada's immigrants, like most of the foreign born who made their way to the frontier, accepted the rags-to-riches myth. They seldom doubted the stories of great natural resources, of limitless opportunities, and of individual freedom. Hard work and thrift blended with enterprise and sound judgment were thought to lead to success. The foreign born did not need to read the Horatio Alger success stories or absorb the boosterism so common to western news sheets. Most arrived already converted to the proposition that they would devote their lives to capitalistic enterprise.

Perhaps the most impressive, if somewhat paradoxical, example of material success was seen in the foreigner who accumulated a fortune so that he might quickly return home. In the same year that the town of Battle Mountain was founded, one of its first citizens, Alexander Melander, sold his interests in a nearby mining claim and returned to Britain with his newly earned wealth.[23] Charles Maunder heard of Tonopah while working as a miner in Wales. He crossed the Atlantic and traveled directly to southern Nevada. Arriving in 1902, Maunder had by July, 1905, discovered an ore deposit, sold it, and left Nevada to return "to the bosom of his family well supplied with worldly goods." [24] After years of work, Chinese Tom of Reno sold his laundry at the corner of Center and Second streets for $15,000. He contacted Father Tubman who had so often befriended him, gave the Irish priest a substantial sum of money to help construct a new church, and left for China to seek out his long deserted wife and family. [25] Madam Foo started her career as an illiterate prostitute; in time she became the wealthiest Chinese in Winnemucca and eventually decided to return to the Orient. But after eighteen months in her homeland she became convinced that Nevada, rather than China, provided opportunity for a woman with initiative and enterprise. Returning to Winnemucca she, along with other Chinese, helped to establish Hong Kong Row, a restricted street west of the Court House where only Orientals of wealth and position were permitted to reside. [26]

The newspapers portray the foreign born as peculiarly original and enterprising in their approach to the business world. There was the advertising program of the German butchers of Virginia City who drove their cattle with names painted on them through the streets so that housewives could order their Christmas dinner by merely calling out the animal's name. The Irishman J. A. Carnahan hastily moved his wife to Reno in late August, 1868, so that his child would be the first born in the new community and would thereby receive fifty acres of land from the city's promoters. "The Fortunate Slovenian," George Perasich, located his vegetable market in Carson City next to the theater and thereby was able to sell his overripe produce to a gang of ruffians who regularly pelted the performers. Noting the large number of the foreign born who wished to be buried in their homeland, a venturesome immigrant in Goldfield announced that for a reasonable fee he was prepared to send bodies any place in the world. There were the ambitious Italians (or perhaps Irishmen engaged in a hoax) who in late 1901 attached a note to a small stake outside of Tonopah.

> We undersigned according to U.S. law claim this fifteen hundred feet ledge, 600 foots wid. Begin at those stake and run to Lone mountains and East to Butler peaks six hundred feets wid. For mining purposes, to have for ourself together to make assessments; and find some rich ore. Guiseppi Rafferti, Pete Pardoni, Garabaldi Jonesi.[27]

The Italians in particular pursued a broad range of economic activity. At first they became charcoal burners, railroad workers, and miners, but by 1906 the Italian businessmen of Reno had accumulated enough wealth to organize an Italian bank. Many of the Italians of western Nevada became leading suppliers of poultry and agricultural produce for the rapidly expanding towns. As early as 1867, one wagonload of G. B. Buggiano's turkeys and chickens from the Empire area brought $600 on the Comstock. But after the successful Christmas sale, Buggiano was attacked and robbed by highwaymen before he reached home.[28] Italian truck gardeners suffered similar hardships when their produce was stolen or destroyed by vandals, or when the irrigation ditches dried up. Giovanni Ghiglieri and Pietro Peceti were constantly involved in law suits because their spirited horses were frightened by the activity in Virginia City. People were injured, property destroyed, and most of the produce lost as the teams would break free of their drivers and charge down the mountainous streets.[29] Italians from the Pine Nut area of Douglas County supplied much of the poultry for Carson City, and during the eighties the Italian Ranch and picnic grounds outside of Eureka became one of the show places of eastern Nevada.

Many nationalities, of course, participated in the provisioning of early Nevada. For years, the Englishman A. Kimber produced large yields of rye, oats, barley, and wheat and supplied western Nevada with flour and grain from his four-hundred-acre field lying north of the Truckee River where Reno now stands.[30] As early as the summer of 1863, the reporters of Virginia City noted the productive capacity of a single Chinese who on a small piece of land east of town supplied the Comstock with a great variety of vegetables. Indeed, the term "Chinese Garden" came to denote freshness and quality throughout the community. Other journalistic phrases like the "French chicken woman" of Carson City, the "Basque apple train" of Eureka, the "Dutch chicken man" of the state prison, and the "French icehouse" of Spring Valley suggest the relationship between certain immigrants and the production or storage of food.

Scores of adventurous immigrants were linked by the newspapers with agricultural or business enterprises in Nevada. Tipperary Jack made his living hunting and trapping along the Humboldt River in the wintertime and growing potatoes at Galena during the summer months. He became known humorously as "the Great American Wolf Hunter from Pertater Gulch." The famed "Irish lemon man" of Newark Valley grew potatoes which weighed four pounds each and with five or six to a hill. Bismark Kirschner pioneered the grocery business in Bodie, Aurora, and Belmont. His close friend Dutch Veaney became the first white man to grow vegetables commercially in the Belmont area, the first producer and marketer of ice cream in Belmont, the first importer of fresh fish (caught in Walker Lake) for central and southern Nevada, and finally, the first weather forecaster of the region. Sometimes Dutch Veaney's fish were transported in the same wagon with Louis Fidanza's wedding cakes. As the longtime operator of the Cristofo Colombo restaurant and bakery in Belmont, Fidanza's "Italian wedding cakes" were sold throughout Nye County. Fidanza's only competitor was Frenchy Mestrieu, actually a Belgian, who owned the Lafayette restaurant across the street from the Italian establishment. Shamrock Shane, also operating out of Belmont, became central Nevada's first hair stylist. As a special blender and eastern Nevada's supplier of coffee, Frenchy Castagnetto received the appellation "Coffee King of Hamilton," and Jolly John, an Irishman, was the first resident of Hamilton to enjoy the luxuries of a plumbing system. Pablo Laveaga, a Mexican, was the first person in Unionville to use gas for illumination, and J. M. Flurshurtz, a German, became the first ice cream maker of Virginia City. The English Beer brothers, with Joseph Beer as senior partner, ran the famous brewery at Empire. Some twenty-five miles further down the Carson River at the French Ranch, over a score of camels were being used by Frenchmen from the Sahara to transport salt from the Churchill County marshes to the Comstock.[31]

Sauerkraut Schell, the garden-farmer of Smoky Valley; Irish Sulley, an early mine promoter at Rhyolite; Scotty Mathewson, a developer of the Carrara marble camp; and Russian Pearley, who devoted a lifetime to operating gambling parlors at Delemar, Tonopah, Goldfield, Beatty, Bullfrog, and Rhyolite, suggest a few of the immigrant types who provided Nevada newspapers with provocative accounts of the local society. The list could be lengthened to include Cockney Dan, who was born in the center of London, enlisted in the Mexican War, and became one of the first persons to settle in Eureka; or Hungarian John, who founded the camp and town of Tybo, grew wealthy, and died a pauper in 1901; or the six members of "Dot Leetle German Band," who walked from town to town throughout much of northern Nevada and demonstrated a remarkable physical, as well as musical, ability.

The immigrant connections of many of Nevada's leading promoters, industrialists, financiers and prospectors have long been recognized. Both the contemporary journalists and more recent novelists have written much about Peter O'Riley and Patrick McLaughlin, the Irishmen who discovered the Comstock Lode, and about Henry Comstock, the Canadian for whom it was named. French John Bishop not only located the mineral wealth at Gold Hill, but his cabin along with one built by a German and another built by an Irishman comprised three of the first four buildings of the camp. Eilley Orrum Bowers, a Scottish-born boardinghouse keeper, became the Nevada symbol for flamboyant wealth; and the Mexican Gabriel Maldonado, onetime owner of the Mexican mine, was for a time the richest man in Virginia City. John Mackay, James Fair, and William O'Brien of Ireland were three of the shrewdest investors on the Comstock, whereas Phillip Deidesheimer, Baron Ferdinand Von Richthofen, and Hermann Schussler of Germany helped to provide the engineering and scientific initiative which made mining profitable. John McCane of Ireland, James F. Lewis of Wales, Adolph Sutro of Germany, and the tenth Lord Fairfax of England have been pictured by journalists and biographers as energetic and industrious foreigners who helped to transform a barren wilderness into a rich and exciting community.

Although the leading Comstock immigrants are repeatedly discussed in biography, fiction, and newspapers, some of the twentieth-century speculators like John McKane, W. G. Cotter, L. E. Chiatovich, John Olson, and John Jones maintained even stronger European ties. All were the product of the Tonopah-Goldfield boom era and most of the men emphasized their involvement with Old World ideas and institutions. In 1905 John

McKane was declared owner and operator of the richest mine in Nevada, but he openly "maintained allegiance" to King Edward. He had twice stood for the Canadian Parliament and as a Scot planned to sit some day as a lawmaker at Westminster.[32] As a onetime captain in the Russian Army and later the discoverer and developer of the mining camp at Golden Arrow, W. G. Cotter had been trained as an engineer in Europe, and while he was not interested in returning to Russia, he attributed his financial success to the knowledge and experience he had received in his homeland.[33] On the other hand, L. E. Chiatovich was considering returning to the Dalmatian Coast when a French friend who was leaving the country gave him a small claim. Chiatovich eventually used the claim as the site for his profitable cyanide plant.[34] John Olson of Denmark discovered the Silver Glance mine, but quickly sold his interests so that he might fulfill a life long ambition to become an assayer and engineer. John (January) Jones followed the pattern of many Welsh miners in that he was lured from camp to camp by each new discovery. He drifted from Cardiganshire to Canada to Colorado and finally to Goldfield where in 1904 he struck the famed "Million-Dollar January Lode." Jones's widely advertised investment organization, which practically guaranteed a $10,000 return for every $100 invested, made him for a short time the most famous prospector in the state and a hero in his homeland. But his propensity for naïve schemes destroyed his business effectiveness and he quickly resumed the life of a prospector.

If pioneering accentuated the materialistic attitudes among the native Americans, the act of immigration seems to have heightened the urge for self-improvement among the foreign born. While the ability to innovate, discover, and accumulate has at times been identified with the American character and the frontier experience, in Nevada the immigrant provided much of the initiative, energy, and persistence required for the making of the state. Of course, the very *raison d'être* for many of the local newspapers was to advertise and promote the new settlements and boom camps. Consequently, immigrant success stories were used to justify editorial claims and prove the economic potential of the community.

Distrust and Discrimination

The newspaper accounts of the immigrant were a compound of myth and reality, bias and objectivity. But the disconcerting mixture seems to reflect the society. In Nevada, as elsewhere, noble ideals were not always translated into efficient action, and stated principles often bore little relationship to actual practice. When aroused, Nevadans could show great feeling for a particular man and yet condemn hundreds of his fellow nationals. In Charles Goodwin's *The Comstock Club,* Yap Sing was viewed as a cook of great merit, yet his employers argued that "all" Chinese should be banished from the state. In 1870, the Irish of the Comstock could literally shower Joseph Gaerens, an injured Cornishman, with silver coins and then devote the remainder of the evening to fighting and maligning his friends and countrymen. In the various immigrant exclusion movements, newspapers often expressed deep-seated racial and national bias. In a few instances, the popular feeling broke into physical violence, and immigrant groups became the object of contempt and abuse.

Linguistic misunderstanding, differences in social habits, and economic competition resulted in surprisingly frank disclosures of discrimination. For example, in 1864, when five Frenchmen built a small house a mile north of Dr. Ellis's hotel at Steamboat Springs, a vigilance committee was formed, and a party of men drove off the foreigners and burned the building. The group of about a dozen men proudly explained that they fired at the Frenchmen as they fled through the sagebrush. One man was killed from a bullet in the back, but the vigilantes assured the community that they had wounded others. A few days later, the confused and frightened foreigners erected another cabin a few miles to the south in Washoe Valley on land claimed by the famous Sandy Bowers. Again the ruffians struck and chased the young Frenchmen into the brush while the cabin was dragged away and burned.[35] In the meantime, a French brigade had been formed at Virginia City and had marched off to assist their countrymen in Washoe Valley, but they arrived too late to participate in the melee and quickly disbanded. Of course, hatred of Frenchmen as such was not the issue. Men like Monsieur Chavel were teaching Mark Twain and Dan De Quille swordsmanship on the Comstock at the time, and a dozen other highly respected Frenchmen resided in the area. Nevertheless, it was the foreignness and incipient danger which the five non-English-speaking youths represented that brought about their undoing in Washoe Valley.

By the late sixties, Nevada's largest and most easily identified non-white group had come under attack and for the following forty years tended to siphon off much of the latent national bias and racial hatred which might otherwise have been directed towards other foreign elements. The Chinese differed from most migrants in that they were imported to dig irrigation canals, lay rails, and perform other menial tasks. As the original purpose for their importation was satisfied, the predominantly unattached males drifted to the mining camps and took up such occupations as were open to them. Unions and worker-oriented groups expressed immediate resentment, and the Chinese were confined to specified types of labor.

The Orientals, however, faced considerable discrimination

even during their first years in Nevada. As early as 1860, E. D. Sweeney, an Irishman, and Robert Fulstone, an Englishman, instituted the famous cry "the Chinese must go." They organized a "committee of safety" for Carson City, marched to the Chinese Quarter west of town, threw the tools and cooking utensils belonging to the Orientals into a pond, "and politely escorted the moon-eyed rascals beyond the town limits." [36]

Illustrative of the scores of confrontations reported in the newspapers was the Woodchoppers War, a demonstration led by the anti-coolie society of Carson City. By 1868 large numbers of Orientals had been hired to augment or supplant the mainly French-Canadian woodcutters of the Sierra. In early May, a group of the unemployed and unemployable, made up mainly of foreign born and led by an Irishman, declared their intention to drive all Chinese out of the state. However, armed guards were rushed from the Comstock, the sheriff of Douglas County equipped a posse, and the governor declared his readiness to call out the militia, so the more boisterous anti-Chinese talk subsided. It was the big companies and wood contractors who enforced the law and supported the rights of the Chinese, for they were profiting from the cheap labor. Consequently, by 1869 many ruffians in western Nevada were ignoring both the capitalists and the legal restraints in their attacks on the Orientals. Perhaps the most famous confrontation occurred in September, 1869, when a group of Comstock miners, dominated by Irishmen, marched out from Gold Hill and frightened the Chinese from their labor on the Virginia & Truckee Railroad.

Even more ruthless was the "Chinese War of Unionville." At eight o'clock one Sunday morning in mid-January, 1869, a band of citizens drove wagons into the Oriental quarter and ordered "all the Chinese living in town" to prepare to move. By eleven o'clock every Oriental in the community had been escorted on foot or hauled in the wagons out of the district. Some were taken the several miles to the nearest Central Pacific Railroad station. No resistance was encountered from the Chinese, or from the sheriff, who was present, or from a single social, religious, or fraternal organization of the town. The following week a judge dismissed all charges against the men involved and over the following months the local *Humboldt Register* bitterly attacked any newspaper that even questioned the legality or Christianity of the Unionville action.[37]

During the seventies and eighties, the papers revealed a constant series of racial incidents, and in the more troubled periods of 1878–1882 and 1885–1886, the conflict became extremely bitter. From Tybo to Tuscarora and from Wadsworth to Wells, there were clashes between Caucasians and Orientals. The state legislature passed numerous anti-Chinese resolutions and made overtures to the national government for Oriental exclusion. All national discussion and international negotiation on the Chinese problem was followed by scores of editorials in the Nevada press. Anti-Asaitc circles, Workingmen's organizations, Caucasian leagues, anti-Chinese phalanxes, and the Ku Klux Klan were formed in communities throughout the state and vigorously endorsed every move to rid Nevada of the "Yellow Peril." Chinese prostitution was condemned and cohabitation outlawed. In the general election of November, 1880, the state, in a declaration of sentiment, voted 17,259 to 193 to abolish further Chinese immigration.

Despite the discrimination, by 1880 the Orientals numbered 18 percent of the population of Ormsby County (Carson City) and 16 percent of the inhabitants of Lyon County (Silver City and Dayton) and had grown to 8.7 percent of the state's overall population. In areas like Carson City, where the anti-Chinese societies met weekly and employers were forced to discharge

118

Oriental labor or face a boycott, there was a deep-seated fear that the Chinese would literally take over economic control of the community. Over the years, French-Canadians took advantage of the situation and tried to expel the Orientals from the Sierra forests and the lumbering trade; the Irish attacked the Chinese when they attempted to enter the mines; the Scots and Basques refused to herd sheep with the foreigners; and in the twentieth century the Japanese, Koreans, Filipinos, Hindus, and Mexicans demanded separate accommodations and employment on non-Chinese work gangs. Almost everyone criticized "the Celestial's" selling of whiskey to the Indians, his use of opium, his buying and selling of females, and his deplorable living conditions.

In early 1879, O. P. Crawford, a Humboldt County assemblyman, failed to support a resolution directed to the United States Congress calling for the exclusion of the Chinese. Although Crawford emphasized that he withheld his vote for legal and constitutional reasons, over 60 percent of the citizens in his home community of Paradise Valley signed a petition which ordered him "like Adam" to get out of Paradise. The petition was published in most Nevada newspapers. It read in part:

> Your constituents—the same who elected and trusted you, and whom you have so outrageously betrayed and disgraced —hereby bid you leave forever the town and vicinity of Paradise, and seek a clime more congenial, in which to peddle your perjured honor and flout your violated oath; and remember, wherever you go, the contempt and disgust of every honest voter in Humboldt County will follow you.[38]

Outbreaks of anti-Chinese hostility continued well into the twentieth century. One of the more famous and destructive riots occurred in Tonopah on the night of September 15, 1903. Homes were pillaged and destroyed, and Orientals injured, driven onto the desert, and even killed. An immediate outcry against the mob violence reached San Francisco and Washington, D.C., and forced the arrest of fifteen suspects who were accused of directing the raid. Over the following weeks, nine men were released from jail, and at the December trial of the remaining six, all were acquitted in a courtroom scene of "wildest enthusiasm." [39]

Although Reno had reacted somewhat more moderately than most communities during the nineteenth century, in November, 1908, the city, with official authorization, destroyed most of the large Chinese quarter and deliberately left dozens of elderly people homeless at the beginning of winter. Chinatown, which occupied valuable property east of Virginia Street and north of the Truckee River, was declared to be unsanitary and "an eyesore to the people of this beautiful city." Pictures of the destruction showing old men on crutches and young women with babes in their arms were reproduced in newspapers throughout the West. The Chinese consul of San Francisco hastened to Nevada, and the Chinese minister in Washington tried to intervene with the federal authorities. Petitions were signed and the Chinese demanded damages from the city, but in the end it was decided that the action had probably saved the community from a major epidemic and that it was a necessary part of a beautification program. Anyway, the "more substantial" buildings, which were mainly houses of prostitution, had not been bothered.[40]

The immigration of thousands of Chinese into the West was one of the greatest of America's many folk wanderings. Much of Nevada's first half-century of history was bound up with the movement. But for the Chinese, the state was never a promised land; rather, it became a land of heartbreak and defeat. The contemporary Nevada journalists recorded the story, but the twentieth century is still waiting for a literary work in which the Oriental's identity is restored, his personality projected, and his aspirations and frustrations effectively dramatized.

The popular image of the prospector with his shovel and burro and the placer miner with his washing pan seriously distorts the actual character of many Nevada mining camps. Rather than pick-and-shovel economies, industrial societies grew up around the great bodies of ore, and rather than isolated camps, complex urban centers often arose. In many ways, towns like Eureka and McGill tended to resemble the immigrant manufacturing cities of Lawrence, Massachusetts, and Passaic, New Jersey, more than the wild west of popular fiction.

The mineral wealth of the Eureka district was first discovered by Cornish prospectors in the mid sixties, and by the late seventies, the peculiar ore mixture of silver and lead, with smaller amounts of iron, silica, antimony, and other minerals, had resulted in the erection of an elaborate and complex smelting operation. Foreigners did most of the work in Eureka. There were the German engineers and metallurgists, the Welsh smelter and furnace builders, the Slavic miners, the French service personnel, and the Italian charcoal burners. Of the 7,086 people in Eureka County in 1880, more than 59 percent were foreign born. Considering the rather large number of American-born children, a survey of the census suggests that approximately 75 percent of all adults in Eureka in 1880 were foreign immigrants. Some 12 percent of the population of Eureka County had been born in Italy. If the charcoal burners in western White Pine County were included, about 14 percent of the population of the district was Italian. Furthermore, the vast majority of the large Swiss population was culturally and linguistically part of the Italian community. By the late seventies, the production of charcoal for the smelters had become almost exclusively an Italian function.

The diverse ethnic population coupled with continuing labor

disputes provoked distrust and criticism of the foreign born. The first major clash occurred during the winter of 1871–72 when the construction of new furnaces led to a charcoal burner's attempt to raise the prices on the fuel. Several contractors, therefore, hoped to reduce the price of charcoal through the employment of Chinese woodcutters, but so much antagonism developed that by June, 1872, they were forced to dismiss the Orientals. At this point many contractors began to encourage the introduction of cheap Italian labor. The action was to prove almost too successful.[41]

By March, 1876, the *Eureka Daily Sentinel* complained that three-fourths of the migrants coming into the area were unemployable Italian immigrants.[42] The burners were consistently viewed as the dregs of the labor market. Their usual ten dollars per week income was less than one half that paid to common mine workers. Muckers and millmen scorned them, and they were forced to live in crude, ill-equipped hovels and dugouts. The community's deep antipathy to the burners was pointed up by numerous indignities, typical of which was the Oliver Stewart affair. While playing in the timber near his Pinto home, Stewart's nine-year-old son claimed an Italian shot at him. Informed of the attack, the boy's mother accosted the Italian and held him at gun point until neighbors arrived. The foreigner was then taken the fourteen miles over the mountains to Eureka and lodged in jail. Unable to pay the $2,000 bond, the Italian remained incarcerated for some weeks, until it became obvious that the boy was merely attracting attention and seeking approval by accusing a member of a hated minority.[43]

By 1878, the Eureka furnaces were consuming in excess of sixteen thousand bushels of charcoal per day at an overall cost for fuel of nearly $600,000 per month. The hills for a distance of thirty-five to fifty miles around had been denuded of piñon, dwarf cedar, and mountain mahogany from which charcoal was made. As a result of greater transportation costs and a mild recession in 1879, the major smelters attempted to reduce the price of charcoal from thirty to twenty-seven cents per bushel.

The charcoal burners' guilds in France and Italy had during the late eighteenth and early nineteenth century developed into secret revolutionary societies which played major political roles in the life of both countries. In Nevada, however, the burners had been slow to organize and it was not until July 6, 1879, that some five or six hundred men met at Colso Tatti's saloon and took the first steps to form The Eureka Coalburners Protective Association.[44] The group resolved to hold the price of charcoal at thirty cents a bushel or after July 9 they would cut off all supplies to the smelters. In addition, they demanded payment in cash rather than in credit at local stores where they were consistently overcharged and defrauded. They also asked that shipping receipts be open for inspection and that there be a careful checking of weights and measures. For a few days, it appeared that the burners' demands would be met, but as feeling mounted, the Italian businessmen and store operators, who at first had supported the association, tended to desert their laboring fellow countrymen in favor of a more restrained course of action.

Of the four original officers of the charcoal union, two were Italian and two German, but the four disassociated themselves from the organization when trouble seemed imminent. Vocal opposition to the burners' demands was not raised by the smelters, but rather by Reinhold Sadler, a German who later became governor of Nevada, and by Joseph Tognini and Joseph Vanina, both Swiss-Italians. All three had contracted at a fixed price to supply charcoal to the big corporations. Therefore, they hoped to reduce the price paid to the burners and, as middlemen, reap the profit. Other Germans and Italians like Joseph Hausman,

Solomon Ashim, Peter Strozzi, Joe Magnini, and Lambert Molinelli were minor community officials or businessmen who rather reluctantly supported the city administration. The sheriff was a young and aggressive Irishman.

A further ethnic factor influencing the course of events during the spring and early summer of 1879 was a series of anti-Chinese, anti-Catholic and antiforeign movements. An article in the *Eureka Daily Sentinel* of March 27 explained, "It is questionable if any town in the United States of the same size as Eureka possesses so many organizations, secret and otherwise, and no less than three have been formed in the past two weeks." One of the three new societies was the American Labor Union. Along with the better established anti-Chinese groups and the Ku Klux Klan it proposed that English-speaking Caucasians "born on the North American Continent" break the monopoly on jobs held by the foreign born of Eureka. The American Labor Union and its kindred societies blossomed into active associations and throughout 1879 urged the exclusive employment of Americans in local industry and in public and civic positions.[45]

During the confusion, the rumors, and the bitterness, the Italians repeatedly used force to stop the loading and transport of charcoal. A sheriff's posse was quickly formed to arrest the troublesome foreigners. Spies were recruited, guerilla-type bands were formed in the hills, and lawsuits became frequent. On August 11, the governor was asked by Sadler, Tognini, Vanina, and others to send in the militia, and newspapers throughout the state demanded that law and order be restored and that the burners be crushed. The most eloquent voice raised for the burners was that of a mysterious writer known as Veritas. Veritas later proved to be Louis Monaco, a twenty-seven-year old Swiss-Italian photographer of Eureka. He noted the "miserable, pitiful state of the poor toiler of the forest" and addressed a plea to the company, the middlemen, and the public officials to rise above the deliberate cultivation of prejudice.

> Throw down your mask, be fair and just, and in atonement for the past be at least humane in time to come. And since you have been made rich by these poor workers, don't raise prejudices or talk of sending an army with guns, bullets, etc.; but it better becomes your duty to send an army of cheese and macaroni to quench the hunger of these poor, famished, desperate wretches, who are really more hungry than ill-disposed.[46]

Joseph Tognini, one of the contracting middlemen, replied to Veritas and, supposing him to be an American humanitarian who did not understand the idiosyncrasies of the foreigners, ordered him to stay out of the conflict. "Veritas is exceedingly funny in his conclusions, when he speaks of cheese and macaroni as opposed to guns and bullets." The burners' union was a "conspiracy" and a "lawless band," and their talk of freedom was "bosh, balderdash and nonsense." Laissez-faire must prevail. "Can you stop the sun from rising or the wind from blowing?" Remember "your sympathy is not wanted" by the "better class of Italians."

> It is perfectly natural that in times of depression and stagnation of business, idle men . . . seek some plausible excuse to foment other idlers, hoping thereby to derive a benefit from the wreck of the fortunes of good citizens. There is a law governing the business conduct of all men, viz: that of supply and demand.[47]

On August 18, in a major confrontation near Fish Creek, three Italians and two Swiss were killed, six other foreigners were seriously wounded, and fourteen were taken as prisoners. The Italian minister in Washington asked for an investigation and the Italian consul and vice-consul at San Francisco hurried to Eureka. After the "Fish Creek Massacre," the resistance of the Italians slowly collapsed, and although trials, law suits, and occasional clashes continued for many months, the burners did not again challenge the pillars of Eureka's economic life.[48]

The Italian War tended to end with the "Fish Creek Massacre," but the immigrant irritation continued for many years. The widespread journalistic attention given to the affair, the prejudice and violence engendered, and the several moving letters of Louis Monaco made it comparable to a Sacco and Vanzetti drama; yet in almost ninety years, there has been neither an adequate literary nor historical treatment of the Eureka Italians.

During the early years of the twentieth century, the copper camps of eastern Nevada were rapidly expanded into a major industrial complex. Radical unions were quickly formed, labor trouble became commonplace, and large numbers of immigrants flowed into the region. The labor organizations objected to the employment of certain foreign nationals in skilled jobs and particularly opposed the company's importation of Greeks and Japanese from the mines at Bingham Canyon, Utah.

In March, 1908, *The Ely Mining Record* declared that "Greeks, Hungarians, Slavonians, and Japanese have been coming into the district by the hundreds." The paper charged that they were migrating "under a guarantee of employment" when it would be a "far better policy for companies to employ home labor . . . and thus give the people who are interested in the upbuilding of the country an opportunity to make a living."[49] About a month later, in a bitter editorial entitled "Cheap Foreign Labor," the *Record* declared, "It is now apparent to all observing people that a systematic effort has been undertaken by the allied interests in this district to supplant American labor by the employment of Greeks." Indeed, the reluctance of employers to

hire the native born had made "an honest American workman
. . . a nine day wonder" in the White Pine area.[50]

Over the following months the Greeks along with Slavs,
Mexicans, Japanese, Italians, Koreans, and smaller numbers from
other European, Latin American, and Asian countries quickly
converted the mining district at Ruth and Kimberly and the
smelter area at McGill into variegated and sometimes turbulent
foreign communities isolated by distance from the outside world.
By 1910, almost 10 percent of the 7,441 persons in White Pine
County had been born in Greece. In the same year, the camp
at Copper Flat on the rim of the pit boasted 233 adults (persons
over sixteen), only four of whom had been born in the United
States and only one (a Swede) in northern or western Europe.
The remaining 228 adults represented fourteen foreign countries.

Deep resentment and fear of the southern Europeans first
burst into the open in 1907, when many newspaper articles and
editorials called for a "White Man's Camp." In January, 1908,
the confusion and violence resulted in the death of three Greeks;
eventually the United States secretary of state, the governor of
Nevada, and several Greek consuls were drawn into an investigation of immigrant conditions. In the meantime the findings of
a White Pine County jury that a Greek was guilty of attempting
to murder a company guard had to be set aside by the judge on
the ground that "racial prejudice was shown in the jury's ver-
dict." [51] While the community feeling was at a fever pitch, some
McGill residents, along with a deputy sheriff, decided to "have a
general cleaning up of all the Greeks." [52] And on January 21,
1908, many of the confused and frightened foreigners were called
from their homes and forced to stand in line while "the good
were culled from the bad." Some eighty-seven who failed the
inspection were loaded into two box-cars and hauled the thirteen
miles to Ely. Since no one wished to pay the rail charges to trans-

port the cold and hungry foreigners further into the desert, they were eventually released.

The greatest tragedy to grow out of the events of 1907–08 was an atomization and feeling of distrust among the foreign nationals similar to that which had developed at Eureka. For example, in an apparent effort to court favor with the authorities, one Greek merchant brought personal charges against several fellow countrymen who had sought food and shelter at his store. Such action destroyed self-respect and pride in national culture and created factions and hatreds within the Greek community. Arms were imported by Greeks to protect themselves from Greeks, resentment led to a further killing, and newspaper headlines like "Greeks are Robbing Greeks" became common.[53]

Throughout the same period, a less well-organized, but equally acrimonious attack was directed against the Japanese. When a drunk shot into a barracks housing Japanese railroad workers, the occupants retaliated by taking the man a prisoner and returning him to McGill. But a local newspaper caption misrepresented the facts by proclaiming "Japs Regarded as Undesirable." When the community learned that a Japanese man was living with a white woman, immigration officials were brought from Salt Lake City for the purpose of deporting the "undesirable." Certain Greeks and Slavs were also constantly faced with the possibility of deportation as a result of being charged with gambling and keeping houses of ill fame, and many journalists seemed pleased with a western Nevada report which claimed that Japanese and Hindu railway workers were rioting.

During the autumn of 1907, when exaggerated reports from Hazen declared that a full-scale race war was being waged along the Southern Pacific railroad tracks east of Reno, several editors became almost ecstatic with delight. One writer argued that "this racial friction should be carefully nurtured and fanned into a

Gold Creek, along with a dozen other
towns in Elko County, long supported a
Chinese store and a small Chinese colony.
It was in Gold Creek that the famed
six-toed Chinaman was hanged and that
many of the older Chinese lived
until well into the twentieth century.
The photograph depicts the town's
Chinese store about 1910. (Courtesy
of Nevada Historical Society)

Soon after the turn of the century
the Basque Bar appeared in Nevada towns
as a recreation and amusement center
for immigrant sheepmen. Among the
approximately 750 persons in the Austin
area in 1910 were some 25 Spanish,
10 French, and 15 Portuguese
sheepherders and agricultural laborers.
They frequented Domingo's Bar.
Domingo Acorda is behind the counter.
The proprietor of a Chinese restaurant
is pictured with the sheepmen.
Picture taken in 1909. (Courtesy
of Nevada Historical Society)

The Italian Benevolent Society
preparing for a parade in
Reno about 1910. (Courtesy
of Nevada Historical Society)

Luigi Capurro married Dominica Gardella
and immigrated to the United States from
Genoa in 1871. Luigi became a successful
rancher near Reno. His infant son died
soon after the picture was taken.
(Courtesy of Nevada Historical Society)

fierce flame of passion by American section bosses—and Irish, too. It will help a lot to solve the Oriental immigration problem that is puzzling this government today. If a war of extermination between the two unnaturalized alien races could be 'rubbed up' on American soil, the desired end would soon be reached, with no fear of demands for indemnity." [54]

Following the lead of eastern and northern Nevada, *The Tonopah Daily Sun* opened a campaign against the foreign born. On July 30, 1907, *The Sun* declared that southern Europeans were "destroying the prosperity of Tonopah" and that American labor had been almost completely "crowded out by the non-English speaking Slavs." [55] George Davidovich, the wealthy merchant and saloon keeper, was accused of conducting the "traffic" in European labor. Since there was another carload "of miners for Tonopah" being recruited in New York City, *The Sun* suggested that immediate and drastic action be taken. [56]

> The facts are that south of Europe miners working here spend no money in the town. After every pay day you can see them lined up in front of the post office, buying money orders and sending 90 percent of their wages to the old country. They live huddled together in shacks and a dozen in a room like Chinamen. Their living is no better than the worst of coolies and they are of as little benefit to the community. They have little intelligence and are low in the scale of civilization. [57]

For over two years, Lindley C. Branson, the Quaker editor of *The Sun*, led the crusade against southern Europeans and Asians. Frequent editorials and cartoons depicted a European giant crushing innocent America, or President Roosevelt refusing to see the evil Japanese as they slipped by him into a beautiful land. Branson's arguments were not novel, but he did provide Nevada with a vocal exponent of the anti-immigration movement. Branson pointedly rebuffed foreign groups in Tonopah which urged tolerance, and he charged Davidovich and other immigrant leaders with receiving fifty dollars for every man they imported and placed in the mines. He explained that northern Europeans of the nineteenth century made good citizens while southern Europeans of the twentieth century made bad citizens. The latter could never be blended into the American character. To them "liberty meant license" and every tree trunk was to be transformed "into a firebrand." According to Branson, the Japanese would never disavow their "allegiance to an emperor beyond the sea." [58]

During the nineteenth century, the few Japanese who had arrived in Nevada had been received with mixed emotions. In many instances they were given high praise, but on other occasions they met with hostility. For example, in August, 1868, a troupe of performers was on a stagecoach traveling from Dayton to Virginia City when a white man ordered one of the Orientals to lower a curtain. The Japanese understood little English and failed to respond. A fistfight ensued and when the stage coach reached Virginia City, a local justice fined three of the foreigners twenty dollars each. The party was among the first of their race to arrive in the United States, and in California their performance had been declared excellent. Nevertheless, after the fines, an unsuccessful performance at Piper's Opera House, and excessive local charges left them without funds, the Pacific Mail Company transported the group out of the state free of charge.[59]

During the first decade of the twentieth century, a large number of Japanese were drawn to Nevada to participate in the railroad building and the new mining boom. At first the sons of Nippon were confused with other Orientals and generally ignored in the large labor battalions. But in January, 1905, they were singled out as a particularly dangerous minority. In that month, the some sixty-five Japanese adults of Reno organized a grand Japanese-American celebration marking the fall of Port Arthur and the military victories over the Russians. Although many community leaders and particularly the administration and faculty of the University of Nevada actively joined the Japanese festivities, the *Nevada State Journal* balanced all favorable and friendly news items with editorials suggesting that Japanese labor should be excluded from Nevada railroad construction and, if necessary, force should be used to bar further employment of the Orientals.[60]

Some weeks later in an article entitled "The Yellow Peril" numerous arguments were advanced to prove that the United States must support "our old friend Russia"; otherwise America would be overrun by Japanese immigrants and the Pacific Ocean by the Japanese navy. "In the name of common sense, then let us cease our maudlin and uncalled for sympathy with the yellow nation at war." America must stop "pulling British chestnuts out of the fire," Russia must win, and the West Coast must have a "Japanese exclusion act." The United States would present the new act "to a nation the fangs of whose resentment have been made helpless by the forces of defeat."[61] Over the following years, much of the Nevada press became even more aggressive in seeking Japanese exclusion. The state laws to prevent the intermarriage of Orientals and Caucasians were augmented and bills were introduced to bar the Japanese from working on any publicly financed project.

The animosity was reflected in outbreaks of violence like the one that occurred at Caliente on the night of June 19, 1906. While several carloads of Japanese railroad workers were being transported to their place of employment along the tracks, the drawbar either broke or was removed, allowing the cars to roll free down the track. The cars eventually crashed into the rear of a train, and, although no one was seriously injured, the Japanese assumed that the affair had been deliberately planned. Fighting broke out, and when a deputy sheriff rushed to the scene, shooting followed. The sheriff was killed and several Japanese critically wounded.[62] With over two hundred Japanese in the area, rumor mongers declared that the Orientals had seized Caliente and that the town had been turned into a fortified stronghold. After the 1906 affair and down to World War I there were repeated suggestions that many of Nevada's Orientals were spies laying the groundwork for Japan's take-over of the American West.

During the early twentieth century, much of the more aggressive anti-immigration sentiment in Nevada was closely tied to unionization, illiteracy, and a strange fear of foreign sabotage. As large numbers of eastern Europeans began to join unions and become effective agitators, labor's anti-immigration sentiment diminished. As communities established schools for the teaching of English to adults, and mine and railway supervisors initiated the policy of posting warning signs in numerous languages, accidents among the foreign born declined and talk of their carelessness and stupidity died away. And finally, when Italy, Greece, the South Slavs, and Japan became America's allies during World War I, fear of an alien political syndicate generally disappeared.

Scores of articles, editorials, feature stories, headlines, and cartoons reflect Nevada's periodic discrimination against various foreign-born groups. Often the newspaper treatment was a conditioned reflex and not an examined premise. Often the journalists noted, but failed to reflect upon, the contemporary problems. Often the foreign born were viewed as part of a monolithic mass of nameless Greeks, Slavs, Italians, and Chinese. Nevertheless, the newspapers offered a vehicle for the exchange of ideas and today they provide historians with a means of inquiry into Nevada society. Unfortunately, the Japanese clash at Caliente, the Italian conflict at Eureka, the Greek episode at McGill, and similar incidents have not been discussed in significant works which would serve those who wished to understand the forces of discrimination in a frontier environment.

Rivalry and Conflict

Perhaps only the instinct of self-preservation or the remnant of some Old World ethic kept many of the young immigrant men from becoming unmanageable in the American West. In early Nevada, thousands of men were almost completely self-governed and dozens of isolated communities were self-directed. Under such circumstances some immigrants were sure to engage in irresponsible confrontation rather than fruitful cooperation, in destructive rivalry rather than creative enterprise.

In a way, the newspapers have created an image of the immigrant in early Nevada by means of their selective reporting. They not only recorded the day-to-day events, but sometimes wove the facts into enduring editorials and vignettes. Obviously, some of the newspaper stories were pointless and incidental in that they were mere tales of violence, but others were absorbed into the life and folklore of the state. Thus an avenue was provided whereby Nevada's immigrants helped to contribute to the formation, extension, and maintenance of a regional character.

Perhaps inevitably, minor conflict and rivalry more often grew out of disputes between two foreign groups than between Americans and immigrants. At least a dozen Nevada authors have noticed the traditional animosity between the Irish and Cornish. The often amusing and exaggerated areas of enmity grew up during the era of the California gold rush and were quickly reflected and even intensified in early Nevada. On the Comstock, Cornish and Irish boxers pounded each other into pulp, and on at least one occasion, the respective trainers engaged in an even more deadly rivalry with pistols.

In July and August of 1870, the Irish and Cornish embarked on a week-long conflict which resulted in Gold Hill becoming known as Bloody Gulch. The trouble started when one group of the Fenian guards attempted to parade on their training grounds at Fort Homestead at the upper end of Gold Hill. The Cornish heckled them from the sidelines and several fights ensued. The disturbance continued over the following days until a major clash occurred in a local saloon. During the melee every door was torn off, every bottle of liquor broken, and, after fists became numb, pistols were introduced. But while a score of men were injured, not a single Celt was killed.[63] Street fights, brawls, and violent conflicts on election night, like the one at Candelaria on November 6, 1888, were accepted with general good humor by the Nevada communities. But incidents like the one at Brunswick Mill on the Carson River were considered far more serious.[64] In April, 1875, some of the Irish revolted against an English factory superintendent and subsequently wrecked much of the machinery at the mill.

The invasion of each other's bars became a common practice on holidays. In both Virginia City and Austin several men lost their lives in the numerous saloon-crashing episodes. At the same time, the Manxmen of Virginia City refused to drink with either of their Celtic kin and erected their own pub, while the more prestigious Scots formed their Caledonian clubs and celebrated Robert Burns's birthday with marked exclusiveness. Yet on occasion, as shown by Alice Ward Bailey in *The Sage Brush Parson,* the Irish, the Cornish, and the Scots could unite as a

Celtic phalanx so that they might more effectively harass any Englishman imprudent enough to argue politics.

One classic example of the Cornish-Irish feud has been noted in several short stories and touched on in at least one full length book, but details of the episode are still buried in old newspapers. As the town of Belmont was settled during the late 1860s, large numbers of Irish and Cornish miners drifted into the area. In April, 1867, a rumor circulated among the Irish work force of the Silver Bend Mining Company that they were to be discharged so that the English-dominated company could employ more Cornishmen. A gang of ruffians quickly decided to take matters into its own hands. One night they seized the general agent of the company, manhandled him, and finally killed a gunwielding passerby who attempted to assist the agent. A protective league was immediately formed, and the Ku Klux Klan organized an "America for Americans" citizens' committee, but further serious clashes were averted.[65]

In February, 1874, John Booth, a longtime newspaperman of Nevada, moved to the rising county seat and soon thereafter founded the *Belmont Courier*. Although an intelligent and balanced editor, Booth was a native of York, England, and occasionally indulged in a friendly needling of his Irish readers. He pointed out that his birth date, March 16, was one day earlier than that of Saint Patrick and that the great saint was really a British emigrant trying to civilize Ireland. Feeling slowly mounted, and in August, 1874, when an Irishman, Richard O'Malley, tried to gain the Democratic nomination for sheriff of Nye County, Booth, although a Republican, threw his substantial influence to the Democrat incumbent, James Caldwell. When O'Malley lost the nomination, and violence was narrowly averted, Booth unwisely explained that it had been illiterates, fire-eaters, and "sellout Irishmen" who had supported O'Malley.

A few weeks later, O'Malley shot and seriously wounded Booth's son, George. Eventually, public reaction forced the leaders of the "Irish faction" to leave town, but by that time, both George Booth and his wife had died, and John Booth had moved to Austin to embark upon his last newspaper undertaking.[66]

The duration of the Irish-English feud at Belmont was somewhat unusual, though international rivalries were not. For years, the Chileans of Virginia City insisted on flying their flag beside the Mexican flag on Mexican Independence day. Consequently, every September the two Spanish-speaking societies prepared themselves for national combat. Such disagreements were commonplace in early Nevada. In August, 1863, the *Virginia Evening Bulletin* carried the caption "An International Scrimmage." A German and an Irishman had provoked a violent disturbance which had in turn grown out of a German-Mexican fight of the previous day.[67] Slavs and Chinese in Carson City cut and mauled each other so often that the court devised a rather perfunctory system of fines. But the clash between Italians and Slavs employed on railroad work gangs proved more serious. In one encounter north of Reno, four Italians were killed in a single night and guards had to be posted to protect the Latins from their former European neighbors. About the turn of the century, Italian railroad laborers at Sparks resisted the employment of the Japanese. After several fights and one murder, however, the Italians slowly grew to respect the newcomers and eventually many worked under Japanese section foremen. In the same period, the Japanese and Chinese of Reno became involved in a conflict over the closing of a brothel. In early 1905, the Japanese organized the Chigin society, in part designed to force all undesirable members of their race out of the city. They were immediately confronted by Tom Dung, a Chinese. Dung not only ran a house of prostitution using Japanese girls, but he had taken one of the girls as his common-law wife. After months of economic and legal conflict the well-organized and aggressive Japanese finally closed the brothel.[68]

During the first decade of the twentieth century, a rash of racial incidents occurred in the Tonopah area of southern Nevada. Newspaper headlines like "Race War at Berlin," "Criminality of the Foreign Born," and "Too Much Nationality" became common. In November of 1903, a *Tonopah Bonanza* caption cried "Murdered by Mexican." At Lone Mountain, a camp some twenty miles west of Tonopah, the Mexicans had killed one of four Italian brothers as the result of a feud over packing wood down from the mountains.[69] In March, 1906, the sheriff of Nye County and a small posse made a spectacular nighttime drive in an early-day automobile to the camp of Berlin. They traveled the seventy-five miles north of Tonopah to restore order in a three-way conflict between Portuguese, Italians, and Basques.[70] About the same time, the sheriff was called to the camp of Clifford fifty miles east of Tonopah to investigate the murder of a union man who had gone to the community to force all Italians to work under union contracts.[71] In August, 1907, the sheriff traveled a hundred miles south of Tonopah to crush the so-called Austro-Mexican War.[72] And in the same month, the deputy sheriff killed Frenchy Lafleur at Atwood (Gold Dyke) sixty miles northwest of Tonopah and was immediately charged with murder by several Frenchmen of the community.[73] The "bloody Miller riots," in which the officials tried to keep Italian strikers from killing Greek strikebreakers, was something of a relief for the sheriff, since it occurred only twelve miles from town.

In the years before World War I, the Greeks and Slavs of White Pine County were periodically involved in serious personal hostility. But almost as often strife broke out between the

Croats and the Serbs. Both had carried their suspicion of the other to America, and each seemed pleased to stage a bloody knife battle, particularly if the affections of a woman or the fine points of religion were in question. Even the Finns and the Swedes agreed upon widely separate quarters in Tonopah, and the clannish Finns and the proud Montenegrins came to blows in several of the isolated mining camps of Nye County. During the era of the Balkan Wars, Greeks and Italians engaged in numerous battles. The Greeks and Turks sometimes had to be housed and employed in different areas, and the Koreans, who were enraged when referred to as Japanese, brought about the death of an American who consistently affirmed the superiority of the Nipponese culture to that of the conquered Korean. However, the most well-defined, hard-hitting, and colorful national rivalry ever experienced in Nevada was the feeling provoked by the Franco-Prussian War.

Anticipating the struggle in which their countrymen were soon to become engaged, the Germans started the conflict on the Comstock by killing a Frenchman during the summer of 1869. On August 12, Maximilian Flaco, a worker at the slaughterhouse at American Flat, drifted into a brewery operated by two Germans. He became belligerent and abusive, and the next morning the Frenchman was found with a crushed skull, lying outside the brewery door.[74] Trouble continued in American Flat, and by the following spring it had spread to other Comstock communities. By July, 1870, both the French and the Germans had organized themselves into committees and commissions. In early August, as the European war got underway, the saloon encounters blossomed into major brawls. On August 4, the *Gold Hill Daily News* announced "A Bloody International Fight at American Flat," and then after a second day of violence, the paper carried the rather prosaic but pointed caption

"Still Fighting" and suggested that man's reason had been un-hinged by dog days.[75] Some two weeks later the *Territorial Enterprise* declared "Another International Battle" to be in progress, and finally on August 17 it announced, "All Quiet on the Rhine." One entire day had passed on the Comstock without a skirmish between the "French and Prussian armies." [76]

The manning of the saloon battlements, however, was not limited to the French and Germans. An article of August 16 read,

> At the brewery in American Flat, night before last, another grand fight of all nationalities took place. Germans, Irish, French, Americans, Spanish, Swedes, Sclavonians, Italians, and English participated on the festive occasion. The representative of Albion appears to have been very closely engaged, as he came out of the fight with one of his 'blawsted' eyes hanging on his cheek and with his 'bloody' nose split open.[77]

The English and Italians generally supported the Prussian cause, and the Irish normally threw their influence to the side of the French. But during the "August Days," individuals often switched sides, depending on who bought the whiskey. On one occasion, a contingent of Scotsmen, a few Mexicans, and a Swede united to defy the remainder of the house. In another instance, a Prussian was found who sang the "Marseillaise." And in yet a third encounter, a Spaniard was stabbed when he did not know which side he was on.

One of the more preposterous episodes was entitled "The Knights of the Geiger Grade." A Prussian exuberant over German successes and an Irishman formerly of the British cavalry quarreled over the proper use of the sabre. They grew angry, exchanged challenges, mounted mules, and from one hundred yards apart the pair of Don Quixotes rushed toward each other. The mules became frightened and only after much effort did the riders get close enough for the Irishman to hit his opponent on the head with a cudgel and thus win the battle.[78] During the months of August and September, 1870, it seemed that half of the population of the Comstock was tilting at Prussian or French windmills.

During the late summer of 1870, the German Sanitary Fund of the Comstock quickly collected funds to purchase a gold and silver brick to be sent to Berlin to be used "for the wounded, and widows and orphans of the fallen." The inscription on the $3,123 brick further explained that "Germany, battling for unity and civilization, commands the sympathy of Republican America. We may not draw the sword, but would help to stanch your wounds. Virginia. Nevada."[79] The brick won the highest prize in a patriotic competition in Prussia. It became the object of a national lottery, was won by a Hamburg merchant, was given by him to the military, and was finally placed on display in the trophy room at the armory in Berlin.

During the autumn of 1870, the Germans conducted a series of Grand Military Balls, but on the night of January 31, 1871, during a "jollification" and torchlight procession through Virginia City, they met with considerable resistance. Much of the crowd appeared unfriendly, and when a marcher retaliated against a boy who had knocked a torch from his hand, the German was escorted to jail.[80]

There was also an abrupt change in attitude on the part of the Italian immigrants. During October and November, 1870, the Italians and Germans attended each other's celebrations and united in rejoicing at their common success in Europe. But when the Germans refused to pay Professor Farini for staging their New Year's Eve party, the Italian-German friendship collapsed, and at least two suicides or murders were traced to the accompanying bitterness.

The Franco-Prussian War was also fought with considerable spirit in Hamilton, where, after the formation of a McMahon Club, there was talk of creating a "Napoleonic Reserve" which would back up the European forces with men and supplies. In the eastern town, the French appear to have been the dominant element, whereas in western Nevada, the Prussians were the more active. In the new railroad town of Elko, the Germans collected forty-five dollars and ordered their country's new flag. It was flown over the town in late August, 1870, so that all could see the flag which was "borne by King William," and was "floating victoriously at the head of nearly a million of warriors." [81] Perhaps no paper equaled the Carson City *Morning Appeal* in pure chauvinistic romanticism. Typical of its articles was a seven-stanza poem on August 28, 1870. After deprecating the flippant, taunting, and conceited attitude of the French and the ruthlessness of the Corsican leadership, the poem concluded with a cry for Germanic support around the world.

> And surely not in vain we now address you,
> You also hear the soul inspiring tale
> For what we fight to-day, it must be conquered
> For all who from the German spirit hail.
> Be French or German! that is now the question;
> The arena even now is entered by the foe;
> Help, brothers, help! help in this mortal combat
> Across the ocean—think of German woe.[82]

Of course many Frenchmen and Germans did not participate in the nationalistic observances. For example, the French-born Nevada newspaperman Andrew Maute, whose father-in-law was a German, was feted by the Carson City Turnverein and was affectionately known as the "Great Bismark." In Belmont and Austin, as well as in Eureka and Reno, the smaller number of French and Germans refused to become involved in the war activities, and most of the German Jewish merchants seemed to ignore the problems of the fatherland.

Immigrant conflict in Nevada as elsewhere throughout the West was more often personal and pointless than organized and nationally oriented. The theme of family strife, with brother set against brother in deadly conflict, was always a newsworthy topic and provided the basis for much journalistic improvisation. Distasteful accounts like that about the four Welsh brothers of Candelaria, who were involved in the crude and wanton killing of each other, or the Irish-Canadian O'Neils of Spring Valley, whose confused feud led to brother being pitted against brother, suggest a hostile and often brutalized society with inadequate legal restraints.

Unquestionably the most famous reenactment of the Cain and Abel drama centered around the Felesina brothers and their experiences as woodcutters in the pine nut area of eastern Douglas County. According to the newspapers, in June, 1874, Giovanni Imperali awakened in the forest to see Domenico Felesina striking his own brother with a hatchet. Later young Imperali watched in shocked horror while Felesina burned the corpse. Fear for his life led Imperali to say nothing of the incident until he had come down from the hills in December, 1874. At that point, Imperali wrote to his parents in Italy and told of the crime. The Imperali and the Felesina families were both from the hamlet of Giosotto, near Milan. Soon after receipt of the letter, Domenico Felesina returned to his Italian home, whereupon the elder Imperali, with his son's letter in hand, went to the authorities.

After the introduction of the Italian police into the affair, the numerous tales and extensive journalistic speculation and improvisation leave the reader bewildered. Felesina escaped from the police in Giosotto and was chased about Italy; Imperali and Felesina were found to be cousins, and the families jealous of each other; and a Felesina brother, Antonio, entered the picture as a wood contractor at Carson City. Antonio absconded with $3,500 paid to him in advance of his wood deliveries and became the object of a Nevada search. When Domenico Felesina was captured in Italy he told the police that while he was in the Carson Valley area he had worked for an Irish wood superintendent by the name of Kelly, an English farmer by the name of Boyd, and a German farmer whose name he had forgotten. Domenico claimed that all would swear to his innocence. Thereupon, the Italian government requested the United States Secretary of State, Hamilton Fish, to ferret out the truth of the case. Fish placed the matter in the hands of the federal officials in Nevada and emphasized that the government of His Majesty, Victor Emanuel II, was anxious to see justice done.[53] In the meantime, Imperali had left the state and with only vague and unauthenticated reports the case was dismissed. The Felesina affair failed to point up the efficiency of international justice, but it did show the close relationship between many Nevadans and their homeland.

Unfortunately the foreign born were often guilty of the violence of which they were accused. Both John McCallum and his Scottish fellow cook John Murphy were to die because they could not agree on the making of Irish stew. In May, 1874, the two Scotsmen were employed by a fluming company near Lake Tahoe. Although both were Scottish-born, Murphy was of Irish parentage and insisted that McCallum learn how to make Irish stew. The Scotsman belittled the diet of the Emerald Isle and, while drunk, seriously injured Murphy in a fight. Murphy walked the fourteen miles to Carson City to see a doctor and a few days later returned to the mountains to even the score. Over the following several days, Murphy stalked McCallum throughout much of western Nevada and finally overtook him in Carson City where, after pursuing his fellow countryman through stores and down alleys, he finally shot and killed him in front of the post office.

The trial of Murphy lasted several months, and, although the execution was postponed three times, the hanging finally took place at high noon on December 29, 1874. Murphy did not know when he was born, but as a boy he had run away from home and enlisted in the British navy. He later deserted and arrived in California in 1849. Murphy worked first as a miner, later as a pugilist, and in the late fifties, he enlisted in the American Army. He deserted in 1860 and made his way to the Comstock, where he became famous as a fighter in Virginia City and later in Aurora. Both Murphy and his manager were involved in shooting affrays with Cornishmen and Manxmen, and in 1864, Murphy again joined the Army, but deserted before his unit left the state. During the late sixties, Murphy became a cook, but devoted most of his attention to "anti-Christian spiritualism." Although completely illiterate, he was a good showman and drew large crowds when he talked with spirits. His final hour-and-a-half sermon was delivered from the gallows before his execution.[84] John Murphy was a braggart, a drunk, a pugilist, a swordsman, and a preacher—a classic example of the undisciplined and emotionally disturbed immigrant who, with an attractive vulgarity and an appetite for pain, created a grave and disturbing element on the Nevada frontier.

The journalists of 1874 intertwined the Felesina and Murphy episodes with a third western Nevada affair—the shooting of the Frenchman Frank Ben by the printer-journalist William Somers. Ben was working in a field in Carson Valley when Somers rode along the road on horseback. The printer dismounted and shot the Frenchman in cold blood. The community was outraged and a move to lynch Somers was thwarted only after he was moved from Genoa to the Carson City jail. But as the months passed, the murderer was made to appear a "giddy-headed" lad who had merely protected his honor after the foreigner had verbally attacked him. One writer suggested that the young man from Iowa might well become another "Mark Twain or Dan De Quille" and that Frenchmen were known for their sharp tongues. Numerous newspaper editorials led the people of Carson Valley and Carson City to reverse their position. A petition signed by several hundred citizens resulted in the death sentence being set aside at Christmastime 1874. Seldom have the violent emotions and mob instincts of a community been converted into bigotry and antiforeign prejudice more rapidly and more completely than in the Ben-Somers case.[85]

Another simple and senseless type of violence which overtook many young and inexperienced foreigners was typified by the Cotton Tibbs affair. In May, 1912, a Basque was shot and killed while eating breakfast on the Adams and McGill Ranch, some thirty-five miles southwest of Ely. The cook, Cotton Tibbs, was known as a troublemaker. His three specialties were molesting Indian squaws, getting drunk, and using firearms. After shooting the young Benifacio Egosque, Tibbs then rode to a neighboring ranch and explained that four Basques had attacked him while he was cooking and that he had fired in self-defense. He volunteered to ride into Ely and give himself over to the sheriff. Tibbs, of course, never found his way to Ely, and the newly arrived Basque died before the name of his home town could be learned.[86] Cotton Tibbs added another notch to his six-gun, and a family in the Pyrenees waited to learn of the accomplishments of their son in the New World. The disappearance of immigrants in the vastness of the American West was a theme reemphasized with depressing regularity through the printing of European letters of inquiry in Nevada newspapers.

Obviously, not all or even a large percentage of the Nevada immigrants were involved in rivalry and conflict. When an English naval officer moved to Virginia City with his non-English-speaking Japanese wife, she was received by polite society and showered with pleasant attention by the entire community. Later, as Nevada was being depopulated during the 1880s, journalists put forth the suggestion that the industrious Japanese might make desirable settlers for the state's sparsely inhabited valleys. Examples of friendship between the foreign born were no doubt more common than the incidents of disagreement. When a Frenchman and a German were temporarily marooned in a mine shaft, they became close friends although neither spoke the other's language and neither was able to speak more than a few words of English. Clearly, the isolation of Nevada's mining camps stimulated mutual trust and interdependence at the same time that it promoted antagonisms.

Even the English-Irish conflict seems to have been more of a masquerade than a deep-seated enmity. The two groups commonly united to oppose the Chinese in the nineteenth century and to oppose immigration from southeast Europe in the twentieth. Of the 1,076 persons living west of A Street in Virginia City in June of 1880, 360 were foreign born, of which 277 were either English or Irish. Twenty-two percent of all the married English persons had Irish spouses. Indeed, over twice as many English men and women had Irish spouses as were married to Americans.[87] While the upper middle class who lived on Virginia City's west side was no doubt atypical of English immigrants to Nevada, their marital patterns suggest how little is known about the habits and the thinking of the foreign born.

The scores of newspaper vignettes provide an invaluable source for studying the rivalry and conflict theme. Some commentators relied on violence and the macabre to attract readers; in general they failed to add dignity or meaning to the lives of the foreign born. Nevertheless, the journalists did report on the activities of frontier immigrants, and while they often recorded minutiae, it is through such stories that the historian can study the manners and the morals of an age. Furthermore, the cumulative newspaper impact serves as a kind of literature in that it expands the consciousness and communicates insights about the life and times of foreigners in Nevada.

Loneliness and Despair

One of the most significant, if often fortuitous, characterizations to be supplied by Nevada newspapers was that of the lost, isolated, or desperate immigrant. Space has commonly been viewed as a manifestation of freedom, and in America, size and distance were generally used as a synonym for affluence and prestige. But space was also terrifying when too vast for human control. Man has shown as great a need for the protection of circumscribed limits as for the freedom of unhampered movement. The American West often forcefully demonstrated that size and distance were more of a liability than a liberation. The Nevada foreign born moved freely from one area to another; however, most communities were too small, too isolated, and too fluid to provide the social and cultural opportunities requisite for the immigrant's happiness and well-being. Several factors helped to create the feeling of despair so often seen in the immigrant.

In the first instance, it was the combination of a destructive physical environment and a peculiarly mobile society which brought misery and death. During the boom decades of the sixties and seventies, stage drivers, prospectors, and others crossing Nevada commonly found exhausted foreigners who had unwittingly attempted to walk the great distances between the mining camps. In June, 1864, four Mexicans left Austin to explore and prospect in the San Antonio district some eighty miles to the south. One of the Mexicans has previously discovered the San Antonio mines, and all were acquainted with the barren terrain; nevertheless, three months later the dried and mummified bodies of three of the group were found on the desert at the southern end of Smoky Valley.[88]

Newspaper accounts and obituaries were often depressingly brief. One sentence told of an Italian's body found on a hillside near Battle Mountain; he had died while crossing the area on foot. An Elko-to-Hamilton stage driver saw a Frenchman dead along the road. He had succumbed of exhaustion while climbing a steep mountain grade. A German was discovered a few miles north of Austin; he was incoherent and had been wandering in the sagebrush for days. The immigrant lived for a week, but never regained his sanity. The frozen body of a Norwegian was found in the snow on the mountains west of Washoe Lake. The only Scotsman in Tybo became ill and started to walk the thirty miles to a doctor at Belmont, but died twenty miles from his destination. A man was discovered dead in a cabin below Dayton; his Swedish passport indicated that he had been in America but a few months. A prospector came across the body of a German fifty miles southwest of Tonopah. The man had apparently died of thirst when only three miles from water. A receipt in his pocket indicated that he had recently been admitted to citizenship in Nevada. An Austrian who spoke Italian died of a heart attack in a saloon in Virginia City. The *Territorial Enterprise* summarized the casualness of the times when

it explained: "He arrived here after the fire—at least no one re-
members seeing him previously to the fire—and nobody seems
to know much about him." [89]

Occasionally, when the papers were short of news, a dead
body could be expanded into a feature story. During the summer of 1874, a bleached human skull was seen along the road a
few miles out of Belmont. After the incident was recorded, interest and speculation mounted, and finally, parts of a skeleton
were brought into town for general inspection. The old-timers
identified several of the front teeth as belonging to a Frenchman
who had disappeared suddenly four or five years earlier. The
editor summed up a thousand unsolved immigrant deaths when
he explained, "It is quite probable that the whole affair will remain a mystery for all time to come." [90] Obviously, not all of
those who became lost or were isolated perished. Two crazed
and naked Mexicans stumbled into Columbus on September 3,
1875. A Slav gave them food and water, and they quickly re-
covered from their nineteen-day walk from Lone Pine, California. Later the same month a Serb dragged himself into Lida.
He had left Pioche thirty days earlier, had quickly become lost,
and had wandered aimlessly across the entire state of Nevada.

In the second instance, it was isolation and loneliness which
led many immigrants to despair and mental decay. An article in
the *Reese River Reveille of* March 21, 1878, typifies the stories of
tragedy. John Booth, the English-born editor of the *Reveille,* was
awakened one morning by the sound of wagons rolling down
Austin's main street. Upon inquiry, Booth learned that the lead
wagon carried the corpse of Madame Pauline Lognoz, wife of
August Lognoz of Ophir Canyon, and that many ranchers from
Smoky Valley and Birch Creek made up the procession. The
scene was not an uncommon one for Austinites during the sixties
and seventies. Persons from the outlying areas tolerated isola-

tion during life, but as a last wish asked to be buried in town where their graves would not be lost to man. Pauline Lognoz's coffin had been filled with snow from the mountains and the wagon had traveled at night so that the body would be preserved on the long trek to the Austin cemetery.

When the Lognozes first opened a store in Ophir Canyon in 1866 they had dreams of becoming wealthy and of returning to France. But the camp had quickly collapsed, and by the late seventies only three French immigrants remained in the isolated canyon to the west of Smoky Valley. After years without either community life or feminine companionship and with no hope of ever being able to return to Paris, the forty-eight-year-old Pauline Lognoz took strychnine and then quietly requested her husband to call in the only other human being in the canyon to be a witness at her death.

John Booth's article revealed that neither he, nor August Lognoz, nor the men of Smoky Valley understood why Madame Pauline committed suicide; to them she seemed richly blessed with American freedom. They reasoned that the excitement growing out of a shipwreck which she had experienced years before had unsettled her mind.[91] Nevertheless, Lognoz wanted his wife buried where she had not been privileged to live, near the civilization of a town. Nor was Lognoz totally unaware of the inadequacies of central Nevada; he renamed his mine in Ophir Canyon the Forlorn Mine, moved to a ranch down in Smoky Valley, and almost twenty years later sold both the ranch and the mine and returned to France to marry a Parisian and become the father of two children.

Only a few weeks after Pauline Lognoz ended her life in Ophir Canyon, the great naturalist John Muir passed through the area on his way up Smoky Valley. Muir was struck by the fact that although Nevada was one "of the very youngest and wildest of the states, nevertheless it is already strewn with ruins that seem as gray and silent and time-worn as if the civilization to which they belonged had perished centuries ago." On his way into Austin he "found no less than five dead towns without a single inhabitant." [92] Of the four hundred or more old camp sites and ghost towns that once flourished in Nevada, none collapsed without bringing ruin or decay to at least a few of the inhabitants. No doubt the uninitiated foreigners, who were unacquainted with the American tradition of denuding the landscape and moving on, suffered the most from the physical and psychological mobility of Nevada life.[93]

Isolation, uncertainty, and failure provided a significant undertone which echoed throughout the Nevada press and which clearly imprinted its shadow on the writings of both journalists and novelists. Although statistics are unavilable, the number of ill or depressed persons who are known to have destroyed themselves gives a depressing twist to the image of the happy immigrant. A recitation of the examples of suicide at any of the state's major houses of prostitution would quickly dispel the myth of gaiety that has tended to surround the oldest profession.[94] When a Swiss farmer and a German saloon keeper committed suicide only a few hours apart in July of 1877, the *Gold Hill Daily News* combined the cases into one article entitled "Self-Murder" and cautioned, in an ill-advised attempt at humor, that self-violence should be undertaken early in the day or the story could not be included in the evening paper.[95] Men and women, the young and the old, and particularly the foreign born, resorted to self-destruction in such numbers that Nevada's suicide rate rose to more than twice that of the national average.

John McIntyre of Donegal threw himself in front of the train three different times before he was finally killed in the switch yards of Virginia City. H. Calaghan took poison but was revived; then he cut his throat but was successfully treated. Before his third attempt at suicide he requested Comstock doctors to leave him alone. An examination by local hospital attendants showed the Irishman to be perfectly sane. After living in Unionville eight years, Mara Spors of Holland had neither provided her husband with a child nor adjusted to the western environment. She became "insane from loneliness" and took an overdose of laudanum.[96] Felix Francis of Switzerland tried to suffocate himself with charcoal fumes, but the house caught fire and two Mexican women dragged him to safety. Francis spoke no English and had neither money, friends, nor relatives; an associate and fellow countryman had been killed in a mining disaster.[97] After working for years to save enough money to return to Italy, a woodcutter finally purchased his ticket in Reno, but in the anxiety and excitement he became so confused that he nearly killed himself by deliberately throwing his body against a brick wall.

Peter Alexander arrived in Nevada in 1867. He worked near Battle Mountain and in Austin and moved on to Hamilton during the summer of 1869. While at Austin, the twenty-four-year-old Scotsman had fallen in love with a prostitute, and when he could not find employment in Hamilton, the girl helped to support him. Facing an inner conflict with his conscience and deeply humiliated and confused, the young immigrant borrowed his partner's pistol and shot himself. His brief note read: "John, I have taken your pistol. I can't get work and am tired of life. Keep my razor and strop. Your pistol you will find with me. The authorities will give it to you. Good-bye friends and home. Peter Alexander, Renfrewshire, Scotland." [98] The day before the Alexander affair, the Hamilton community had been told of a Canadian prostitute who took poison because her German procurer threatened to desert her, and a few days later, a Chinese prostitute committed suicide when her male partner gambled away her earnings and then forced her out onto the street. Also in the same week, both a Cornish and an Irish miner had died at Hamilton after taking poison.

While many immigrants were optimists and opportunists as they started the long trek west, thousands were to die with their spirits crushed by failure, defeat, and despair. On May 10, 1843, Frances Reynolds married W. G. Woon at Tenbury Wells, Worcestershire. A few years later, they emigrated to the United States and during the early fifties moved on to California. In 1860, they arrived on the Comstock and for fifteen years lived in a small cabin overlooking the Ophir mine. The Woons buried two children in England, three died at sea or while traveling across the plains, others died or were killed in California and Nevada. When the Woons twelfth, youngest, and only living child was killed in the mines during early 1875, the mother had him buried near her cabin home. She became incoherent while visiting the grave, and thirty-two years and seven days after her English wedding she was officially declared insane by the authorities at Virginia City, Nevada.[99]

A less dramatic manifestation of disappointment and loneliness can be seen in the scores of immigrants who returned to their homelands. Of course, notice was seldom given of the departures unless they became associated with a newsworthy incident. After years of laboring in Nevada, Ferdinand C. Alexander boarded the train in Virginia City in June, 1876, to return to his wife in Bordeaux, France. He had saved $500 in coin, plus gold notes and some stock certificates. However, he suffered a heart attack near Steamboat and died before reaching Reno.[100] But even more pathetic was the case of Paul Tichard who, in his anxiety to proceed toward France, refused to wait for the train at Wells and started hiking down the track. In either confusion or despondency, he jumped in front of a train and was killed. A generation after the death of Alexander and Tichard, other Frenchmen, along with their Spanish cousins, faced an even sterner test of isolation as sheepherders on the broad Nevada range. Dominique Laxalt echoed the despondency of hundreds of Basques when he explained how his friends Peyo and Garazi went insane from loneliness. But after Garazi was returned to the Pyrenees, he soon regained his senses and was not troubled again. According to Laxalt, the experience showed that home-sickness could totally destroy even the sturdiest of the Basque sheepmen.[101]

In many instances, emotional disaffection and psychological discontent were factors in promoting immigration. When per-plexed or bewildered Europeans settled in capricious Nevada, they seldom became permanently attached. Rather they carried their emptiness with them and continued their search for an El-dorado. Such persons were temperamentally incapable of giving the new land a fair trial. Even when economically successful, they often believed their lives to be as barren and as purposeless as the soil. Such immigrants could not undergo the shock of be-ing uprooted and of living in a strange and seemingly hostile environment. Many became homing pigeons who would will-ingly ignore adversity, material loss, and danger in an attempt to seek more familiar surroundings. Some immigrants found it difficult to become a part of the American society and impossible to become a part of the strange life of Nevada. Basic human in-stincts and innate traditions did not permit them to belong, to participate, to adjust. They lived and worked in the community, but could never grow roots with which to anchor themselves. They easily mastered the details of local life, yet found it im-possible to fill the emotional void which emigration had created.

Nevada also swarmed with foreigners who had not exercised

good judgment in immigrating to the West. Thousands had thrown themselves blindly against the unknown and trusted to luck that the results would be satisfactory. They quickly awakened to the painful realization that their imagination had run away with their judgment. Many immigrants were psychologically ill-equipped for either the life of a recluse tucked away in a mountain valley or that of a riotous miner stranded in a turbulent boom camp.

Obviously thousands of immigrants were diminished by their environment. They were shackled, they were deprived, and they were subjected to a kind of geographical injustice. But their lives have been provided with a deeper meaning by the journalists who noted the hardships and reported on the hostile conditions. In the twentieth century, the plight of the immigrant has been reemphasized by some of the West's best authors. It is not that the journalists and novelists have enhanced the lives of the foreign born or ameliorated their despair, but rather that they have recorded the migrants' experiences and directed popular thought so that society can more fully appreciate the dimension of the immigrant suffering and the awesome toll taken by the frontier.

[1] Ray Allen Billington, *America's Frontier Heritage* (New York: Holt, Rinehart and Winston, 1966), p. 80.

[2] For an example, see *Gold Hill Daily News,* July 20, 1868, p. 3, col. 1.

[3] *Ibid.,* August 3, 1869, p. 3, col. 1.

[4] *Nevada State Journal,* September 19, 1885, p. 2, col. 2.

[5] *Gold Hill Daily News,* December 26, 1863, p. 3, col. 1.

[6] *Nevada State Journal,* September 27, 1904, p. 4, col. 2.

[7] *The Silver State,* October 16, 1897, p. 3, col. 1.

[8] *Morning Appeal,* March 29, 1879, p. 3, col. 2.

[9] *Ibid.,* May 23, 1879, p. 3, col. 3.

[10] *The Silver State,* July 18, 1881, p. 3, col. 1.

[11] *Eureka Daily Sentinel,* March 11, 1879, p. 3, col. 2.

[12] See the *Reese River Reveille* for July and August, 1877, for numerous articles on Herhily.

[13] *Gold Hill Daily News,* July 27, 1868, p. 3, col. 1.

[14] *Morning Appeal,* January 5, 1873, p. 3, col. 2.

[15] For two of the more complete articles on Chinese Mary, see the *Carson Valley News,* May 22, 1875, p. 3, col. 1, and the *Borax Miner,* April 1, 1876.

[16] *Nevada State Journal,* March 2, 1880, p. 3, col. 3.

[17] See a series of articles in the *Morning Appeal* between June 10, 1879, and November 21, 1879.

[18] *Territorial Enterprise,* April 20, 1871, p. 3, col. 1.

[19] *Ibid.,* September 17, 1871, p. 3, col. 2.

[20] *Eureka Daily Sentinel,* June 8, 1878, p. 2, col. 2.

[21] *Tonopah Bonanza* (Weekly), September 26, 1903, p. 2, col. 2.

[22] *Morning Appeal,* November 20, 1879, p. 3, col. 3.

[23] *The Elko Independent,* September 11, 1869, p. 3, col. 2.

[24] *The Tonopah Daily Sun,* July 16, 1905, p. 1, col. 6.

[25] *Reno Evening Gazette,* October 4, 1906, p. 5, col. 2.

[26] *The Silver State,* February 25, 1875, p. 3, col. 1.

[27] *Tonopah Bonanza* (Weekly), November 23, 1901, p. 4, col. 3.

[28] *Territorial Enterprise,* December 27, 1867, p. 3, col. 1.

[29] *Ibid.,* February 7, 1879, p. 3, col. 3.

[30] See a series of articles in the *Territorial Enterprise* during May and June, 1866, and climaxed with the report of July 3, 1866, p. 3, col. 2.

[31] *Morning Appeal,* September 10, 1870, p. 3, col. 1; and *Territorial Enterprise,* September 9, 1870, p. 3, col. 2.

[32] *The Tonopah Daily Sun,* April 29, 1905, p. 1.

[33] *Ibid.,* July 21, 1906, p. 1.

[34] *Ibid.,* July 15, 1905, p. 1.

[35] *Gold Hill Daily News,* April 11, 1864, p. 2, col. 1, and April 15, p. 3, col. 2; and *Virginia Evening Bulletin,* April 11, 1864, p. 3, col. 1, and April 12, p. 3, col. 2.

[36] *The Daily Nevada Tribune,* February 19, 1879, p. 3, col. 5.

[37] *Humboldt Register,* January 16, 1869, p. 3, col. 2.

[38] *Gold Hill Daily News,* March 15, 1879, p. 2, col. 2.

[39] See the *Tonopah Bonanza* (Weekly), September 19, 1903, and other issues through December, 1903.

[40] *Reno Evening Gazette,* November 11, 1908, pp. 1, 8.

[41] See numerous articles in the *Eureka Daily Sentinel* between September 17, 1871, and June 22, 1872.

[42] *Eureka Daily Sentinel,* March 10, 1876, p. 3, col. 3.

[43] *Ibid.,* October 10, 1875, p. 3, col. 3, and October 17, p. 3, col. 2.

[44] *Eureka Daily Leader,* July 7, 1879, p. 3, col. 3.

[45] *Eureka Daily Sentinel,* March 27, 1879, p. 3, col. 3.

[46] *Ibid.,* August 15, 1879, p. 3, col. 3.

[47] *Ibid.,* August 16, 1879, p. 2, col. 3.

[48] See the *Eureka Daily Sentinel* and the *Eureka Daily Leader* during July and August, 1879, for daily reports on the conflict.

[49] *The Ely Mining Record,* March 21, 1908, p. 4, col. 1.

[50] *Ibid.,* April 18, 1908, p. 2, col. 1.

[51] *White Pine News,* May 30, 1908, p. 1, cols. 3–4.

[52] *Ely Daily Mining Expositor,* January 22, 1908, p. 1, cols. 6–7.

[53] *White Pine News,* June 2, 1908, p. 1, col. 1.

[54] *Ely Daily Mining Expositor,* October 29, 1907, p. 2, col. 2.

[55] *The Tonopah Daily Sun,* August 10, 1907, p. 2, col. 1.

[56] *Ibid.,* August 7, 1907, p. 2, col. 1.

[57] *Ibid.,* July 30, 1907, p. 1, col. 2.

[58] *Ibid.,* August 24, 1907, p. 2, col. 1.

[59] *Territorial Enterprise,* August 29, 1868, p. 3, col. 1.

[60] *Nevada State Journal,* January 8, 1905, p. 2, col. 1.

[61] *Ibid.,* February 28, 1905, p. 2, col. 2.

[62] *Caliente Load-Express,* June 30, 1906, p. 4, col. 3.

[63] *Territorial Enterprise,* August 4, 1870, p. 3, col. 1.

[64] *Morning Appeal,* April 3, 1875, p. 3, col. 3, and April 7, 1875, p. 3, col. 2, and other entries over the following weeks.

[65] See the *Weekly Silver Bend Reporter* for April and May, 1867.

[66] See the *Belmont Courier* for August and September, 1874.

[67] *Virginia Evening Bulletin,* August 11, 1863, p. 3, col. 1.

[68] See the *Nevada State Journal* and *Reno Evening Gazette* for January, February, and March, 1905.

[69] *Tonopah Bonanza* (Weekly), November 28, 1903, p. 1.

[70] *The Tonopah Daily Sun,* March 7, 1906, p. 5, col. 3.

[71] *Ibid.,* January 27, 1906, p. 4, col. 2, and January 29, 1906, p. 1, col. 1.

[72] *Tonopah Bonanza* (Weekly), August 17, 1907, p. 1.

[73] *Ibid.,* August 24, 1907, p. 1, col. 5.

[74] *Gold Hill Daily News,* August 13, 1869, p. 3, col. 1.

[75] *Ibid.,* August 4, 1870, p. 3, col. 2, and August 5, p. 3, col. 2.

[76] *Territorial Enterprise,* August 17, 1870, p. 3, col. 1.

[77] *Ibid.,* August 17, 1870, p. 3, col. 2.

[78] *Ibid.,* September 13, 1870, p. 3, col. 2.

[79] *Gold Hill Daily News,* September 14, 1870, p. 3, col. 1.

[80] *Ibid.,* January 31, 1871, p. 3, col. 1, and February 1, p. 3, col. 1.

[81] *The Elko Independent,* August 24, 1870, p. 3, col. 1.

[82] *Morning Appeal,* August 28, 1870, p. 2, col. 3.

[83] Confused accounts of the Felesina affair appeared in most western Nevada newspapers. Perhaps the clearest report is to be found in the *Carson Valley News,* May 8, 1875, p. 2, col. 1.

[84] See numerous articles in western Nevada newspapers between May 12 and December 30, 1874.

[85] See the *Morning Appeal* from May through December, 1874.

[86] *White Pine News,* May 19, 1912, p. 1, col. 1.

[87] See Enumerator's Report, Census of 1880, Storey County, Nevada.

[88] *Reese River Reveille,* September 15, 1864, p. 1, col. 2.

[89] *Territorial Enterprise,* January 11, 1876, p. 3, col. 2.

[90] *Belmont Courier,* July 11, 1874, p. 3, col. 2.

[91] *Reese River Reveille,* March 21, 1878, p. 3, col. 2.

[92] John Muir, *Sheep Trails* (Boston: Houghton Mifflin Company, 1918), pp. 195–96.

[93] Grant Smith Papers, University of Nevada Library, Reno, Collection 229, Box 2.

[94] See article from *Gold Hill Daily News* of September 5, 1876, entitled "Gilded Sin."

[95] See article from *Gold Hill Daily News* of July 20, 1877, entitled "Self-Murder."

[96] *The Silver State,* November 30, 1877, p. 3, col. 1.

[97] *Territorial Enterprise,* June 4, 1869, p. 3, col. 1.

[98] *The Daily Inland Empire,* August 25, 1869, p. 3, col. 2.

[99] *Territorial Enterprise,* May 18, 1875, p. 3, col. 2.

[100] *Gold Hill Daily News,* June 30, 1876, p. 3, col. 2.

[101] Robert Laxalt, "Basque Sheepherders. Lonely Sentinels of the American West," *National Geographic,* June, 1966, p. 880.

5

===

Immigrants in Fiction

America has been represented as a land of wealth, as a society of powerful democratic tendencies, and as a benevolent reservoir of human concern. The image was sometimes authentic and sometimes illusory, but it provided a new dimension for the masses of Europe and it spurred a migration that only harsh laws could circumscribe. A score of immigrant odysseys were worthy of a Homer. There were the Puritans seeking a place to worship in New England, the Quakers finding a haven in Pennsylvania, the Huguenots escaping to South Carolina, the Irish fleeing from the famine, the South Chinese stealing away from chaos, and the Scandinavians leaving a stifling conservatism. And the twentieth-century pageant of Russians driven by pogroms, Italians lured by jobs, and Greeks impelled by overpopulation has added new features to America's diverse image.

In a less sweeping, but no less dramatic and illuminating way, the immigrants to Nevada and the Far West supplied the journalists and novelists with scores of plots, characters, and scenes. The migrants who pushed on to the forbidding wastes of the Great Basin, much like those who settled in the crowded urban slums or on the lonely Midwest prairies, preserved some of their native social order. Only gradually did they emerge from the valleys, deserts, and mines as a new breed of Americans.

If America reshaped the immigrants, so did the immigrants reshape America. For generations, painting, sculpture, music, architecture, and drama reflected, absorbed, and responded to the immigrants. Foreign-born characters were from the first accepted as "normal and natural" features of American literature. For several decades following the Revolutionary War, the English were most often cast as unwanted trespassers. Both James Fenimore Cooper and Nathaniel Hawthorne saw British officials, Army officers, and royal governors as dangerous antagonists and transient aliens on a tyrannical mission. While political differences with ancestral England were repeatedly emphasized, there was no criticism of Anglo-Saxon institutions and little objection to a further infusion of British blood. Indeed, by the end of the century, authors like John Hay in *The Bread Winners* (1884), Pierton Dooner in *Last Days of the Republic* (1880), and Richard Grant White in *The Fate of Mansfield Humphreys* (1884) suggested that American society was being overrun by non-Anglo-Saxon immigrant hoards.[1]

By the turn of the twentieth century, all of the major nationality groups had organized foreign language publications and thereby had greatly stimulated the production of immigrant literature. For example, a 1910 bibliography listed 1,158 Swedish-American newspapers and journals that had been founded in the United States.[2] The periodicals were sporadic and generally were short-lived, but they provided a cultural transition for thousands of immigrants and helped to create a multi-ethnic literary heritage. In many of the urban-oriented publications, the problems of the proletariat and those of the foreign born became interchangeable. Immigrant novels based on ghetto life and social protest soon followed. Abraham Cahan's *The Rise of David Levinsky* (1917), Anjia Yeziersha's *All I Could Never Be* (1932), and novels by Leo Rosten, Elias Tobenkens, Nelson Algren, and Louis Adamic noted the big-city immigrant or his children in the transition to and collision with the "American way" of life.

The Middle West, and particularly the Great Plains, also provided a rewarding setting for foreign-born fiction. Hjalmar H. Boyensen's *Falconberg,* published in 1878 and dealing with a Norwegian settlement in Minnesota, has been seen as the first truly immigrant novel.[3] Many works, like Johan Bojer's *The Emigrants* (translated from the Norwegian in 1925) and Velhelm Moberg's work also entitled *The Emigrants* (translated from the Swedish in 1951), follow the Boyensen theme. They, along with Willa Cather's *O Pioneers!* (1913) and *My Antonia* (1918), Ole Rölvaag's *Giants in the Earth* (1927), and novels by Ruth Suckow, Herbert Krause, Hamlin Garland, Stewart Englstrand, Feike Feikema, and many others, make the Missouri and upper Mississippi river valleys the setting for much of America's best immigration fiction. Although the Scandinavians and Germans predominate as literary subjects, the Bohemians, Jews, Russians, Irish, Dutch, Icelanders, Welsh, and other ethnic types are also frequently woven into the stories.

The Columbia River has tended to command attention from writers of the Pacific Northwest. Archie Binns, Vivien R. Bretherton, Ernest Haycox, and Stewart Edward White have celebrated the Scottish, English, and French-Canadian personalities associated with the Hudson's Bay Company and the early trek to the Columbia River country. Nard Jones also wove the Irish, Germans, Italians, French, Welsh, Japanese, and Chinese into his study of the river. In a series of stories entitled *Team Bells Wake Me* (1953), H. L. Davis found the Oregon valleys lying along the Nevada border to be filled with uneducated Mexican herders, stupid Swedish farmers, scrawny Basque sheepmen, ignorant Scottish highlanders and assorted Italians, French-Canadians, Finns, and Chinese. The early immigrants, according to Davis, had methodically corrupted the native Indians.

> First their country had been traversed by French-Canadian fur-traders, who liked them and intermarried with them to have a place on their trap-line to sleep. Later came American missionaries, who, though not in favor of intermarriage themselves, imported retinues of Kanaka flunkies from the Hawaiian Islands to prove that they really could convert somebody, and the Kanakas intermarried busily and hatched mobs of children. Still later several crews of Chinese tie-cutters imported by the railroad, stirred themselves into the mixture, along with a few caravans of horse-trading gypsies, some Mexican sheepherders, and two or three early-day Negroes who, to judge by the general pigmentation of the tribe, must have been miraculously powerful and persistent. All was accomplished in the name of peace, friendship, religion, and racial understanding, and the result was these cattle-drivers, of whom the men were all thieves and the women all prostitutes.[4]

Writers about California's foreign born have been so numerous and their work so varied that a brief assessment fails to suggest the breadth of their scope. Some of the better immigrant books have tended to be concerned with the depressed minority groups. There was the Chinese theme centered around San Francisco, the Mexican theme drawn from the Los Angeles area, and the more recent Japanese theme relating to the Central Valley. Versatile authors like Idwal Jones built stories around a Chinese boy, a French chef, a Welsh gold seeker, and a European wine maker. Famous writers from Helen Hunt Jackson to Jack London, Evelyn Waugh, William Saroyan, Upton Sinclair, and John Steinbeck evolved a kind of immigrant motif in an attempt to develop the plural vision of both the insider and the outsider.

A reasonably balanced picture of the literary response to the foreign born in Nevada can be gained by looking at some fifty authors of widely varying artistic merit and range of orientation. Four or five of the novelists stand out as writers of considerable emotional vigor and authority, and the remainder are useful inasmuch as their works correlate local trends and immigration patterns. Several of the major literary themes drew heavily on immigrant characterization. Unfortunately, much of the literature is relatively obscure; therefore, a brief summary of the more pertinent works will perhaps help the reader place the immigrant in a broader perspective.

Western Motif

Whether described by Crevecoeur, Jefferson, Cooper, or Tocqueville, the frontier was credited with a rudimentary, but virile, form of American democracy. Although greatly oversimplified, the concept came to provide a guiding principle which influenced American thought and the writing of western stories. Authorities like Henry Nash Smith have argued that the ability of the frontier to produce epic literature seldom extended beyond the agricultural lands of the Great Plains and did not include the drama of the cowboy. Nevertheless, by the end of the nineteenth century, the cowboy had emerged as an exotic figure, and although often reduced in fiction to a subliterary and melodramatic stereotype, he became a legitimate offspring of the western frontier experience.[5]

One of the first writers to elevate the cowboy western to a position of respectability, if not social significance, was Owen

Wister in *The Virginian* (1902). He was joined by Emerson Hough (*The Covered Wagon, Fifty-Four Forty or Fight*) and others. Bertha Muzzy Bower and Harry Sinclair Drago quickly accepted the Wister approach and became prolific popularizers of the West and at the same time exploiters of the immigrant theme. Bower and Drago adopted Wister's aphorism that the western was an American story and "an expression of American faith," and yet both sensed the presence of the foreign born in the West and commonly wove immigrants into their Nevada novels.

In 1906 Bower created Chip for the novel *Chip of the Flying U*. Later, in *The Flying U Ranch,* Chip was married and began to share the spotlight with an Irish-Spanish cowpuncher. The two characters continue through other Bower works until in the 1920s Chip was acclaimed "the most cuddled, the most admired, of all the cowboy heroes."[6] Starting in 1921, Bower hoped to repeat her success by creating a lovable, laughable, baffling Irishman, Casey Ryan. But Casey Ryan, as a variant of the rebellious shanty Irish and the comic stage Irish, never quite achieved Chip's popularity. Nevertheless, Chip and Casey Ryan made Bower a successful writer. In *The Cowboy and His Interpreters* (1926), Douglas Branch selected Bower as one of the four novelists who formed a special literary "constellation." According to Branch, Bower was one of the "aristocrats of cow-country fiction." Of the over sixty Bower novels, at least ten are given southern Nevada settings, and during the 1920s, when she developed Casey Ryan, her works, along with those of Drago, tended to dominate the Nevada western.

Casey Ryan (1921) and *The Trail of the White Mule* (1922) were not immigrant novels, but they were based on the life of a pugnacious Irish immigrant. They were not Nevada-oriented, but both were set in Nevada. Known from Colorado to Montana to California, Casey Ryan had become the most notorious stage-driver to roll out of the West. But it was at Lund, Nevada, that Casey first attempted to use an automobile in the furtherance of his transportation business. In carrying foreigners to the mines of eastern Nevada, Casey's qualifications as a driver were constantly called into question, and on frequent occasions he was compelled to use his "Irish fists" to keep the "Bohunks" in the conveyance. Casey's fights, his prowess as a driver, his matrimonial pursuits and his operation of a garage at a desert oasis were designed to prove that he was the greatest braggart and had the kindest heart in the state.

Eventually Casey married, and, in the process of being tamed, he moved from Tonopah to California. In *The Trail of the White Mule,* he became antagonistic and depressed by the conventions of Los Angeles life. Even the deliberate breaking of the speed laws and the delightful brawls with Irish policemen provided only limited excitement. Consequently, Casey took up prospecting and returned to the Nevada-California border country near Las Vegas. As a fighting, foolish, and friendly prospector, he was injured, jailed, starved, shot, beaten, and almost drowned before he rather reluctantly turned to bootlegging and the interstate transport of liquor. He often found the latter occupation stimulating.

Always the optimist, always reckless, always unmanageable, Casey Ryan became the New York City Irishman of humor and song transported to the wild West. Other Bower novels of the Nevada era depicted drunken Bohunks, frightened Englishmen, rheumatic Scots, and assorted Swedes, Mexicans, and Chinese. According to Bower most of the foreigners were "synthetic Americans with a foreign tongue." But as a true Irishman, Casey Ryan was seen as the true American. He understood and could instantly absorb the independent spirit of the West. Bower's foreign characters are endowed with a frivolous and raffish air and are often cast in purposeless and unemotional plots, yet the humor is always simple, homespun, and wholesome, and neither the settings nor the immigrants are machine-made.

Most of Bower's Nevada stories reflected "the pure open stretches of God's country," and most of her heroes tended to ricochet off into irrelevant adventures. They never demonstrated world-weariness, world-hatred, perverse indulgence, or nihilism. They even felt sympathetic towards respectability, virtue, piety, and conventional behavior. Occasionally mystery and suspense were added to the drama. In *The Voice at Johnnywater* (1923), a pleasant, weak-willed Englishman named Frank Waddell fled from his prosperous desert ranch near Beatty because of mysterious and frightening voices. Although the Englishman never appeared in the story, his desertion of the ranch and the accounts of his nervousness and fear created a sense of urgency. Bower employed no sex in this novel, no psychological coloring, no cynicism, no pessimism, no shooting, no Indian raids, no badmen, no social misfits, and no poverty. There was merely the saga of a nice, self-sufficient, all-American boy who changed from Hollywood movie actor to Nevada ranch overseer and who, through perseverance, unraveled the enigma that drove Frank Waddell back to England.

Although many writers have adapted Basque immigrants to literature, Harry Sinclair Drago was the first to stress their emotional, intellectual, and social integration into the Nevada environment. Within a thirty-year period ending in the early 1950s, Drago published more than one hundred books, used some sixteen or seventeen pseudonyms, wrote a hundred short stories, did almost two-score movie scripts, and served (throughout the early 1920s) as a newspaper columnist. In 1926, he settled in Hollywood and became a writer for Tom Mix. But Drago found cowboy movie making a synthetic experience with the only authentic western features being the horses and the landscape. He later declared: "the western motion picture was trash" and the self-perpetuating western television shows are their "shoddy but legitimate offspring." [7] But Drago viewed the western novel as a significant achievement.

During the early thirties, Drago deserted Hollywood for the familiar country of northern Nevada where he had already set three of his stories. While living at Winnemucca, he carefully studied the topography and researched the history of Humboldt and Elko counties. Indeed, he laid the groundwork for his fiction with greater care than either his mentor Owen Wister or his southern Nevada contemporary B. M. Bower. Drago also made a serious attempt to depict the unpicturesque, usually shabby, unlettered, loyal, tireless, and fearless cowpuncher much as he believed him to be. While he felt at home with many of Nevada's immigrant nationalities, he often forsook the human and the distinctive for the conventional and the accepted. While he revealed much about the Basques, he was more interested in using them than in interpreting them. Nevertheless, with the inclusion of foreign-born characters, Drago's fiction was raised above the dull predictability of many drugstore westerns. He, more than most writers, captured the sensibilities of traditionally stable people confronted with the nondirection of the mobile western society.

As two cowboy ruffians drifted across northern Nevada, in *Whispering Sage* (1922), they were attracted by the lush prosperity and semi-isolation of Paradise Valley. They frequented the Basque bar and frightened the one-eyed Mexican bartender into revealing the secrets of the community. With the key information the gunmen secured valuable water rights and the assistance of an overly ambitious and half-confused American rancher by the name of Acklin. Acklin was intrigued by, and at the same time jealous of, the dignity, the culture, and the thrift shown by the Basque gentry. During the hot, dry summer, Acklin financed the building of a dam in a nearby canyon, and all irrigation water was diverted from the Basque lands.

José Arrascada, a wealthy and realistic ranch owner, led the Basques' legal attempt to fight back. They warned Acklin that he could not bribe the sheriff or turn public opinion against them. "You might get away with this grab in Germany or Russia, or back East in the coal country, with only a lot of Bohunks to fight you," but neither western justice nor the Basque immigrant could be intimidated.[8] They had wrested a grudging foothold from the desert and had learned determination and how to respond when faced with disaster. The Basques were not to be humiliated nor would they "bend the knee" like so many Mexicans. "He [the Basque] was no Latin. In his veins was the blood of the gypsying Celt."[9] They would neither yield to the unjust demands of Anglo-Saxon society, nor succumb to its forms like patronizing Latins.

After weeks of bitter conflict in which José was killed, Basque livestock destroyed, and their people branded "Bascos and Greasers," the immigrants were on the verge of defeat. Fortunately, the conspirators fell to fighting among themselves, and an undercover lawman from Wyoming who had fallen in love with José's daughter restored order and even taught the Basques a few of the cardinal virtues of frontier democracy. In addition to being an action-packed western, *Whispering Sage* emphasized the pride and the independence, but also the clannishness and the group snobbishness, of a minority people. Assimilation of the Basques seemed to be resisted more often by their own leaders than by the Americans among whom they had settled.

In *Smoke of the .45* (1923), a stranger drifted into a railroad hotel operated by an overbearing Irishman and an industrious Basque. Within a few hours, the stranger was found murdered and two cowboys who were in town (Winnemucca) at the time were accidentally drawn into the affair. They eventually became curious and determined to investigate the peculiar circumstances surrounding both the death and the coroner's inquest. As Johnny Dice pursued various clues, his Basque friend, Tony Madeiras, played a series of unpopular roles in an effort to flush out the killer. Thinking Madeiras cowardly and disloyal, fellow cowboys and community groups heaped scorn and insult upon the Basque in much the same way the Irishman cursed and abused his Basque partner at the railroad hotel.

Drago's most plausible and mature Nevada novel was *Following the Grass* (1924). As a fictionalized account of an exciting historical movement, the story was both trenchant and meaningful. The eldest son in a Spanish Basque household migrated to Mexico, but later journeyed on to California where other members of the family joined him. During a drought in the mid sixties, the small party pushed on from the Feather River country into northern Nevada. As the Basques made their way east, they suffered from both natural hardships and personal insults. They almost perished on the desert, they were attacked by Indians, they were labeled Mexican Greasers, and they were hated by cattlemen because they kept sheep. Although able to endure the natural perils, the family found it frustrating and demoralizing to face the "hostility, hatred, and contempt" of fellow human beings. Finally, as Angelo Irosabal entered Paradise Valley, he was met by David Gault, who ordered his son to shoot the "greasers." The youth, Joe Gault, hesitated because Angelo carried a child, Margarida Irosabal, in his arms. Joe and Margarida were later married, thereby defying the ordinances of both families. In addition to the rejection by their parents, the young couple was forced to face years of drought, marauding Indians, recurring sickness, and failing fortunes.

The plot in *Following the Grass* was topical and incisive; the foreign born became a viable and realistic element. Although repeatedly assailed by the brutal forces of man and nature, Drago's immigrants did not grow insensitive. Rather, they grew into leaders like Angelo Irosabal. Although blind to the future needs of his people, Irosabal stood as a heroic figure who merited the position of Basque chieftain. Unfortunately, Drago's Basques became trite and superficial when they were pictured as "lovers of solitude" and "driven to clannishness" by Nevada bigotry; and they merely served western sentimentality when they "crossed frowning seas," "broached high hills," and "prospered in barren deserts."

In 1933, Drago returned to the Nevada setting with *Desert Water*. The story centered around the rather colorless conflict between a large interstate cattle company and several local ranchers whom the company was attempting to displace. The Basques were cast in a passive role as "clannish and timid." They tended to stand aside and merely watch while the Yankee bullies fought and killed. In addition to the Basques, there was the usual quota of Chinese cooks, Scottish blacksmiths, and other immigrant characters, but none of them emerged as viable personalities.

Clearly Drago used the Basques more to enrich his westerns than to convey a social message. Yet his Basques absorbed the western ideal of political democracy and social and economic equality. For the sake of personal independence, Drago's Basques withstood the many deprivations and stoically accepted the isolation and the exhaustion exacted by the natural environment. They remained steadfast in their oversimplified convictions despite conflicts with Indians, ruffians, and Yankees. Furthermore, the Basques were truly free because, differing from many immigrants, they did not recognize the problem of assimilation. They carried no psychological burden of marginality and they did not consciously emulate or strive for admittance into the dominant society. Drago tended to suggest that the Basques were not outsiders, since there was no local society which they wished to enter. They, therefore, suffered from the inhumanity of their fellow man and from the vicissitudes of nature, but they did not suffer the conflict of values and loyalties which destroyed the happiness and lowered the efficiency of so many immigrant groups. José Arrascada, Angelo Irosabal, and other Basque leaders accepted the opportunity afforded them in Nevada, they competed successfully, they achieved wealth and respect, and the fact that they were still thought of and treated as Basque was reason for pride rather than embarrassment.

In *Secret of the Wastelands* (1940), Drago changed his perspective from the Basque to the Chinese and from northern Nevada to a mythical *Lost Horizon* setting in the southeastern part of the state. At the time of the passage of the Chinese Exclusion Bill, the Orientals had been forced out of many Nevada communities. In their wandering in the wastelands, Drago's Chinese discovered a fertile agricultural valley unknown to either the Indian or the white man. Rich mines were found in the hills surrounding the valley, and the Chinese yearly extracted a small quantity of precious ore. Through a network of Chinese agents, the gold and silver were exchanged for needed supplies, which were mostly imported from China. The Wu-tai-shan Company of Reno and the lovely Carlotta Soong secretly managed the outside purchases for the hidden colony.

When a few professors decided to undertake an archaeological expedition into southern Nevada, the handsome Jim Morningstar was employed as the scientists' guide. Morningstar's father had helped to drive the Chinese from a central Nevada community and had been responsible for the death of Carlotta's Mexican mother. Carlotta therefore hated Morningstar, and she feared that the expedition might expose the secret colony. But Morningstar and his Irish partner, Sulphur Riley, proved to be the friends of the Chinese and ultimately became the saviors of the colony. Carlotta fell desperately in love with her erstwhile enemy, but in the end she stood silent as her hero rode out of Shangri-la accompanied by a female scientist.

The characters in *Secret of the Wastelands,* as in most westerns, invite and command strongly polarized emotions. Ethical contradictions are seldom tolerated, and attitudes are clear and unmistakable. Drago pictures the Chinese as potent western cowboys who, when reared in isolation from white men, acquired remarkable physical prowess and normal self respect. But he also touches on the tremors which could have brought severe racial conflict to Nevada. While he sings the glories of the rugged West, he clearly echoes the repression suffered by the Basques, the Chinese, the Mexicans, and other minority groups.

Harry Sinclair Drago was neither a cowboy nor an immigrant. He failed to underscore what a cowboy might do in a given situation and his ear for dialect was imperfect. He was overly influenced by the myth of the West and his simplified view of the foreign born sometimes narrows rather than expands the reader's sensitivity to Nevada's human problems. Nevertheless, through his Basque characters, Drago often captured the aspirations and the temper of a people. He revealed the tensions surrounding the settlement of many immigrants, and he attracted readers with a mixture of mystery, belligerence, sentiment, and color. As one of Nevada's first extensive literary popularizers, Drago blended the foreign born into the state's history and geography.

The Basques and the Chinese are the foreign-born characters

used most often in Nevada westerns, and both nationalities were often subjected to the crude passion and the irrational action of cowboy ruffians. Works like those by Charles H. Snow and Clair Cave suggest the violence to be found in most of the subliterary publications. Snow, a blind man with five pen names and author of as many as eighteen westerns in a single year, often employed Nevada settings and utilized immigrants. Typical of his nearly four hundred novels was *Nevada Gold* (1937), in which two degenerate cowboys malign a Chinese restaurant operator at Battle Mountain for not providing them with free meals. In Clair Cave's *Wild Peach* (1937) the perennial "dark, and dirty and ragged" sheepherder drifted through the dry hills of southern Nevada. He was loathed as a transient by the cattlemen and indiscriminately labeled a "Basco," although he eventually appeared as a friendly and rather clever Mexican who eked out a meager existence on the fringes of society.

The hatred directed toward the Chinese, the confusing of Basques with Mexicans, and the clashes between American cattlemen and foreign-born sheepmen were commonplace literary artifices. But the constant fight for survival was basic to the lives of many of the rural immigrants. To endure, resist, and prevail against overwhelming odds appears as the leading immigrant theme in the Nevada westerns.

The Bonanza Feature

Nevada was born of a mineral discovery, and the mining industry quickly became the key to the state's economic prosperity. Mining terms like strike, stamp mill, high-grade, drift, placer, lode, ledge, and bonanza became fever-tinged words in the local vocabulary. The color and boisterousness of the boom camps and the unsettled nature of the prospectors created the codes and customs by which society was measured. For over a generation the Comstock, in particular, dominated the economic and political life of the state, and for almost a century it inspired historical and literary attitudes as well. Only slowly did the less well-publicized mining centers of central, eastern, and southern Nevada create the atmosphere of excitement and struggle around which popular novels could be woven. Most of the books dealing with the bonanza idea owe more to ambition and enthusiasm than to an artistic sense or a critical literary perspective. The stories are often romantic in backdrop, extravagant in approach, and sympathetic in purpose. However, the desolate locale and the fragmented society commonly show through the literary overstatement, and the foreign-born characters tend to provide their own dimension by which immigrant history may be judged.

Several female authors have drawn relevant portraits of immigrant life in the early-day camps. Mary M. Mathews lived in Virginia City for nearly a decade before her return to Buffalo, New York, in the late seventies. In 1880, she published *Ten Years in Nevada: Or, Life on the Pacific Coast*. Mrs. Mathews was an opinionated, self-conscious, naïve, and overly critical middle-aged Victorian. However, she set the stage for her narrative with a pointed sketch.

> I will now give the reader an introduction to the inhabitants of Virginia City. They are the same as all other mining towns, composed of all classes, and they are of every nationality under the sun. Americans, Scotch, Irish, English, French, Germans from every German State in the Old World; Spanish, Mexicans, Norwegians, Italians, Piute Indians, and John Chinaman—he being the worst of all, and is truly the curse of the Pacific Coast.[10]

Clearly Mary Mathews was not an impressive literary stylist, but in the course of her long narrative she portrayed a dozen different immigrant characters with whom she had lived and among whom she had worked.

Miriam Michelson knew the same Virginia City that Mary Mathews did; she saw it as a child, however, and the impressions were more indelibly etched. As she matured into a popular novelist she borrowed heavily from her childhood memories, but although the daughter of German-Jewish parents, she built her best Nevada story around an Irish-Catholic household. *The Madigans,* published in 1904, was in part autobiographical, in part a children's book, and in part a feminine tale with a humanitarian bent.

The plot was woven around the observant, perceptive, and somewhat rebellious eleven-year-old Cecelia Madigan, who was used by the author to decry the vulgarities of Virginia City life. On one occasion the child was shocked when she peered through a knothole in a board fence at the rear of Lally's barn-like opera house. The German entrepreneur was staging a female walking match for the benefit of the city's male spectators. After six days, only the gaunt and tense Frenchwoman, La Tourtillotte, and the plump and sluggish German woman, Van Hagan, were still moving around the circular track. Both had removed excess clothing, which did not detract from the spectators' coarse pleasure.

Miriam Michelson had no doubt observed far more sensual spectacles during her Virginia City childhood, and she chose the walking contest as a decorous way to strike out against those cruel amusements which involved "poor sexless, half-maddened" foreign women. She saw them as having been divested of even a "sickly remnant" of dignity, and thus caught on life's treadmill, they "tottered around and forever around." [11]

The Madigans, much like Mathews' *Ten Years in Nevada,* links morality with economic opportunity and associates the idea of a second chance with the intervention of benign fate. Indeed, the leading Irish characters eventually achieved happiness less because of their own exertions than because of a srange turn of luck in the Comstock wheel of fortune.

Many Comstock novelists like Zola Ross, Lillian Janet,[12] Todhunter Ballard, William Carroll, and Octavus Roy Cohen embraced the immigrant to help portray basic historical themes. During the early fifties, Cohen took a brief holiday from his detective fiction, theatricals, and humorous tales about Negroes and turned to Nevada for *Borrasca* (1953). In the novel, a small troupe of performers, several of whom were German, entered Virginia City during the summer of 1868. Rudolph Kleinman, star of the show, had traveled with the company for the express purpose of reaching the mines and becoming wealthy. Heinrich and Heide Kramer, a contentious juggling team from Berlin, had become discouraged with show business and tired of life in general. Understandably, the theatrical organization quickly fell apart when it reached Nevada, and Cohen devoted the remainder of his story to the introduction of historical figures of the era. Many of the famed foreign-born residents, from Eilley Orrum Bowers to Father Manogue, were forced into a series of plots built around mine disasters, love affairs, and fortune hunters. Cohen thus typified the many writers who, after a few weeks in Nevada, reshaped the legend of the great Bonanza and recast its most dramatic and exuberant characters.

Perhaps the longest roster of immigrants found in any Comstock novel was created by James M. Cain in *Past All Dishonor* (1946). Cain, better known as the author of *The Postman Always Rings Twice, Double Indemnity,* and *Mildred Pierce,* followed his typically hard-hitting, fast-paced, and violent style. In *Past All Dishonor,* his fascination with evil and his attempt to jolt and shock the reader seems well fitted to Virginia City life. The refinements of civilization are often stripped away, and men and women reveal their true nature. Roger Duval was sent to California by the Confederacy to gain information which would promote the southern cause. He quickly traced the Union's monetary strength to the flow of bullion from Virginia City and immediately laid plans for the interruption of mining operations. But agent Duval was easily distracted by a house of prostitution run by foreigners with Confederate sympathies, where *Maryland, My Maryland* and *Dixie* were sung in German, and where the French and Creoles provided drinks and entertainment. Morina, the former wife of a Venezuelan army general, was not only the establishment's highest-paid prostitute, she was also a southern sympathizer.

Duval had met Morina in California, where he had fallen hopelessly in love with her, and although shocked by her profession and her vulgar performance for the male clientele, he determined to marry her. In the meantime, Duval's pro-Confederate Mexican associates attempted to disrupt the mines by forming a labor union and promoting a strike. A pro-North Welsh mine superintendent led the opposition. Distracted by his burning love for Morina, by his association with a fourteen-year-old Irish prostitute, and his interest in a half-blood Chinese prostitute, Duval deserted his own labor union, only to be attacked by a Swedish prolabor sympathizer. Eventually, Duval and Morina returned to California, where they tried to sabotage a shipment of precious ore. They failed, and, as the story ended, they were left with the certainty of capture and their devastating love for each other.

Once labeled "a suspenseful exercise in disbelief," Cain's work taxes the reader's credulity, but it is sustained by its disassociation from the mainstream and by a Hemingway type of boldness. Despite a weakness in plot, most of the immigrant characters are well cast. Irishmen and Italians, Chinese and Mexicans,

Welshmen and Swedes, Frenchmen and Germans, and assorted South American parade through *Past All Dishonor* with a cheap and flippant air that is both spontaneous and engaging.

Past All Dishonor tended to typify the Comstock stories in that there was much action and much confusion, but often little purpose. Cain and other authors noted the lawlessness, the sordidness, and the audaciousness, but they overlooked the backbreaking labor, the squalor, and the extremes of nature. Most of the writers saw the immigrant to some extent, yet the paucity of truly creative or unconventional themes suggests the superficiality of their research. In Nevada life, the spectacular and the bland, the pure and the corrupted, were often indissolubly blended, and the truly realistic and artistic works were those which explored and exhibited life without disjoining it. Fortunately, the corrosive features of even the more hackneyed westerns did not cloud the role of the immigrant character or of the ethnic groups.

Mark Requa wrote about central Nevada camp life rather than that of the Comstock, and instead of seeing the immigrant in a sordid context or as an alien torn between hope and despair, he reflected a broad and uncluttered frontier egalitarianism. Requa's only significant book, *Grubstake* (1933), was a labor of love shaped by his childhood memories and lifelong experiences in Nevada. His father had risen rapidly in the Virginia City and San Francisco business world to become a significant figure in railroads, oil, and mining. As an engineer, young Mark directed railroads and mines in eastern Nevada and devoted considerable time to the development of various Herbert Hoover enterprises. He managed Hoover's bid for the presidency in 1928, and five years later dedicated the Nevada novel to his longtime friend. *Grubstake* was set in the general locality of Eureka in 1874 and was designed to reflect one of the great boom areas of the Nevada mining frontier. The suggestion that central Nevada represented a cosmopolitan potpourri at that time was no exaggeration, for in 1880, 4,216 of the 7,086 people in Eureka County (almost 60 percent) were foreign born.

In *Grubstake,* when an old prospector named Shorty Paterson discovered a rich body of ore north of town, he instinctively realized that the local German assayer, Hans Randt, could not be trusted to give him an honest assay. Shorty was correct. Randt returned an unpromising report to the prospector and at the same time sold the correct information to William Patrick, the town's Irish boss and saloonkeeper. A Fourth of July celebration provided Patrick with an opportunity to try to get Shorty drunk and thereby learn the location of the mine. Requa was as much interested in the sights and sounds of a mining town as in the development of his characters. Consequently, he devoted a third of the book to the intrigue and color surrounding the celebration. During the festivities the children of a local Chinese restaurant owner won a prize, the Mexicans became involved in a knife battle, and the drilling contest was won by an Italian team (the Cornish took second place and the Irish came in third). As the crowd left the reviewing stand, there were "Indians; Chinese; foreigners, mostly Cornish, Welsh, and Irish . . . it was the typical western mining town crowd of the years of the gold rush." [13] Eventually, William Patrick and his Cornish helper, Nick Trevethan, were outsmarted by Shorty Paterson and his Scottish helper, John Macklay, and the wealth passed to Shorty and, through him, to the deserving "little people" of the community.

Although the basic plot of *Grubstake* was commonplace, facets of the story were unique. In the one-room school of thirty children, there were Chinese, Mexicans, Slavs, Italians, Cornish, and other foreign migrants. As a restaurant owner, the Chinese

Sam Hing was accepted as a leading businessman of the town; Mexicans frequented the saloon with complete equality, and even the bad men were not really very bad. *Grubstake* is of interest to the student of ethnic cultures, not because it engages in social criticism, but because it seems to suggest that no social criticism is necessary.

Anne Burns also focused on the central Nevada mines, but her work differed from *Grubstake* in that she attempted to interpret the more traditional and formalized literary types. *The Wampus Cat* (1951) borrowed heavily from the local history of both Eureka and Virginia City and absorbed themes from numerous contemporary works. In using the John Mackay legend, Miss Burns cast Pat Burke as a forthright Irishman who had risen from rags to riches within five years after his arrival in America. His Cornish maid, Chatty Silvertooth, who had also been in America only five years, provided the inevitable Anglo-Hibernian contrast. The Cornish woman, with her respect for rank, position, and culture, reflected middle-class mentality, whereas the Irishman would "toady to nobody." Yet even Pat Burke—much like James Mallory in John O'Hara's *Butterfield 8* —had his moments of introspection. "I know how I look too. I look exactly what I am. An Irish Mick, lousy with money, trying to be—well, what Chatty calls a fine puss gentleman. God forgive me." [14]

The handsome, twenty-eight-year-old Ronald McKistry, an English metallurgist from Cambridge, provided a second contrast as he dealt with the crude Irish miners who derisively dubbed him Lord Renfrew. The overriding fear of borrasca in the English-owned and Irish-operated mines, the tension as a result of a strike initiated by the Italian charcoal burners, and a deep Celtic anxiety that a dangerous mountain lion (wampus cat) might enter the snowbound town provided the story with a tragicomic sense of foreboding. The Irish accused the Welsh of being purveyors of superstition, the English metallurgist outraged the Cornish miners by supporting the striking "Dagos," and Burke orated on the Irish contribution to British greatness. Eventually, Burke, lightheartedly and within a period of a few hours, lost his fortune, regained it, and lost it again. In *The Wampus Cat,* the traditional eastern lace-curtain Irish were combined with Comstock legend and the whole imposed on a central Nevada setting. Pat Burke, as well as the other foreign born, too readily conformed to the popular stereotype and too often repeated timeworn clichés. The work failed as a comedy and as a character study, but it accurately reflected the Celts as a rather paradoxical immigrant group who were within reach of the American dream and yet who remained self-conscious, ill at ease, and often the butt of local humor.

The southern Nevada mines have not excited a literary output comparable to that stimulated by the northern part of the state. However, the twentieth-century boom camp of Tonopah quickly drew the attention of Aileen Cleveland Higgins and thereby became the setting for southern Nevada's first novel. The author never visited the state, but rather described the new mining town as she came to know it from brief articles in newspapers and magazines. *A Little Princess of Tonopah* (1909) was among the first of the famed Little Princess Series of childrens' books authored by the imaginative housewife of Perry, Illinois.

Jean Kingsley, the motherless heroine of the novel, accompanied her engineer-father to Tonopah soon after the first great ore discovery. At first, Jean's experiences appear to be light, pleasant, and purposeless, but in time, they add up to an ethnographic report on the town. Upon arrival in Tonopah, Jean and her father lived in a tent and ate their meals at Charley's Inn, a Japanese restaurant operated by Jiro Imado. Jean learned many of the peculiar aspects of Oriental art and philosophy by observing Mr. Imado. Next, she made friends at the bakery shop operated by Max Sluven and his industrious wife. Max's love for good music, his pervasive homesickness, and his stubborn persistence led Jean to a fuller appreciation of the German character. Soon the vibrant Jean had made friends with an Irish priest, with neighborhood Chinese servants, with the daughter of a French engineer who had recently arrived from Chile, with a Spanish-speaking schoolmate, and with an Italian fruit peddler.

Jean found her schoolroom "just like a picture book. There are so many faces, and they are all different." [15] There was the Irish boy who never knew his lessons, the Japanese boy who was afraid to recite in class, and the Spanish girl who performed gypsy dances. But it was the homesickness of many of their parents which most impressed Jean. The sensitive foreign adults found Tonopah ignorant of Wagner and Verdi, disinterested in folk songs or harvest festivals, and incapable of truly enjoying leisure, wine, or friends. The immigrants seemed to long for the old villages, for the old houses, for the smell of new-cut hay, and for the beauty of grapevines loaded with fruit.

Aileen Higgins suggested that a western boom camp needed traditional culture as well as material progress. She sensed, but never criticized, many of the dehumanizing forces at work in the camp. While essentially a children's book, *A Little Princess of Tonopah* was the first broadly inclusive literary approach to the immigrant of twentieth-century Nevada.

Taken together, the bonanza literature of Michelson, Cain, Requa, Burns, and Higgins was a strange blend of fact and fiction. The authors were romantic novelists in that they did not attempt to compile an objective record of events and personalities, and they let their foreign-born characters escape into an exciting and precarious boom-camp world of drama and anarchy. On the other hand, they were historical novelists in that they used facts to gain critical and moral assurance. They accurately placed their immigrants in aspiring and violent mining towns. They showed them to be weary of life and desperately home-sick and they conceded that often they were pawns in the hands of fate.

The Isolation Mystique

Writers have found it easier to feel compassion for the plight of a single man than for that of thousands. This has proved espe-cially true when the life of a man comes to less than his effort seems to merit. Several novelists have successfully portrayed the loneliness and injustice endured by individual immigrants. Their works provide a tactile impression of the locale—of the dry earth, the arctic winds, the blazing sun, the desert rocks. They also portray the more subtle meanings of isolation—the passive indifference, the group exclusiveness, the social preju-dice.[16]

In following the theory that the most intimate is the most universal, Walter Van Tilburg Clark sought out details of local life and formed them into a picture of early-day western society. Clark's first major novel, *The Ox-Bow Incident* (1940), was a western in the tradition of Owen Wister, Zane Grey, and Henry Sinclair Drago. But his examination of life and of man's aliena-tion from culture and society raised questions about the entire frontier myth of democracy and justice. The *Ox-Bow Incident* was a morality play. It emphasized the disorder which resulted when the frontiersman severed his roots with the past and found himself outside the law, unable to maintain his stability. Although Clark introduced only one foreign-born character in

The Ox-Bow Incident, the single immigrant graphically portrayed the impossibility of remaining a detached individualist in early Nevada.

Three misfits were tracked down and hanged by vigilantes for the supposed murder of a man later found to be alive. One of the misfits was a bitter, talented, and rebellious Mexican from Sonora. The youngest of the three refused to believe that the mob was serious. As a weak man, he died many deaths before hanging. The oldest was so completely demented that he never quite realized what was happening. But the Mexican immediately sensed the brutality and sadism of the leader of the vigilantes. The immigrant symbolized the outsider at a time when the tribal pride of the majority had to be sustained. To protect himself against the injustice that he knew he must suffer, he had cultivated a burning resentment for the Gringos. The Mexican understood western morality and knew a mob could be carried, willy-nilly, by a current of avarice or hatred. In short, he expected the injustice that he received.

Resigned to his fate, at first he refused to speak. But pride and hatred overwhelmed him. He emphasized his superiority by declaring himself fluent in ten languages and by removing the bullet from his own thigh after being wounded in an attempt to escape. The leader of the mob, of course, could not allow the foreigner to retain his poise or self-respect. Before being hanged, the proud Mexican, who had known what was to happen from the first and had steeled himself against weakness, was reduced to a cringing wretch. Seldom have the glories of the new western man, happily isolated from the forces of traditional society, seemed more hollow.

Many of Clark's immigrant characters in one way or another were physically cut off or intellectually alienated. Gwen Williams, "a black mucker's daughter," in *The Track of the Cat*

(1949) found herself isolated with the tormented Bridges family. Invited to the Bridges' ranch home to lay plans for her marriage to Harold, Gwen suffered a series of affronts and insults. She was humiliated and finally made angry when father Bridges had to be reassured, while in a drunken stupor, that she was to marry Harold, and not his favorite son Curt. "Better. Much better. Curt marry some decent American girl now, not little foreign whore."[17] And Curt, while tracking the cat, repeatedly thought and muttered about the "little Welsh bitch." Harold's brothers died in a vain attempt to destroy the cat which killed their livestock, and the resultant pall of melancholy and isolation which permeated the Bridges household was expressed in the mother who worshipped an introverted god of death and the father who escaped with alcohol. Mother Bridges, in particular, had fallen victim to the western malady of joylessness. The family thus epitomized Van Wyck Brooks and Lewis Mumford's image of the frontier as a product of dour, barren, and ingrown Puritanism.

But Walter Clark saw loneliness as a personal thing and a product of town as well as of country life, and he saw injustice as a human characteristic and an attribute of society as well as of geography. The arrival of millions of southern and eastern Europeans toward the end of the nineteenth century changed the ethnic composition of American cities as well as the attitudes generally held toward foreigners. For instance, when Clark was attending public school in Reno following World War I, there was a miniature immigrant city across the tracks south of the playground. In 1920, Commercial Row and Center Street could boast of 1 Armenian, 2 Russian, 3 German, 3 Syrian, and 4 Polish merchants, plus a Turkish tamale man, a Persian silk shop, and a Rumanian who sold surplus army supplies, as well as Greek restaurants, Chinese laundries, Italian barbershops, and assorted foreign tailors, watchmakers, and jewelers.[18] Clark sensed the loneliness and injustice suffered by this new wave of immigrants as they settled in Nevada's urban centers and decaying mining towns.

The City of Trembling Leaves (1945) was a narrative dealing with Timothy Hazard and his life and loves in Reno. It was almost inevitable, therefore, that the work would touch on the foreign-born shopkeepers or on their children. Jacob Briaski was a good music student and a friend of Timothy while the two were in elementary school. His parents kept a combination clothing store and hock shop near the speakeasies, flop-houses, and taxi-dance spots on Commercial Row. They "were short, fat, sad people, who spoke broken English."[19] Both boys were dedicated to music, and Jacob's father read and pondered over the Talmud and the philosophers. He also loved fine musical instruments and regularly carried the better ones left in his shop to his home upstairs. To him, the infinite story of life could be felt and explained in music.

As a small, lonesome boy, Jacob grew up with little more than his talent for music. After years of dedication, his San Francisco music instructor informed him that he could never become a great artist, so Jacob removed a six-shooter from his father's shop window and killed himself. Like ten thousand other boys from central and eastern Europe, he had lived for the day when he could escape from the moribund region of the city, from "the ersatz jungle, where the human animals, uneasy in the light, dart from cave to cave under steel and neon branches."[20] The artificiality of the jungle could not meet the basic needs of the truly sensitive lad. He, like the Mexican, was caught in a hopeless web. The Mexican could not escape from the cowhands on the rugged frontier, and Jacob could not escape from himself and the indifferent society.

Luigi and Maria in *The City of Trembling Leaves* were also cut off from the advantages of American life. The story of Luigi's Bar in Tonopah leaves the reader with an honest sadness for the immigrant who could not escape from the labyrinths of a dying town. Although Luigi's Bar attracted a number of people on "Sunday afternoon, or sunset, or night," the town was obviously decaying and the day was coming when "the fellows don't come no more." Nevertheless, Luigi remained a good citizen. He had a sign over the cash register declaring that he was an American; a banner on the wall said "God Bless America"; and he would not allow fellow Italians to "talk good" about Mussolini. But the bar was cut off and dying, and the death was not understood, even by those who were a part of it. "Luigi's was no longer enough in itself, but a small place at the bottom of the main street of Tonopah, Nevada, and Tonopah on its mountain was surrounded by night, and filled with the rattling lamentation of the wind." [21] Nevada, with its waves of Irish, Greeks, Slavs, and Italians, and with its four hundred ghost towns, has known many bars like Luigi's.

As life has become economically secure and physically comfortable, modern men seem to have decided that God is dead and that the universe is meaningless. But Robert Laxalt, through the character of his father, moves back to an era when life was hard, and suffering the common lot, and when men agreed that God was wise and good. Laxalt underscores the almost medieval kind of faith and simplicity which led thousands of immigrants to settle on the wind-swept, sun-drenched, high lonesome wastes of Nevada.

Sweet Promised Land (1957) was both a personal memoir about the author's father and a landmark for the immigrant sheepman. The book created an image of the Basque sheep-herder, much as Hamlin Garland's *Main Traveled Roads* created an image of the Plains farmer. Laxalt knew Nevada and sheep as well as Garland knew the prairies and the farm. Both were saddened by the hardships suffered by their parents; hardships which as children they too had experienced, but could never share. Both present their subject with honesty and yet with deep emotion; both became backtrailers so as to better understand where they had been. In one case, the image of the idealized independent farmer collapsed, and in the other, the myth about the subhuman or the superhuman vagabond sheepman was discredited. The Basque sheepman, much like leatherstocking frontiersmen of a century earlier, had become literary subjects who were often viewed as a class apart, on the fringe of civilization. When Laxalt's father, after revisiting his childhood home in the Pyrenees, turned from relatives and friends and walked down the hill intent on returning to his Nevada home, he and hundreds of other Basque immigrants, whose thoughts he typified, suddenly became Americans.

Like so many other European youths, Laxalt's father had planned to remain in America for "just a little while; just enough time to make some money and go back." He postponed the return for forty-seven years. When he first arrived in America he experienced some derision, bullying, and fun-making because of his speech, habits, and clothing. But strange examples of fair play and human kindness slowly eroded away his determination to hurry home. The primitive society suddenly brought him self-identification when a group of cattle rustlers killed his sheep dog and then, in a moment of remorse, gave him a horse as payment for their heedlessness. The youth recognized the open range as a harsh and cruel place, and yet he became grateful for the small favor of acceptance, and in the end, he was bound to its vast loneliness.

In *Sweet Promised Land,* Laxalt looked back over his father's life without reticence, without manipulated tragedies, without incrimination, much as the life was lived. Nowhere did he find his father truly alien, nowhere was he superfluous, nowhere was he nostalgic or passive. In leaving kinfolks, after the visit to the beloved Pyrenees, the father refused to glance back and suddenly his son understood.

> I saw the West rising up at dawn with an awesome vastness of deserts and mighty mountain ranges. I saw a band of sheep winding their way down a lonely mountain ravine of sagebrush and pine, and I smelled their dust and heard their muted bleating and the lovely tinkle of their bells. I saw a man in crude garb with a walking stick following after with his dog, and once he paused to mark the way of the land. Then I saw a cragged face that the land had filled with hope and torn with pain, had changed from young to old, and in the end had claimed.[22]

As an intimate biography of an immigrant, *Sweet Promised Land* spoke not only for the Basque sheepherders, but, as a reviewer has suggested, "for the Italians and the Yugoslavs, for the Swedes and the Irish, the Portuguese and the Greeks." [23]

Laxalt's allegorical novel, *A Man in the Wheatfield* (1964), resembled *Sweet Promised Land* in that it was drawn almost exclusively from the author's youthful experience and imagination. Although *A Man in the Wheatfield* was given the unlikely setting of an isolated western community composed entirely of Italian immigrants and their immediate descendants, the broad demographic and historical outlines were sound. As early as 1880, parts of the Carson Valley to the east of Carson City had become a predominantly Italian community. For example, in that year 43 of the 69 persons residing in New Jerusalem were Italian-born. Twenty years later, 52 of the 110 people in the

town of Sutro were from Italy, and for over forty years some
one fourth of the approximately 500 residents of Dayton were
Italians. Fortunately, the distinct culture and folkways of the
Italians were not lost on young Laxalt as he grew up in an immigrant home in Carson City.

When Smale Calder bought Bandoni's garage and gas station and settled in the town, his action created much concern
since he was an "American." And "except for the lonely farm
tramps who came through in planting and harvest times . . . or
the occasional curiosity seekers . . . [the townspeople] were not
used to Americans." [24] Unfortunately, Calder was also a lover
and keeper of snakes and a protector of insect life. These and
other peculiarities quickly engendered hostility and fear among
the townspeople. The village priest, Father Savio Lazzaroni,
could have preserved order and maintained sanity within the
community had he not been beset with apprehension and ren-
dered impotent by self-doubt and a belief in omens. Consequently, the priest realized after it was too late that Calder was
not the Devil incarnate as he had supposed, but rather was a
man whose extreme simplicity had cloaked him in purity.

Had it been given a different turn, *A Man in the Wheatfield,*
with its allegory and use of the Devil, could have become an
Italian morality play. This notion raises the question of the extent to which foreign folkways and European superstitions were
retained in a liberalizing and uninhibited environment. The
novel further suggests the wealth of almost totally unexplored
lore available in a study of immigrant practices and customs.
Edmund Burke once suggested that superstitions were the religion of the poor in spirit. Yet surely society, history, and literature would be impoverished without them. To what extent and
in what ways were the Old World beliefs in myths and miracles
sustained on the frontier, and in what form were they trans-

mitted to the second generation? Under what circumstances and how often were immigrant superstitions absorbed into the thought of the West? What mental accommodations did foreign-born groups make to the Nevada physical environment? Finally, was it the isolated rural settlements or the crowded urban tenements which most effectively retained their foreign temperament?

The immigrant character of *A Man in the Wheatfield* tends to suggest that despite the atomistic effect of mining on the Comstock, railroad building along the Carson River, and the magnetism of urban centers, many Italians in and around western Nevada were reluctant to give up their intimate and personal relationships for the casual and segmented existence on the outside. Certainly not all immigrants wished to assert their individuality by abandoning their traditions and customs for a lonesome anonymity. The often exaggerated attitude concerning the determination of foreigners to accept Americans forms and values is thrown open to question. Strange as it seems at first, Laxalt has shown that it was perhaps as easy to cultivate a ghetto mentality in the desert as in New York City.

One of the most imaginative and explicit attempts to link the isolation of the Nevada West with the cosmos and with mankind was offered by George Stewart in *Sheep Rock* (1951). Stewart's fictionalized account of a black, rocky protuberance with a hot spring located in the desolate wastes of northern Washoe County carried the same mythical undertones as his *Fire* and *Storm,* both of which were set in the nearby Sierra. It was Stewart's sharp sense of the complexity of nature and of man, of the many layers of time and experience that somehow coexist and can be contracted into a moment, that made his fiction dramatic and unconventional. Actually, *Sheep Rock* was a phantasmagoria of things seen, envisioned, and invoked in the imagination. The work made use of geology, biology, and anthropology to convey a sense of the timelessness of nature and the pricelessness of primeval terrain.

One of the tragic injustices at Sheep Rock centered around Private Smithson and the mongrel military outfit to which he belonged. Troop C was a cosmopolitan Army unit made up not only of the customary Irish and Germans, but also of Jews, Mexicans, and Englishmen. Smithson, a Cockney, had served with Her Majesty's Lancers, and when a fellow cavalryman deserted he was selected to pursue the fleeing soldier. Smithson found the deserter's decapitated head floating in the hot spring at Sheep Rock, and the entire troop, with sadistic vengeance, tracked down the small band of starving and frightened Indians who had inhabited the spot and exterminated them.

Stewart's introduction of the immigrant into the frontier cavalry was historically accurate and psychologically convincing. For example, in 1860, four of the six noncommissioned officers at Fort Ruby were foreign-born; in 1870, 69 of the 135 soldiers stationed at Fort Halleck were foreign-born; and in 1880, 30 of the 56 soldiers stationed at Fort McDermitt were foreign-born.[25] But in a broader sense, *Sheep Rock* was a microcosm of the larger world. Through the use of time and space, Stewart showed the caprice of man. The grandeur of the world was underscored by capturing the mystery, the emotion, and the legacy of one arid and deserted spot where men of many nations fought, dreamed, and died with only the remotest evidence of purpose.

By the late 1930s, the crude but vibrant southern Nevada mining society described by Aileen Higgins in *A Little Princess of Tonopah* had disappeared. Mine exhaustion and economic depression had driven all human life from a hundred once-prosperous towns. Edwin Corle's *Coarse Gold* (1942), followed the story of Coarse Gold's founding by Sam Branahan in the

Frank Bell, born Toronto, Canada, served as Nevada governor, 1890–1891. (Courtesy of *Nevada Highways and Parks Magazine*)

Reinhold Sadler, born Czarnikau, Pozen, served as Nevada governor, 1896–1903. (Courtesy of Nevada Historical Society)

John Edward Jones, born Montgomeryshire, Wales, served as Nevada governor, 1895–1896. (Courtesy of Nevada Historical Society)

John P. Jones, born of Welsh parents in The Hay, Hereford, was U.S. senator from Nevada from 1873 to 1903. (Courtesy of Special Collections, University of Nevada Library, Reno)

It is not known how the beautiful Circassian girl Zobedie Lut made her way to the Comstock in the late sixties. Circassian women had for centuries provided the Sultans of Turkey with their harems while Circassian men provided them with their cavalry. Miss Lut was a "performer." (Courtesy of Doten Diaries, University of Nevada, Reno)

Chang Woo Gow, born in China of part Japanese ancestry, had grown to a height of eight feet by the time he was twenty-four years old. By 1870 he had become Europeanized and actively supported the French of Virginia City in the Franco-Prussian War. (Courtesy of Doten Diaries, University of Nevada, Reno)

Irish songs and plays were particularly popular in early Nevada. Kathleen O'Neil, "Kitty from Cork," was one of the most idolized singers and dancers of the late sixties. (Courtesy of Doten Diaries, University of Nevada, Reno)

Although only four and one-half years old, James Speight of London excited the theater crowds of Virginia City with his instrumental accomplishments in the spring of 1872. He died of a heart attack some two years later. (Courtesy of Doten Diaries, University of Nevada, Reno)

During the mid-sixties
Madame Rose Picor of
France operated the
Boule D'Or on C Street,
Virginia City. It was
justly famous as one
of the most exclusive
restaurants in the West.
(Courtesy of Doten
Diaries, University
of Nevada, Reno)

John Millian.
(Courtesy
of Nevada
Historical
Society)

Death Any Afternoon

The personable Frenchman John Millian was hanged
at Virginia City at 12:42 P.M. on April 24, 1864.
He had been convicted for the murder of one of
the West's most publicized courtesans, the English-born
Julia Bulette. Millian was accompanied to the
scaffold by the famous Irish priest Father Manogue
and delivered a final oration in French. The week
following the execution, the *California Police Gazette*
added this woodcut to their lengthy coverage of
the affair. (Courtesy of Nevada Historical Society)

There were 8,000 to 10,000 Chinese working on the
Central Pacific Railroad in Nevada during 1868–1869.
The photograph was taken in mid August, 1868, at a campsite some
sixteen miles southwest of present day Lovelock. (Courtesy
of Chinese Historical Society of America, San Francisco)

By 1920 there were only 689 Chinese
in Nevada and only a few who had
participated in the construction
of the Central Pacific. Three of
the old timers were honored in 1919
in a semicentenary celebration.
From left to right: Took Wong,
Chao Lee, Cue Ging. (Courtesy of
Amon Carter Museum, Fort Worth)

Mexicans, Scots, Chinese, and Portuguese all worked
as Nevada sheepherders, but by the twentieth century
the Basques had become the dominant nationality in this
lonesome occupation. The photos show Jean Pierre Laxalt
and his flock of sheep above Lake Tahoe in 1946.
(Courtesy of Gus Bundy)

Adolph Sutro at Sutro, Nevada.
Born in Aachen, Germany, in 1830,
builder of the Sutro tunnel, and one
of Nevada's leading engineer-promoters,
Sutro eventually became mayor of
San Francisco. (Courtesy of California
Historical Society, San Francisco)

nineties and its collapse and depopulation to one resident by 1942. The lucky Irishman who discovered the ore, the Maltese bouncer at an Italian bar, the foreign prostitutes, and the Chinese laundry were all included in the typical boom-camp pattern, but the key or thread in the life of the town was more artistically and meaningfully drawn.

Christian Wick had rediscovered the ghost camp, over a hundred miles from Las Vegas and long lost in the desert waste, and in an attempt to reshape his own life had become the old camp's single resident. When he explored the local cemetery, he found among the sagebrush and greasewood four crude markers still standing, and he began to wonder about the lives of those who once inhabited the town. One of the markers carried the inscription "Sing Loy. Born in China. Died in Coarse Gold."

In the 1890s, Wing Sing, an enterprising laundry operator, had saved his money and, according to custom, bought a slave girl or wife for $200. Nine months later the Chinese family was expecting a baby, but the money saved for the occasion suddenly became unavailable with the closing of the local bank. Without the money, Wing Sing was afraid to summon the local doctor. Perhaps it did not matter, for the physician was in a house of prostitution, drunk. Sing Loy died in childbirth. A mob which had originally formed to protest the closing of the bank decided instead that Wing Sing had deliberately killed his spouse and ought to be lynched. The confused, frightened, and grief-stricken Chinese finally hid in the corner of a boxcar and on May 8, 1900, escaped from the cursing, rock-throwing, drunken citizenry of Coarse Gold. The "good people" of the town buried Sing Loy and placed the crude wooden headboard on her grave.

Much to Christian Wick's consternation, forty-two years

later, tungsten was discovered at the old mine, and almost over night Coarse Gold was rebuilt. No one remembered the mob which had chased "the Chink" out of town, and as a bulldozer knocked down Sing Loy's grave marker, and a highway was built across the cemetery, the "good people" of 1942 were humming a new slogan:

> We're gonna have to slap
> The dirty little Jap
> And Uncle Sam's
> The man to do it! [26]

As a serious historical novelist, Edwin Corle not only told the truth about the past, he also showed its relevance to the present. He demonstrated that each new generation tends to reflect and not correct the evils of the old. Throughout the constant confrontation between innocence and depravity, refinement and brutality, *Coarse Gold* refrains from making moral judgments and does not speculate on man's path to redemption.

But the barren frontiers of southern Nevada have attracted the allegorical and the anagogical along with the episodic and the tragic. In over fifty books, the team of Frederic Dannay and Manfred B. Lee, better known as Ellery Queen, have gone far to create the form for the American detective story. In *And on the Eighth Day* (1964) they combined mystery with utopianism and used the great desert expanse as their setting. The leader of the settlement at Quenan Valley near the California-Nevada border was a visionary but non-Christian ascetic who seemed equally adept at conversing with the spirits and presiding over a farming and handicraft community. (One is reminded of Father George Rapp and the founding of New Harmony in 1815.) The colony's only contact with the outside world was through Otto Schmidt's country store, which was located several miles from prosperous Quenan Valley. Schmidt's German relatives often sent him books, which he sometimes traded or sold to the colony leaders. When a traveler, motoring from Los Angeles to New York, lost his way and discovered first the country store and then the settlement, he quickly sensed the peculiar blending of many Old World influences and traditions. Martin Luther, Philipp Melanchthon, Russian sectarianism, and the desert life of the ancient Hebrews could all be felt in the rude cornucopia where change was frozen and even time stood still.

After eight days in the valley, the outsider discovered that the holy, prophetic book which the colonists were trying to interpret was actually a black-lettered, archaic-looking copy of *Mein Kampf;* he simultaneously found that selfishness and greed pervaded the communal order, much as it did in communities in the outside world. When the twelve councilmen became convinced that the intruder was not a possessor of occult powers who could read the book of prophecy, he was allowed to continue on his journey. As he was departing, he saw an aviator parachute to safety on the desert floor; even as the airman descended, the colony leaders declared the dark skinned man under the white canopy to be their new savior.

Ellery Queen chose the panorama of Nevada as the ideal setting for a modern-day, or perhaps timeless, mystery play. He revealed a form of social thinking which strove to replace the lawlessness, the sordidness, and the glamour of the world with a medieval type of communal protection. The very space and desolation of the West provided a new magnet for the old doctrines and ideologies. But while many foreign-oriented groups planned or attempted communal settlements in Nevada, most quickly discovered that they could neither maintain a disciplined society within, nor isolate themselves from the popular environment without. In real life, the prophets have found Nevada to be peculiarly inhospitable to both communal living and religious asceticism.

Of course, most immigrants never envisioned themselves as heroes destined to slay the mysterious dragon of loneliness or alienation. They sought a better life for themselves and for their children. Despite the romanticizing of later novelists and historians, the average migrant was not an Edward Bellamy fictionalizing on the happiness of coming generations. He wanted success and accomplishment in the foreseeable future. Furthermore, the foreign born demanded not only material success but emotional integration. Most immigrants did not wish to wander; they sought to draw upon their traditions, to merge into the community, and to grow roots.

One of the threads running through Nevada literature touched on the individualistic, optimistic, and vital nature of the foreign born. But another thread revealed the geographical isolation, the personal desperation, and the human negation experienced by many immigrants. The chastening counter theme pointed up unsettling forces like the accelerated life cycle of the mining camps, the accepted patterns of discrimination, and the malevolence of nature. Such sobering undertones provided sensitive novelists with their most poignant insights into the lives of Nevadans.

The Reminiscence Syndrome

During the five decades since World War I, and particularly during the 1930s, the sluices of nostalgic memorabilia were opened, and the readers of Nevada literature were required to navigate as best they could a torrent of reminiscence, dramatized recollections, and autobiographical essays. In some of the works the immigrant theme predominated, and in others the foreign born were used extensively as a device for emphasizing the extraordinary diversity, manifold tastes, and diffuse society which prevailed in early Nevada. Works on the Comstock, like those by C. B. Glasscock, George D. Lyman, William MacLeod Raine, Miriam Michelson, Wells Drury, Harry M. Gorham, Vardis Fisher, Swift Paine, and others, tended to reinforce accepted opinion and were often discursive in their evaluations. A few books, like Fisher's *The City of Illusion* (1941) and Paine's *Eilley Orrum: Queen of the Comstock* (1929), are fictionalized biographies, and most of the literature, whether touching on Eilley Orrum Bowers, Adolph Sutro, John Mackay, Chinese coolies, Mexican vaqueros, French restauranteurs, or Austrian nuns, provided description, characterization, and occasional insights into the social nuances of the foreign born.

A few of the immigrants of the Comstock era have become fabled, nearly mythical figures. While not acquiring the heroic stature of Johnny Appleseed, Davy Crockett, or Paul Bunyan, the exploits of John A. (Snowshoe) Thompson have, nevertheless, been the source of considerable regional fame. Dan De Quille, in the *Overland Monthly* of October, 1886, laid the basis for a legend which was exploited by several writers including Adrien Stoutenburg, Laura Nelson Baker, and Evelyn Teal. Both Stoutenburg and Baker in *Snowshoe Thompson* (1957) and Mrs. Teal in *Flying Snowshoes* (1957) molded Thompson into a delightfully stubborn, square-head Norwegian who accomplished his feat of carrying the winter mail over the Sierra because of his Old World ancestry and early training.

On the whole, the reminiscences and autobiographical novels have failed to show a healthy skepticism toward the apocryphal tales of the old days. Nor have the authors responded with sufficient flexibility to the extremely complex environment of the Comstock. Only two or three biographical works were courageous enough, or brash enough, or erudite enough to entertain forceful judgments. Most writers who based their stories on highly subjective recollections were overly charitable and commonly fell short in their attempt to analyze and interpret immigrant life.

However, by combining stark realism with romantic imagery, Flannery Lewis, in *Sons Go Down* (1937), produced one of the most moving biographies of the era. The author's grandmother Flannery arrived in Nevada when only seventeen years of age—"the first decent white woman" of the district. To her somewhat prejudiced Irish–New England eyes, it seemed that everyone "considered himself something besides an American,"[27] and yet she quickly sensed the heavy line which divided the immigrants. Those from southern Europe were foreigners because they had a "heavy" accent, followed "peculiar" customs, and often had "swarthy" complexions. Northern Europeans accepted supervisory positions in industry and believed in the philosophy of natural superiority. They became Americans, whereas their fellow migrants from South and East Europe remained aliens.

As grandmother Flannery grew older, she saw, but did not care to understand, the constant movement of people into and out of the city. Various waves of migrants came in, performed their functions in mines, on the railroads, or in laundries, and disappeared. Lewis, with a kind of humorous despair, suggests his inability to convey either the true feelings of his grandmother or the true essence of a crumbling society. By the 1930s Mrs. Flannery, at ninety years of age, had become symbolic of the Comstock in that she was left only with her memories and kitchen walls covered with outdated calendars from Italian grocery stores.

Lewis made his grandmother into a gallant, delightful, and stubborn woman who, much like Virginia City, continued to endure. His picture of a decaying town with dead minds and buried dreams cut through Comstock history both vertically and horizontally. Leading journals favorably compared parts of the story with works by Jonathan Swift, Daniel Defoe, Margaret Ogilvie, and James Barrie, and one reviewer praised the novel as "something that will endure because of its deep humor and its truth." [28]

In part, Nevada was settled like the rest of the West by diffuse waves of interesting people. But Nevada differed from much of the country in that it suffered several periods of severe depopulation, only to be resettled by a second and even a third wave of migrants. Consequently, the foreign born have been a subject for inquiry not only for their arrival and initial adjustment, but also for their mobility and exodus. Much of the fiction published between the wars was deeply influenced by the departure of thousands of people. Yet, few of the writers seized upon the topic or developed a meaningful idiom such as Hamlin Garland's "back-trailers." During the thirties, Flannery Lewis exploited the topic of decay, and by so doing he presented a new focus for Comstock literature and suggested a new way to look at the Nevada immigrant.

The foreign born of central and southern Nevada also attracted the autobiographers. During the 1880s, several young Englishmen migrated to the American West to become Methodist missionary preachers. Thomas Leak, James Whitaker, and many of the other Yorkshiremen first settled in Nevada, but later pushed on to California. George Wharton James of Lincolnshire, however, determined to present his Calvinistic-Methodist doctrine to the sinners of Eureka. The true story of James's life is perhaps more fascinating than the novel written about him. He arrived in Battle Mountain in 1881, and after seven years of preaching in northern and central Nevada and

California, he suffered a physical and emotional collapse. Upon recovery, James adopted a new philosophy, and for the remainder of his long life, he emphasized the natural human freedom of the American West as contrasted with the tradition, discipline, and religious control which had chained so many European minds. He became a man of all talents interested in astronomy, geology, and art; he was a Chautauqua lecturer, an editor of journals and newspapers, and the author of over forty volumes on science, philosophy, politics, and the humanities.

In *The Sage Brush Parson* (1906), Alice Ward Bailey wove her plot around James's early evangelistic experiences in central Nevada. She realistically portrayed James, or Clement Vaughan, as he became known in the novel, as a sympathetic, somewhat troubled, and sensitive Englishman whose strength and courage was drawn from the buoyant atmosphere of the American southwest. In Nevada, the grey clouds of his Calvinistic doubt disappeared, and an "Italian-like sun" cleared his thoughts, brightened his prospects, and allowed for his physical and mental rejuvenation.

After arriving in Battle Mountain in May, 1881, the scholarly parson traveled up the Reese River to the home of English friends at Galena and Lewis. The little knot of devoted British Methodists urged Vaughan forward in his missionary work and helped him to rebuild his faltering faith. They were successful, and after Vaughan preached for a few weeks at numerous mining camps in northern and central Nevada, he determined to carry the word of God to the growing city of Eureka. The Episcopalians detested his democratic manner and his policy of allowing "any ignorant son of Cornwall or Cork" to interrupt him in the middle of a sermon.[29] The Irish made him the butt of repeated pranks and local ridicule. Finally, Vaughan was drawn into a formal debate on British foreign policy, in which the Scots, Welsh, and even the Cornish allied with the Irish in a jubilant twisting of the English lion's tail. By pretending to be of Irish descent and smothering the Celts with kindness, Vaughan not only won the debate, but was made the honored guest at a banquet given by the Hibernian Society.

At the pinnacle of acceptance and achievement, Vaughan's neurotic wife arrived from England and quickly destroyed his prestige and effectiveness as a community leader. Her carefully planned suicide pointed to murder by her husband, and the parson was tried and reluctantly convicted by a local jury. After an impassioned plea by friends, Vaughan was granted a governor's reprieve only a few minutes before he was supposed to die. And although he was subsequently asked to continue his work in Eureka, he silently and sadly rode out of the valley into the sunset.

The transporting of the Celtic-English conflict from Europe to Nevada and the extension of England's Primitive-Methodism to the western mines became major themes in *The Sage Brush Parson*. But the most compelling issue was the personal search for meaning and the values and happiness to be found in western society. Like Beret Holm in *Giants in the Earth,* and scores of other frightened immigrant women, Mrs. Vaughan could not fathom her husband's transcendent vision of America and thereby allowed her insane fear to destroy him.

Isabel Fields, Nora Bowman, Zua Arthur, Helen Croft, and Anne Hawkins were western-oriented women biographers who saw none of the moroseness and morbidity used by Alice Ward Bailey in *The Sage Brush Parson*. Indeed, after seventy years of zestful living, Isabel Fields sketched a blithe and wholesome picture of the foreigners of Nevada. Mrs. Fields, stepdaughter of Robert Louis Stevenson and for years his secretary on the island of Samoa, was a poet, painter, and writer, and the wife and mother of leading American playrights. Clearly, her best artistic production was the autobiographical memoir *This Life I've Loved* (1937). Born in Indianapolis in 1859, she was taken by her mother to Austin in the late sixties. Her father had preceded them to the Nevada mines. Mrs. Fields's re-creation of the English and Welsh children with whom she played, her recollection of the artificial birds ingeniously designed for the Queen's birthday, and the drinking of toasts to Victoria Regina's health are among the memories which served to make *This Life I've Loved* an international favorite.

During the late 1950s and early 1960s, several biographical essays were set in eastern and southern Nevada. Nora Linger Bowman in *Only the Mountains Remain* (1958) developed the character of a Polish gardener who lived with the family on their isolated ranch in eastern Elko County. Zua Arthur in *Broken Hills* (1958) presented the life of her Cornish-born husband-prospector as he moved throughout the state, and Helen Downer Croft in *The Downs, the Rockies, and Desert Gold* (1961) followed her husband's family from the English Downs to Colorado and on to Goldfield.

Of considerably more historical impact was Anne Hawkins's thoroughly researched novel based on the Pony Express. *To the Swift* (1949) was set in the fast-moving, short-lived era when English Bob Haslam carried the mail from Friday's Station near Lake Tahoe to Buckland's, seventy-five miles to the east. Many foreign-born riders like John Fisher, Jack Keetley, Elijah H. Maxwell, William Page, Alexander Toponce, and Howard Egan covered parts of the Nevada route, but none were as colorful as English Bob. As the author attempted to blend the elements of fiction into her historical facts, the story tends to become improbable, but because Robert Haslam approached the Nevada sands with the same thoughtless daring that many of his fellow countrymen approached the sea, "a runt of an Englishman" was enabled to become "a hero of the desert."

Neither Frank Crampton, Paul Ralli, Axel Johnson, nor Charles Ryan attempted to shape their autobiographical stories around the attitudes of the foreign born. But immigrants were instinctively woven into the fabric of their work. The literary judgments of the authors may be open to question, and their characters may be underdeveloped, yet their immigrants are never self-consciously inserted or tediously superficial.

Frank A. Crampton built his Goldfield reminiscences around the Cornish mining phrase *Deep Enough* (1956). Paul Ralli's *Viva Vegas* (1953) was in part sketches and vignettes depicting the writer's migration from Cyprus to England to the United States to Mexico and finally to Las Vegas. Axel P. Johnson's *Smuggled into Paradise* (1958) was the account of the author's illegal entry into the United States from Sweden, his experiences in the Louisiana sugar fields, and his subsequent migration to Nevada. And Charles O. Ryan's attractive autobiographical essay, *Nine Miles from Dead Horse Wells* (1959) concentrated on a small, manageable, immigrant-centered incident in the life of the author.

Ryan redeveloped an age-old superstition, first brought to the West by the foreign-born miners. Supposedly there were Johnny Knockers and Piskeys who haunted mines, and ghosts, ghouls, and ill omens for which underground workers should be on guard. As an inexperienced employee of the Scheelite Mine near Rawhide, Ryan was assigned to an Italian hard rock miner for training. Along with the trivial annoyances of garlic breath and Italian cigars, he learned of the deep-seated superstitions of the immigrant workers. Within a few weeks after his arrival at the mine, Ryan sensed a mounting but intangible uneasiness. A few days later, the foreman's wife visited the mine and was escorted through the underground passages—an action that, according to the superstitious foreign born, would lead to the most serious consequences. The stage seemed set for a major incident. As the tension and fear spread, the Italians and several of the Irish refused to enter the shaft, and later the same day tragedy struck in the form of a devastating cave-in which even enveloped buildings and vehicles above ground. Other immigrants who had narrowly escaped death boycotted the project, and the story ended with no explanation for the bizarre series of events and no evaluation of the premonitions and instincts of the foreigners.

If a scenario writer were asked to compile a composite narrative from the score of biographies and reminiscences he might start with Helen Croft's scene of "ragged, burly men from Ireland, Scotland, and the English countryside" forming "noisy throngs" as they took ship for America.[30] Upon arrival in Nevada the immigrant would probably engage in prospecting as did the Cornish-born Joe Arthur. And as in the Arthur story, a Greek might contest the mining claim at Verdi, a Cockney help to survey another at Fairview, and a Nova Scotian and Italian become mining partners at Eureka. Slowly the immigrant in the hypothetical memoir would come to accept Nevada—its irreverence, its illusions, and its vision of the future. The drama would probably end in a Frank Crampton-like surge of sentimental neutralism with the author implying that he had made the correct decisions and that much was right with the world. Or, if the plot was to show realism, the final scene could include a Flannery Lewis touch. A proud and stubborn and heroic immigrant would refuse to see the obvious decay—the decay of himself, of his mining town, and of his social traditions. Or, if there was to be a fatalism of the George Wharton James–Clement Vaughan dimension, the scene might close with the immigrant engulfed in tragedy, suffering from mental or physical collapse, and numbly riding into the darkness. Most Nevada authors of sunset reminiscences have preferred the first conclusion. They have not wished to recall the harsh realities of evening or speculate on the black void of night.

Two Images of Nevada

For the past half century, Nevada has been associated with a wide range of amusements, tourist attractions, and permissive institutions not known elsewhere in the United States. A particular group of authors, therefore, has tended to stress the external environment, the elusive topics of sin and sex, and the hackneyed themes of divorce and gambling. Reno and Las Vegas in particular have inspired much ephemeral and patronizing literature. Very few of the publications which view Las Vegas as America's gambling mecca attempt to analyze the local society. *Gambling in Nevada, 17 and Black, Las Vegas: City Without Clocks, It Only Hurts a Minute, Las Vegas: Playtown U.S.A., No House Limit,* and similar books seldom cast the immigrant in a major literary role.

In the case of Reno, much immigrant material became available even in the first years of settlement. As early as 1870, only two years after the town was founded, there were Arabians, West Indians, and seven Australians living in the community. Ten years later, the village boasted a scattering of immigrants from widely diverse areas like Jamaica, Malta, Borneo, Chile, and South Africa. By 1910, the city's 10,867 people represented over thirty nationalities, including 43 persons from Asian India and 15 from Turkey. By 1920, its population of 12,016 was drawn from more than forty regions or countries, including small groups from the Philippines, Syria, Korea, and Brazil. In the same year, 5.5 percent of the 18,627 people in Washoe County had been born in Italy.[31] Few inland, isolated, and nonindustrial communities have attracted a greater variety of immigrants. They were drawn from every class of society and from every major race, religion, and nation. Despite the unimaginative nature of many of the Reno centered novels, immigrant characters have not become stereotyped. Even mediocre writers effectively used the foreign born in a wide variety of roles.

The wealthy Europeans and the foreign-born aristocrats who traveled to Reno have provided the city with its most unusual immigrant feature. They helped to make the community known as the most cosmopolitan little city in the United States. In Lilyan Stratton's *Reno,* published in 1921, a portrait painter from the Royal Academy of London, a millionaire's mistress from Morocco, and other equally sophisticated immigrants were introduced. Thirty years later, Latifa Johnson found the same type of foreigners in *Sheila Goes to Reno* (1950). Clare Boothe's play, *The Women* (1937), emphasized the aristocratic foreign divorcees, and even writers of Reno mystery stories have seized upon the motif. Helen Arre, Ross Macdonald, Zenith Brown, and Hazel Payne used the unfathomable Chinese, the inexplicable Basque, and an enigmatic descendant of Oliver Cromwell in their curious Reno mysteries.

In Hazel Payne's *Well-Dressed Corpse* (1953), the corpse becomes a device for introducing the reader to Reno's worldly atmosphere. Julie Barclay, a member of a prominent family, awoke one night to find herself staring at a corpse propped up in her chaise longue. Julie began to reflect upon her associates and neighbors, wondering who might have wished to involve her in the murder. Only two houses away was the palatial home of an Italian expatriate, Count Sessini, and his footman Tito. Julie's close friend Sybil de Ciannti had been born in Cairo before drifting into Reno; Sybil's father was an Italian count who had divorced his French-Canadian wife. Julie and Sybil enjoyed gambling and had become acquainted with an exotic Chinese fan dancer, the Maharaja of Indore, and the Portuguese daughter of a railroad baron. The police caught the murderer just as the last of Reno's famous foreign-born dignitaries was catalogued.

The light, yet subtle, autobiographical tale by the youthful Frederic Siebert introduced humor into the theme of the wealthy cosmopolitan immigrant. As a native of Reno and a graduate of the University of Nevada, Siebert became a Rhodes Scholar and later a student at St. John's University, Brooklyn, where he died in 1929. While at Oxford Siebert composed a playful, simply written work, which characterized three bourgeois Americans in Paris and the subsequent reaction of two of them when they returned to Reno. *George, Wimple, and I* was published in 1929, shortly after Siebert's death.

George Wiltsbobber was a Reno lawyer; the narrator of the story was a University of Nevada English teacher. The two were companions on a trip to Paris where they met a Rhodes Scholar by the name of Wimple. As the three traveled about Paris, they analyzed the social and cultural life on the basis of their Nevada background. Upon returning to Reno, George became particularly enamored with the international types and with European ladies seeking a divorce. In one instance, George was retained by an attractive French divorcee whom he proudly escorted to a local French restaurant for a successful evening. The following day, George was dumbfounded to receive a note from the divorcee which explained that he and the restaurant manager had provided such an authentic French atmosphere that the client had become homesick and was foregoing the divorce to return to Paris. *George, Wimple, and I* exposed the sham of the tourists and the foolishness of the traveling set and also pointed up the comic sentimentality of Reno's rich, aristocratic, and temporary foreign-born residents.

No consistent immigrant theme can be pieced together from the fragmented and often negative comments of a dozen of the more popular Reno novels. Such books often wind along a serpentine of lascivious imputations, but generally fail to relate the immigrant to the moral experience of the community. Works like Cornelius Vanderbilt, Jr.'s, *Reno* (1929), John Hamlin's *Whirlpool of Reno* (1931), Faith Baldwin's *Temporary Address: Reno* (1940), Larry Schrader's *Reno Round the Clock* (1954), and Max Miller's *Reno* (1941) introduce Italians, Germans, Basques, Chinese, and other immigrants but they neither explain them nor relate them to the city or the state.

Miller's novel was typical of the "Nevada directory" approach. After *I Cover the Waterfront* (1932) became a best seller, Miller turned to full-time writing and during his fourth trip to Reno, compiled a narrative about aspects of local and regional life. As a journalist who had reported on the vigorous and sometimes brutal habits of men from Montana rodeos, Australian prize fights, and the San Diego docks, Miller was capable of catching the lusty force of Nevada's past. While he understood the hearty and rugged life, he offered little by way of immigrant characterization.

A score of comic, mystery, and serious writers made Reno into a floating mirage which everyone enjoyed and everyone wrote about, yet no one seemed to think worthy of possession. Although the city was active, it retained a distorted image. In half a century, the authors changed little. A few of the works were held together by their virtuosity and a few by their description, but more were filled with pretense and make-believe. Nevertheless, the theme of international sophistication, wealthy immigrants, and foreign-born aristocrats endows Reno literature with a singular approach to the western immigrant.

Sherwood Anderson once charitably suggested that Reno and all of Nevada had suffered "rather terribly" at the hands of writers. He advanced the notion that Reno was one of the great cities of America, not because it attracted attention, but because it was capable of exuding a charm and creating new attitudes. But Anderson went even further when he attempted to readjust the community's image by emphasizing the independent Basque sheepherders. He believed that the Basques had supplied an attitude of mind which had helped Nevada to become the "repository of nature's greatest and most rugged values." [32]

Anderson's view of the ubiquitous Basque immigrants came to be shared by Erskine Caldwell during his numerous visits to the state. Both Caldwell and Anderson "went on the road" to rediscover America and its people. Caldwell devoted the entire Nevada section of *Around About America* (1963) to the Basque sheepmen, and portrayed the northern part of the state as a region which nourished their peculiar temperament. After crisscrossing the Great Basin many times, he concluded that, although originally drawn to the West as herders, there were by the 1960s more Basque than American millionaires in northern Nevada. Clearly, Caldwell's few days in Winnemucca provided him with only a superficial knowledge of the society, but his extensive use of the Basques in portraying rural Nevada typifies the focus of much of the recent literature.

Since World War II, a variety of novelists have seized upon the mounting interest in the Basques. Many writers have exploited the group to give authenticity and color to their Nevada themes. In *Tonopah Lady* (1950) Zola Ross used a turn-of-the-century Reno street scene to introduce her chief character and, rather incidentally, to demonstrate the fraud once practiced on the newly arrived and confused Basque immigrant. While the episode showed the mischievousness with which non-English-speaking foreigners were confronted, its chief purpose was to provide a setting and backdrop for the story which was to follow.

On the other hand, the motivating force in Kenneth D. Scott's *Frozen Grass* (1960) was the tragic Basque incident historically known as the "Last Indian War." In early 1911, four vaqueros were killed in northern Washoe County, and the discovery of the murder and the pursuit of a ragged band of Indians across northern Nevada added another dreary chapter to the long conflict between red men and white men. Since three of the four murdered men were from the Pyrenees, the new immigrants played a dominant role in the fictionalized story as well as in the last major clash in the winning of the West.

Three novels can be used to illustrate the manner in which Basques have often been treated in literature. *The Lord's Valley, No More Giants,* and *Scarf Cloud* were focused on different problems in different parts of Nevada, yet the Basques were forced into surprisingly similar social molds. The Basques finally escaped their role as sheepherders when in 1963 the Nevada school teacher Virginia Wilson Lee cast Bruno Baratto as the sire in an experiment in artificial insemination. In *The Lord's Valley* (actually Smith Valley), Dr. Ladell Knight, the descendant of an old Nevada family, attempted to guide her nephew, Kimbert Knight, into an engagement with Pamela Stuart. But her wishes were ignored, and Kimbert eloped with Echo Baratto, the lovely daughter of rancher Bruno Baratto. When, in bitter humiliation, the jilted Pamela spoke of the Baratto home as "that filthy, stinking, Basque's cabin," the ambivalent position of the Basques in the community slowly began to emerge.[33] Later, when the doctor urged the pregnant Echo to have an abortion, the girl accused her of bigotry, of ignoring the greatness in Basque antiquity, and of believing that the blood of Saxon and Basque would not mix. Dr. Knight was finally forced to explain that she had impregnated Kimbert Knight's mother with sperm donated anonymously by Bruno Baratto and that Echo and Kimbert, therefore, were half-brother and sister.

A similar tragedy unfolded in a first novel by the English-woman Joaquina Ballard Howles. Mrs. Howles was reared on a Nevada cattle ranch and returned in spirit to the land of her youth in *No More Giants* (1966). The story pointed up a rural family's subservience to the landscape, as well as to a medley of intangible fears and hatreds. Jenny had grown up in the shadow of a selfish and neurotic mother, a confused and unimaginative father, a weak brother, and a mentally depressed aunt. The un-happy family lived on a dry, windswept ranch twenty miles from town (Winnemucca). Slowly, the girl began to realize that her parents detested each other and that neither was capable of loving her. During the summer that Jenny became fifteen, her father, who disliked Catholics, sheepmen, and foreigners, was forced to hire three Basques to help with the farm work. The desperately lonely girl quickly succumbed to the approaches of one of the Basques and spent most of the warm summer nights with him in the willows back of the house. Jenny's frantic affec-tion eventually frightened her timid lover away, and his morose and insensitive brother attempted to become her next partner in the willows. Jenny's search for her handsome but indifferent lover and her experiences in a Reno home for unwed mothers pose age-old questions about man and society. The crude, cruel, distorted, and futile lives which slowly emerge out of the igno-rance, isolation, drought, and depression of rural Nevada of the 1930s provide *No More Giants* with shafts of stark realism.

Robert Lloyd Pruett's novel *Scarf Cloud* might have had a

greater popular appeal had it been published in 1940 rather than in 1947. The plot was built around German espionage and a Basque sheepherder in World War II, but by the late forties, the story lacked the emotional impact and topical immediacy which war hysteria could have supplied. Duggary Garth, a gentleman farmer from Carson Valley, became a pilot for the Air Transport Command, and between flights he returned home to oversee his ranch. While on leave, Dug learned that one of his sheepherders, Roberto Muchado, had been accused of killing an Indian colleague and had fled into the hills. Dug located the young Basque in the mountains and slowly pieced together the puzzling incident.

One day, a small airplane had circled low over the valley, and while men waited on the ground, the pilot had attempted to throw a package to them. The packet had caught on the tail of the plane and fallen in the hills where the Indian had found it. In a futile attempt to retrieve the packet, the men from the valley killed the Indian and shifted the blame to his partner Roberto. With shrewd detective work, Dug located the German crew of the aircraft and German agent No. 63, the director of sabotage for whom the packet of papers was intended. After several cloak-and-dagger episodes in which the German population of Carson Valley was brought under suspicion, the mystery was solved, the Basque freed, and the case closed by the FBI. The German agents had settled in Carson Valley years earlier so that they might at the proper time carry out the orders of der Führer. The German-born sheriff, his deputy, and the other German immigrants of the community were totally unaware of the infamous plot.

Pruett's analysis of Roberto's thoughts and actions follow an oversimplified image of the Basque people. "It is strange about Bascos like Roberto from the Old Country. They seem imbued with an unconquerable fear of the unknown and, as a consequence, isolate themselves in a bold camouflage of ignorance." [34] Pruett's German agents also emerge as dim amalgams of strutting, heel-clicking, accented bores. But *Scarf Cloud* pointed up the geographical, historical, and ethnic relationships which made up a Nevada community, and the book emphasized the too-often ignored fact that the people in all of the isolated valleys west of Denver were not carbon copies of each other.

Lee, Howles, Pruett, and Ross cast the Basques in supporting roles; their stories were not built around the immigrants, but rather engulfed them. The Basques were pictured as newcomers, as an unknown element who received a mixed reception. However, after pointing to the suspicion and the fear, the authors sought to demonstrate that the alarm was generally unjustified and that most of the confusion resulted from misunderstanding growing out of a changing environment. The Basques were seen as a distinct minority who, although temporarily living on the fringes of society, were rapidly emerging in Nevada life. Therefore, integration was desirable, inevitable, and not really in question.

Almost uniformly the literature cultivated the image of the free, independent, and perplexing Basque sheepherders. Writers used them to lean their events upon, to give color to the local setting, to emphasize the particularity of the region, and to provide subtlety and urgency for their plots. But in general, the image seekers have not pushed their Basque theme too far. The corrosive relationships growing out of a feeling of ethnic inferiority and the personal pique stemming from emotional tensions have not been magnified beyond realistic bounds. Rather, the Basques and other immigrants have provided the literati with an enviable and often dramatic field for popular exploitation.

[1] For a discussion of Anglophilia and the immigrant, see Cushing Strout, *The American Image of the Old World* (New York: Harper and Row, Publishers, 1963), pp. 132 ff.

[2] Franklin D. Scott, "Literature in Periodicals of Protest of Swedish-America," *Swedish Pioneer Historical Quarterly,* October, 1965, p. 193.

[3] Henry Steele Commanger (editor), *Immigration and American History: Essays in Honor of Theodore C. Blegen* (Minneapolis: University of Minnesota Press, 1961), see article by John T. Flanagan, "The Immigrant in Western Fiction," p. 80.

[4] H. L. Davis, *Honey in the Horn* (New York: Harper and Brothers, 1935), pp. 245–246.

[5] The western story is currently being investigated as a type of major social document. For an evaluation of the western, see C. L. Sonnichsen, "The Wyatt Earp Syndrome," *The American West,* May, 1970.

[6] Douglas Branch, *The Cowboy and His Interpreters* (New York: Cooper Square Publishers, Inc., 1961; first published in 1926), p. 238.

[7] *Ibid.,* p. ii.

[8] Henry Sinclair Drago, *Whispering Sage* (New York: A. L. Burt Company, 1922), p. 180.

[9] *Ibid.,* p. 80.

[10] Mary McNair Mathews, *Ten Years in Nevada: Or, Life on the Pacific Coast* (Buffalo: Baker, Jones and Co., 1880), p. 169.

[11] Miriam Michelson, *The Madigans* (New York: The Century Company, 1904), pp. 246–248.

[12] Lillian Groom and Janet Cicchetti were joint authors of *City Beyond Devils Gate.* They used the pseudonym Lillian Janet.

[13] Mark L. Requa, *Grubstake* (New York: Charles Scribner's Sons, 1933), p. 133.

[14] Anne Burns, *The Wampus Cat* (Boston: Meador Publishing Company, 1951), p. 14. Mallory said: "I want to tell you something about myself . . . First of all, I am a Mick."

[15] Aileen Cleveland Higgins, *A Little Princess of Tonopah* (Philadelphia: The Penn Publishing Company, 1909), p. 199.

[16] In discussing the foreign born, the Roman Catholic Bishop of Reno once explained: "They pitted themselves against the deserts and the mountains, against the burning heat and the searing cold and their features became as pitted and cragged as the volcanic rock that tore their boots to shreds. In this land of far distances their eyes acquired a remote-

ness as though forever searching for the horizon beyond. . . . Some of them conquered; more of them failed. But whatever their fate, they became a part of Nevada. This bleak, inhospitable, strangely beautiful land became their home."

[17] Walter Van Tilburg Clark, *The Track of the Cat* (New York: Random House, 1949), p. 180.

[18] See Enumerator's Report, Census of 1920, Washoe County, Nevada.

[19] Walter Van Tilburg Clark, *The City of Trembling Leaves* (Garden City, New York: The Sun Dial Press, 1946), p. 33.

[20] *Ibid.*, p. 12.   [21] *Ibid.*, p. 667.

[22] Robert Laxalt, *Sweet Promised Land* (New York: Harper & Row, Publishers, 1957), pp. 118–119.

[23] *Miami Herald* (Florida), September 22, 1957.

[24] Robert Laxalt, *A Man in the Wheatfield* (New York: Harper & Row, Publishers, 1964), p. 12.

[25] See Enumerator's Report, Census of 1860, St. Mary's County, Utah Territory; Census of 1870, Elko County, Nevada; and Census of 1880, Humboldt County, Nevada.

[26] Edwin Corle, *Coarse Gold* (New York: E. P. Dutton and Company, Inc., 1942), p. 118.

[27] Flannery Lewis, *Suns Go Down* (New York: The Macmillan Company, 1937), p. 60.

[28] See *The Book Review Digest* for 1937, p. 600.

[29] Alice Ward Bailey, *The Sage Brush Parson* (Boston: Little, Brown and Company, 1906), p. 201.

[30] Helen Downer Croft, *The Downs, the Rockies, and Desert Gold* (Caldwell, Idaho: The Caxton Printers, 1961), p. 19.

[31] See Enumerator's Report, Census of 1870, 1880, 1910, and 1920, Washoe County, Nevada.

[32] Boyd Moore, *Nevadans and Nevada* (San Francisco: H. S. Crocker Company, 1950), p. 150.

[33] Virginia Wilson Lee, *The Lord's Valley* (New York: Pageant Press, Inc., 1963), p. 133.

[34] Robert Lloyd Pruett, *Scarf Cloud* (Minden, Nevada: The Nevada Printing and Publishing Company, 1947), p. 87.

6

Short Stories and Biographical Essays

Short stories, folklore, and the exploits of semilegendary figures grew from a blending of fact and fantasy and the adaptation of older tales to a new environment. Such stories and myths helped to create an image of the West and formed the basis for widely held attitudes on frontier society. Whether the episodes were entirely fictional like those centered around Paul Bunyan, or in part verifiable as in the case of Davy Crockett, they found a permanent place in the popular imagination. Nevada, like the other states of the West, produced folk heroes eligible for the temple of Valhalla, but the great majority of the characters used in short story writing were not of a mythological nature. Popular taste and easy availability led most authors to rely upon old newspapers and interviews with early settlers. A majority of the stories reflected a rough hilarity and an uninhibited life, others suggested a fearless determination and an unconquerable spirit, and a few depicted a bleak outlook and a barren landscape.

The majority of Nevada's short stories derived from some historical event in which the legend lived but the social significance was lost. Like most westerns, the tales emphasized crime and retribution. They were simple and direct, crude and popular. Facts were used as long as they did no violence to the writer's instincts, and the literary license taken by the authors seldom blemished and never deformed the local history. Of course, the value and the validity of the events depended on the outlook of the reader, and frontiersmen were notoriously receptive to entertainment and story telling of every kind.

Oft-Told Tales

A wide range of writers has fictionalized Nevada's past, but works like those by W. A. Chalfant have tended to embody the most traditional and popular lore. Chalfant's *Tales of the Pioneers* (1942) and *Gold, Guns, and Ghost Towns* (1947) reproduced dramatic episodes associated with the frontier. The author grew up with the tales he told. Born in the newly founded boom camp of Virginia City, he was introduced to newspaper life by his father. The family later moved to Independence, California, where young William joined the elder Chalfant in the publishing trade. By the time of his death in 1943, Bill Chalfant had become the dean of California's newspaper editors. His two volumes include stories set in Nevada and eastern California and emphasize amusing incidents and legendary and historical accounts generally drawn from the files of the old newspapers. The large number of foreign-born characters used by Chalfant points to the high percentage of immigrants in the area, as well as to the contemporary journalist's search for color and the spectacular.

Of the many books of Nevada short stories, seven volumes stand out as manageable collections which lend themselves to immigrant research and analysis. Six of the seven volumes borrow heavily from newspaper accounts and are made up of the Chalfant type of vignette; one book, Ralli's *Nevada Lawyer,* embraces a more modern and versatile theme. The works provide an opportunity for an investigation into the use selected writers have made of Nevada's various nationalities. Statistics cannot prove the worth of literature, but empirical data can be useful in measuring and documenting the attention given to the foreign born. In short, the immigrant involvement in, and stimulus to, Nevada literature can be measured by seeing how frequently they appear in that literature.

Clel Georgetta's *Wool, Beef, and Gold* (1956) comprised thirteen human-interest stories set in the vicinity of the author's ancestral home in eastern Nevada. As the grandson of a French army officer who immigrated to Eureka, Georgetta grew up in an area and among the people about whom he wrote. With both French and Swiss customs influencing his homelife, and with a constant infusion of immigrants into eastern Nevada, he became sensitive to the foreign impact on the folklore of the state. Of the thirteen stories in *Wool, Beef, and Gold,* two were centered around foreigners, two others introduced foreigners as major figures, and three spoke or dealt indirectly with ethnic groups. A Chinese cook, a Mexican sheepherder, a Spanish nobleman, an English bride, and a band of Gypsies typified the diversity of Georgetta's immigrant characterizations.

In "A Pair of Shoes," Antonio Saville was a cultivated drifter who became, in turn, Spanish nobleman, American jockey, and western ranch hand. His touch of refinement made it easy for him to seduce Lila, the wife of Basque rancher Domingo Etcheberren. In careless indifference, Antonio borrowed a friend's horse to facilitate his nocturnal visits with the lady, thereby implicating the friend. After much confusion, Domingo sorted out the facts and then killed the aging Don Juan in a gun battle. The action emphasized the basic similarity between the moral code of old Spain and that of the new West.

"They Die in the Spring" also employed Basque characters, but Rick Novarra and his English wife were forced to cope with issues more complex and involved than an illicit love affair. As a

Nevada Basque, Rick met and married an English girl while he was a soldier in Europe during World War I. The two made the long and, for the bride, somewhat frightening journey from England to a sheep ranch two hundred miles from a railroad in central Nevada. Although the Englishwoman married Rick mainly because of a psychological problem (she had failed to have a child by her first husband), she adjusted to the Basque-American society, overcame the hardships and loneliness, and eventually became a successful writer and interpreter of the region. Georgetta's foreign-born sketches were of a piece, motivated instead of merely researched, and planned instead of merely reproduced. They did not deal with the taming of the Nevada frontier, but they used the frontier as a canvas against which the tales were told.

Nell Murbarger's *Ghosts of the Glory Trail* (1956) appeared in the same year as *Wool, Beef, and Gold*. The works differed markedly in style, but were similar in content. *Ghosts of the Glory Trail* was aggressive and quick, and devoted in large measure to ghost towns and to the miners who inhabited them. Murbarger's introductory paragraphs suggested the focus for her work and presented the characters to be used in her vignettes. For centuries the remote land of Nevada knew only sagebrush and jackrabbits, and then suddenly it became flooded with "prospectors, mining engineers, surveyors, opportunists, long-line skinners, faro dealers, tradesmen, painted women of the night, bullwhackers, saloonkeepers, assayists, Chinese, Indians, Cousin Jacks, Yankees, Chileans, [and] Mexicans. . . ." [1]

Of the book's thirty-eight episodes, twenty-eight were set in Nevada. Five of the twenty-eight were immigrant oriented, and four of these five focused on the Chinese. Murbarger's frequent treatment of the Chinese theme resulted in part from the historical period in which her anecdotes were set and in part from her search for humor. Most of the accounts were drawn from the nineteenth century when the Chinese loomed large as a factor in Nevada life and thought. As early as 1870, 7.4 percent of the entire population of the state had been born in China; it rose to 8.7 percent in 1880, and leveled off at 6.0 percent by 1890.[2] In 1880, almost two of every five foreign-born men in Nevada were Chinese. Such captions as "Where Ghosts Wear Pigtails," "Tybo was Allergic to Orientals," and "Six-Toed Chinaman of Charleston" reveal Murbarger's jocular approach. The one non-Chinese immigrant plot emphasized the rugged character of an Englishman with an Indian wife who lived in southern Nevada for over three-quarters of a century. In addition to the five tales based on an immigrant theme, nine other stories in *Ghosts of the Glory Trail* referred to foreign-born groups or used immigrants as secondary characters.

Murbarger's second volume of short stories, *Sovereigns of the Sage,* was published in 1958. It followed the pattern of *Ghosts of the Glory Trail* in that each anecdote was built around a single incident and developed only one or two characters. The tales were too short to offer a secondary or related theme and too direct to suggest nascent ideas or an interpretation of society. The nationality of characters was not stressed unless they were of particular significance to the plot. Of the fifty semifictionalized vignettes comprising *Sovereigns of the Sage,* thirty were set in Nevada. Nine of the thirty were immigrant narratives or used the foreign born in supporting roles. Again, the Chinese appear most often, but members of at least ten other nationalities also were introduced.

"Seventy Years in a Country Store" and "Man Who Lived in Borax Marsh" typify the use Murbarger made of the immigrant. The first tale revolved around the life of August D. Lemaire, a Frenchman who became a storekeeper in Battle Mountain in 1880. Over the years, he served Chinese laborers, Basque sheepmen, Welsh ranchers, Portuguese farmers, and assorted foreign-born drifters. The equable Frenchman became a relevant and sustained force in a discordant and volatile society. The second immigrant tale, "Man Who Lived in Borax Marsh," portrayed an artistic and romantic German who devoted his life to chasing rainbows. After several years as a prospector, he sought steady employment at a motion picture studio in Hollywood, but the lure of the desert drew him back to Columbus, Nevada, and Borax Marsh. When not painting, he prospected for gold and finally devised an intricate engineering plan for locating and refining the metal. Like many another fanciful prospector, he died in poverty convinced that he was the heir to riches.

Taken together, Murbarger and Georgetta employed immigrants in some fashion in about half of their Nevada stories. They did not, however, emphasize the same nationalities. Georgetta favored the Basques, while Murbarger more often observed the Chinese. In a total of fourteen essays using immigrants in *Ghosts of the Glory Trail,* the Chinese appeared in twelve, Mexicans in four, English in three, Germans in two, Irish in two, Slavs in two, Chileans in one, and Canadians in one. Murbarger's foreign born were natural and engaging and revealed the tough and stubborn quality necessary for survival on the frontier. Georgetta's foreign born, on the other hand, demonstrated that in remote Nevada, tradition, culture, and background were constantly threatened by the struggle, passion, and audacity of the new society.

Between 1946 and 1951, Harold's Club of Reno prepared weekly fictionalized newspaper advertisements based on Nevada history and folklore. Each item appeared as a brief, manageable anecdote designed for popular reading. The stories were too slight and uncomplicated to allow for contradictions or subtlety in their characterization, and deep emotional expression was never attempted.

In 1951, 204 of the dramatized advertisements were incorporated into a book of vignettes and issued as volume one of *Pioneer Nevada*. The illustrated tales tended to emphasize Nevada's rugged landscape, aggressive inhabitants, and exciting history. They were direct, muscular, violent, spectacular, and humorous. The subject matter ranged from romantic yarns about Spanish outlaws with their hoards of gold to courtroom scenes where Chinese swore an oath over the carcass of a chicken. One of the more dramatic plots dealt with the Indian brave who saved the lives of two German prospectors because he, too, had been born in Germany. Equally as imaginary was the report of six hundred Cornish women who were left widows in eastern Nevada after their husbands died from breathing "Delmar Dust." Other stories centered around the "Italian Wars" in eastern Nevada, and the tar and feathering of an Italian merchant at Eureka. The clash between Irish and Cornish laborers in Belmont and the unity of Irish and Cornish miners when they drove the Chinese from a railway construction site on the Comstock were only slightly fictionalized incidents drawn from Nevada newspapers. Of the 204 entries found in volume one of *Pioneer Nevada,* thirteen were immigrant stories, fifteen used foreign-born characters in secondary roles, and twenty-two others referred to foreign-born persons or ethnic groups.

Volume two of *Pioneer Nevada* (1956) incorporated the historical and fictionalized sketches which had been published between 1952 and 1956. Of the 159 single-page accounts, nine were immigrant centered, and eight used the foreign born in secondary roles. Most of the immigrant-oriented tales in volume one and all of those in volume two were confined to the era before 1885. The plots tended to emphasize Mexican ore discoveries,

French activity along the Humboldt River, Chinese railroad construction, and Irish mining ventures. The Slavs, Italians, Greeks, Japanese, and other nationality groups were generally overlooked.

Both volumes of *Pioneer Nevada* concentrated on action and anarchy in the wild West and generally ignored the corporate complexity of community life. The tales were too short to be plotted, too popular for satire, and too quick for character motivation. They failed to invite or command strongly polarized emotion. There was neither bitter hatred nor true admiration. But the abbreviated incidents capture and reproduce the contemporary milieu, and they point up the extent of immigrant involvement in every day life. Furthermore, they punctuate the ethnic and occupational diversity of the immigrants. *Pioneer Nevada* mixed myth with fact, blended human attributes into the physical environment, and suggested the pattern of immigrant assimilation into Nevada society.

Jean McElrath's *Aged in Sage* (1964) was designed as a work of "humorous memories . . . modified with a modicum of history." [3] Most of *Aged in Sage*'s thirty-six short stories were set in Elko County and the remainder in adjacent counties in northern or eastern Nevada. Half of the accounts referred to immigrants. Some eight were immigrant-dominated, while four others cast foreign-born characters in significant secondary roles. Several of the plots used persons from two or three foreign countries, but of the eighteen stories built around foreigners, the Germans dominated in four, the Basques, Chinese, and Irish each in three, and the Italians, English, Welsh, Mexicans, and Canadians in one each. In addition, Swedish, Swiss, Cornish, Portuguese, and Hungarian characters were scattered throughout the tales. The shooting of a Basque herder by a native cowboy in "Sheep Claim" illustrated the ethnic problems of the open range and reemphasized the Basque involvement in the age-old sheepman-cattleman conflict. Accounts of Billy the Kid and his life among Mexican friends in Elko County, the shooting of the badman Sam Brown by a German farmer, and the Basque who was tricked into a badger fight were old Nevada folk stories.

The badger fight long remained one of eastern Nevada's most beloved and hilarious entertainments. Perhaps both to conceal their nostalgia and to demonstrate their independence, the frontiersmen developed loud and pungent amusements. The fun was often in the form of a hoax, designed to bewilder those not in on the secret. The outsider, and particularly the immigrant, provided an ideal subject. In McElrath's story, the Basque Alec Sepulvada prided himself on his great strength and daring, so it was relatively easy to inveigle him into pulling a badger from a barrel so that it might be attacked by an English bulldog. After extensive preparations were made and a large crowd had assembled near Elko's Commercial Hotel, Sepulvada jerked the rope which was to drag the badger from its den. A white china "thundermug" sailed out to greet the unsuspecting and easily humiliated foreigner.

Much has been written about the Atlantic crossing and the overcrowded steerage of immigrant ships, but for Europeans bound for the American interior the overland journey often proved equally difficult. After surviving the voyage with its dangers of typhus and dysentery, after escaping exploitation by bond brokers, forwarding agents, and boarding-house runners, most immigrants bound for Nevada still faced the hazards of ship, rail, or stage travel and the very real problem of not being able to speak the native language in a totally alien environment. Elderly Basques still remember that upon leaving Europe they knew the names of only two American cities—New York and

Winnemucca. For thousands of such persons the traumatic experience of migration was not the arrival in New York, Chicago, or even Omaha, but rather the ordeal of locating friends or relatives in the peculiarly mobile and isolated mining camps of the West.

One of the more intrepid and indefatigable of McElrath's immigrant characters was the Spanish youth in "The Cock Crowed in Basque." The annals of American history are filled with accounts of spectacular heroism and examples of incredible determination, but few frontiersmen demonstrated higher resolve than that shown by Ramon Oyarbide and his partner Pedro as they traveled from their Pyrenees homeland to the mines of Berlin, Nevada.

Ramon and Pedro followed a traditional route by first sailing for England, where, after the usual confusion, they embarked at Liverpool for New York. During the ocean voyage and the rail trip across the United States they suffered only minor hardships. In crossing Nevada, however, the railroad conductor forgot to transfer them to a branch line at Battle Mountain and did not discover his error until they had traveled over 200 miles west and were nearing the California border. Callously set off the train with their luggage, the two youths followed the railway tracks back to Reno, where they eventually caught a Carson and Colorado work train and were carried 150 miles southeast to the town of Luning. Since neither of the migrants spoke English, the Italian-born station agent at Luning drew a crude map showing the desolate 63-mile trail over the mountains to Berlin. Having no concept of the distance, the terrain, or the climate, Ramon and Pedro started the trek on foot. They quickly became lost and consumed their meager provisions; Pedro collapsed of thirst, and Ramon had resigned himself to death on the desert when in the still morning hours he heard a rooster crow. The sound

226

led him to an isolated stage station and the help of its Swiss proprietor. Although the migrants finally arrived at Berlin, Ramon followed the traditional Basque pattern and quickly deserted the central Nevada mines for the northern Nevada grasslands. He eventually achieved prosperity and respect as a rancher.

Jean McElrath mixed fable and fabrication to produce vignettes in the western tradition. The tales made no attempt to reveal the complexity of man's subconscious or the raw and corrosive violence of an isolated society. Rather they were carried along by their zest, adventure, and the rediscovery of the casual and pragmatic relationships of westerners. McElrath, like most Nevada short-story writers, used immigrants freely in her work. The brief anecdotes suggest the course by which some of the foreign born were initiated into Nevada life and the strange paths by which they became community leaders. Even the boisterous and oversimplified accounts of love, violence, pathos, and exploitation helped to provide an understanding of the immigrant.

Of the seven compilations of short stories under consideration, only Paul Ralli's *Nevada Lawyer* (1949) dealt with immigrants caught up in twentieth-century urbanization. Ralli was born ethnically a Greek and legally an Englishman on the ancient island of Cyprus. He migrated by stages, first traveling to Europe and later moving to the United States. He worked as a laborer, lumberjack, steelworker, actor, and lawyer, before becoming city attorney for Las Vegas. Scattered through the forty-seven chapters of *Nevada Lawyer* were approximately one hundred semifictionalized accounts of experiences with local associates and famous or interesting clients. The vignettes were uniform neither in length nor in method of presentation, but the parade of foreign-born clients through Ralli's Las Vegas office gave the book international flavor.

227

Numerous Mexicans, some rich, some poor, and some romantic, sought Ralli's services. There was the Greek woman whose husband invariably beat her when business declined, and the Irish woman who refused to forgive her Italian husband of adultery until she could participate in a similar experience. There was the clever English defendant who flattered the judge by addressing him as "m'lord," and the Italian, thirty years younger than his wealthy wife, who eloped with his step-daughter. There were Irishmen with their customary lack of respect for public officials, and wealthy Greek and Italian gamblers with their flair for the mysterious. Many of the tales were told with tongue in cheek, and most were designed to show the variety and excitement of Las Vegas life. Ralli seldom supplied trenchant comments on society, but he explored the legal labyrinths of a gambling mecca and he noted the city's attraction for the foreign born.

Collections of essays with Nevada settings range from the idealistic and sentimental *In Miners Mirage-Land* (1904) by Idah Meacham Strobridge to the penetrating and subtle *The Watchful Gods and Others Stories* (1950) by Walter Van Tilburg Clark. But the seven volumes under consideration seem to typify the use made of the immigrant by most short-story writers. Clel Georgetta in *Wool, Beef, and Gold,* Nell Murbarger in *Ghosts of the Glory Trail,* and Jean McElrath in *Aged in Sage* used foreign-born characterizations in some half of their Nevada stories. Considering the popularity of the Indian, the cowboy, the outlaw, and other peculiarly western themes, the immigrant motif was surprisingly vital to Nevada authors. Of course, the plots were not designed to arouse a special interest in immigrant problems, or to stimulate concern over immigrant failures, or to inspire a greater appreciation of immigrant contributions. The foreign born were used first because they were there and the writer subconsciously, or artistically, or realistically, sensed their presence; and second because they afforded a natural and yet unique link between Nevada and the entire world outside. The immigrants gave a story greater universality at the same time that they provided authors with unique material for character study. The immigrant also supplied color and culture, variety and vitality to what would otherwise have been a less complex, less diverse, and less reflective literature.

Historical Biographies

The place of the immigrant in Nevada literature could be assessed, or placed in perspective, if similar literary surveys were available for other western states. In the absence of comparable studies, perhaps fuller meaning can be supplied by relating the immigrant of the short story to the immigrant of historical biography. In the final analysis the acuteness of any phenomenon can be seen best through a multifaceted lens. In Nevada there has been a peculiarly close relationship between reflective research and creative writing, between history and literature.

Over the half century in which Nevada was absorbing most of her immigrants, four chroniclers compiled almost two thousand biographical essays. The historical biographies failed to offer sophisticated insights into the national origins or the settlement patterns of the people. And the subjects in the biographies were drawn mainly from a select economic and political class which was quite distinct from those commonly used by novelists. Few of the personal sketches were designed as sensitive literary interpretations; rather, the biographers often sought to sell their books by mentioning as many local residents as possible.

But despite the commercialism and the amateurism, the selectivity and the insensitivity, the biographical case studies provide data which can be correlated with details drawn from the seven volumes of short stories. In brief, something can be learned and many questions posed through the assessment of the historical profiles. For example, did a higher percentage of Nevada's foreign born or of its American born achieve recognition? Did the biographical historians or the writers of fiction most often note and utilize the immigrants? Did the practitioners of the two disciplines discover the same national groups, observe similar immigrant characteristics, and follow analogous ethnic themes?

Although poorly organized and badly written, the first major history of Nevada has proved the most original, inclusive, and useful study yet produced. Edited by Myron Angel and published by Thompson and West, *History of Nevada: With Illustrations and Biographical Sketches of Its Prominent Men and Pioneers* appeared in 1881. Two hundred and eight biographical accounts were scattered throughout the work. Forty-six, or 22 percent, of the sketches dealt with immigrants. The forty-six included fifteen Germans, eleven Irish, seven Canadians, four Scots, four English, two Welsh, one Austrian, one Spaniard, and one Frenchman. Nine of the forty-six migrants were married to persons of the same national origin, nine had American-born mates, eight were single, one was married to a person of a different foreign nationality, and the marital status of nineteen is unknown.[4] The forty-six immigrants were engaged in six basic occupations: eighteen were in agriculture, nine in the professions, seven in business, four in mining, four in government service, and four worked as skilled craftsmen.

It should be emphasized that the forty-six immigrants noted in the biographies were included because of their attainments, and not because they had subscribed to the history. Although only 22 percent of the sketches dealt with immigrants, 29 percent of the 962 prepublication subscribers were foreign born.[5] Even more significant, there was no correlation between the biographies and the purchasers of the volume.[6]

Despite the wealth of social material contained in *History of Nevada,* the narrative sections of the book gave no special thought or notice to the immigrant. The one exception was in the reoccurring references made to the Chinese. The book was written before the foreign born had been isolated for study and before they were recognized as a unique phenomenon basic to America's rapid development. Angel included many of the English- and Germanic-speaking immigrants in the biographies, but he failed to identify the large foreign-born population or to sense the heterogeneous quality which the migrants had contributed to Nevada life.

The last 450 pages of Thomas Wren's *A History of the State of Nevada, Its Resources and People* (1904), were given over to 381 brief biographical essays; 128, or slightly over 33 percent, dealt with foreign-born subjects. As in Angel, the Germans led the list with 32 biographies. There were 29 Irish represented, 21 Canadians, 17 English, 5 Danes, 5 French, 4 Scots, 3 Poles, 3 Italians, 3 Swiss, 2 Welsh, 2 Portuguese, 1 Australian, and 1 Mexican. Of the 128, 66 were married to a spouse of the same nationality, and 12 were married to a spouse of another European nationality; 95 had arrived in the United States as adults (over sixteen years of age). At least 22 of the 128 came directly from their homeland to Nevada, and 27 others arrived in the state within five years after migrating to the United States. Only 3 of the 128 were in the country over twenty years before locating in Nevada.

Since the majority of foreigners migrated as adults, married European spouses, and traveled more or less directly to the state, their Nevada home life unquestionably reflected their European speech and culture. Indeed, 6 of the 128, after settling in Nevada, were sufficiently tied to the Old World that they returned home and only after further reflection re-entered the United States and again located in Nevada.

Eighty percent of Wren's foreign born had at some point in their career engaged in mining; however, only 10 of the 128 accepted mining as their terminal occupation: 51 were employed in agriculture, 46 in business, 11 in crafts or services, 8 in government service, and 2 in the professions. One hundred became at least nominally active in politics: 67 as Republicans, 23 as Democrats, 7 as Silver party members, and 3 as Independents.

Although writing 128 biographies about immigrants, Wren, like Angel, tended to be unaware of the unique human transitions and adjustments which his sketches suggested. Since over one third of his "important" Nevadans were foreign born, he presented evidence of a major ethnic influx and a grand international fusion, but he failed to evaluate his findings. The provincial tone of Wren's work and the political conclusions at which he arrived seldom drew on the wealth of diverse social material at hand.

Sam P. Davis, longtime editor of the *Morning Appeal* and author of *The First Piano in Camp,* published his massive two volume *The History of Nevada* in 1913. Davis devoted several chapters to the development of literature, drama, religion, medicine, and education, but despite the book's considerable social and cultural orientation, the foreign born were not recognized as interesting contributors to Nevada life.

In the second part of volume two, Davis included 495 biographies of outstanding Nevadans, of which 104, or 21 percent, were foreign born. The nationality of the 104 followed the pattern set by Angel and Wren and even further emphasized the Germanic leadership within the state: 40 were German, 20 Canadian, 18 Irish, 7 English, 6 Danish, 4 French, 3 Swiss, 3 Welsh, 1 Norwegian, 1 Austrian (Yugoslav), and 1 was from Bermuda. Seventy-eight of the 104 came to the United States as adults and 49 arrived in Nevada within five years after migration. Only 5 lived in the country twenty years or more before arriving in Nevada. Thirty-two were married to spouses of the same nationality, and 6 to spouses of another European nationality. Thirty-eight chose American-born spouses. By 1913, business had replaced agriculture as the major occupation of the migrants: 38 were in business, 29 in agriculture, 15 were artisans or service personnel, 9 were in mining, 7 in government service, and 5 in the professions. In addition to the 104, at least 45 other biographical sketches dealt with American-born persons whose parents had migrated from Europe to Nevada.

The Davis volumes further emphasized the pattern of selection established by Angel and Wren. Although the Germans, Irish, and English had for decades ceased to be the major immigrant groups in Nevada, their representation among the "prominent" elements of the state remained constant. Few of the Italians, the Greeks, the Slavs, or the Orientals had gained positions of influence and respect.

Out of a total of 836 biographical sketches carried in James G. Scrugham's *Nevada: A Narrative of the Conquest of a Frontier Land* (1935) 163, or 20 percent, dealt with immigrants from twenty-one countries.[7] Of the 163 foreign born, 116 had migrated as adults, and 45 had traveled directly to Nevada. Thirty-three others were in Nevada within five years after their arrival in the United States, and only 11 had lived twenty years or more in the United States before settling in the state.

The number of immigrants married to foreign-born spouses had decreased from earlier biographical lists. Only 39 of the 163 had immigrant spouses of the same nationality, and 9 were mar-

233

ried to immigrants of a different foreign nationality. The political sentiment of the leading immigrants remained constant, with approximately twice as many being affiliated with the Republican as with the Democratic party. Forty-six of the 163 were engaged in business, 42 in agriculture, 22 were artisans or service personnel, 21 were in the professions, 16 in mining, 8 in government service, and 7 in unidentified occupations.

While never consciously aware of the foreign born, Angel, Wren, Davis, and Scrugham provide biographical guidelines which suggest the immigrants' place in Nevada life. In the selection of 1,920 "leading" Nevadans in the fifty-four years between 1881 and 1935, 441, or approximately 23 percent of the total, were foreign born. The overwhelming majority of the immigrants included in the histories were from Canada and northern Europe, with Germany providing the largest number of subjects. Most of the foreign born arrived in Nevada as adults, within a few months, or at most a few years, after leaving their homeland. A large number migrated with (or later chose) a spouse who was also foreign born. Those included in the biographies tended to be agriculturists or businessmen, and they were generally devoted to the principles of the Republican party.

Clearly, the beliefs and activities of the 441 migrants were shaped in part by their background, traditions, and foreign experiences. But it would seem that neither they nor others of their class and station provided the truly meaningful and exciting characters around which many of the best immigrant short stories were woven. Most of the foreigners included in the biographical entries led no social or political revolution, provided no hostility to power abused or justice thwarted, and attacked no idols in the pursuit of truth. They were not among the subdued in the "Italian Wars" of Eureka, or among the quelled in the "Japanese War" at Caliente, or among the suppressed in the

234

Chinese encounter at Gold Hill, or among the accused in the Basque shooting at Gold Creek.

Among the 441 biographies, there were only two Basques; yet the Basques have provided the focus for more Nevada fiction than any other ethnic group. There were only two Mexican biographies; yet the Mexican in *The Ox-Bow Incident* revealed much about man and about the Nevada frontier. The Chinese were repeatedly employed by Nevada authors; yet none of the biographical essays was devoted to a Chinese. And conversely, 115 of the 441 accounts were about Germans and 84 about Canadians; yet the Germans and Canadians produced little inspiration for major Nevada writers.

Rather than historians and biographers it has been journalists and novelists who have provided the fullest record of the Nevada immigrant. Some of the short-story writers, as well as several novelists, allowed their intuition or their insight to transform immigrants into meaningful and artistic figures. By exploiting the past they have helped to preserve it. The few authors who challenged the old interpretations, probed for a new realism, and noted the ethnic transmutation of the society are obviously indispensable. But scores of lesser writers and journalists have also discovered the rich heritage bequeathed to the state by immigrants. Many of the bad books about active men and many of the dull stories about interesting lives have served a purpose. Their loose ends are an antenna by which imaginative writers and social historians receive signals from a dim and poorly charted past.

Nevada's foreign nationalities tended to fall into three categories. The interest and training of the observer seems to have determined what he saw. The Canadians and northern Europeans received the bulk of the historical and biographical attention, but much less notice by the short story writers. The Basques, the Chinese, and the Mexicans were generally ignored by the biographers but were often developed as literary characters. The Italians, Portugese, Greeks, Slavs, and Japanese were strangely neglected in both biographical history and in the short stories. The latter nationalities often represented a human flood surging into the state, but they received neither scholarly nor imaginative treatment. For example, at the turn of the century, Nevada was attracting a larger per capita Italian migration than any other state in America. Yet, only 10 of the 441 biographies dealing with foreigners, only 6 of the 125 short stories using immigrant characters, and only one of the 40 major literary works portraying immigrants introduce an Italian. The figures typify the literary and historical oversight and imbalance that has long perplexed immigration studies.

[1] Nell Murbarger, *Ghosts of the Glory Trail* (Palm Desert, California: Desert Magazine Press, 1956), p. 2.

[2] Peterson and Lewis, *Nevada's Changing Population,* p. 26.

[3] Jean McElrath, *Aged in Sage* (Private Printing, 1964), see Dedication.

[4] For the purpose of marriage statistics the English, Scots, and Welsh are considered one nationality.

[5] There were 986 subscribers, but 24 were organizations.

[6] Among the foreign-born groups, the Germans led in purchasing the study with seventy-one prepublication orders. They were followed by the Irish, the Canadians, and the English. But Danes, Swedes, Australians, Portuguese, Italians, Poles, Swiss, and three South Americans also subscribed to the history, and not a single immigrant from any of these eight nationalities was included in the biographies.

[7] Canada furnished 36, Germany 28, England 27, Ireland 15, Denmark 13, Italy 10, Scotland 7, Switzerland 5, Yugoslavia 3, Portugal 3, Sweden 3, France 2, Norway 2, Australia 2, Mexico 1, Wales 1, Spain 1, Finland 1, Lebanon 1, Austria 1, and Syria 1.

7

The Frustrated and the Fulfilled

Both foreign and native observers of American life have suggested that the New World attracted and bred a race of restless wanderers. In Nevada, the seemingly compulsive movement from camp to camp, district to district, and in and out of the state was more pronounced than in many other regions of America. Despite Nevada's generally un-European-like terrain and its geographical isolation it drew a uniquely high proportion of immigrant settlers. Indeed, in periods of great demographic confusion and mass activity, the foreign-born migration outnumbered the American-born influx by as much as ten to one. Although Nevada was an isolated and mountainous state, the immigrants were drawn from all echelons of society, from widely varied professional and occupational groups, and from most of the countries of the world. Traditionally, the migration to the western mines was predominantly male; however, by the time Nevada had been formed into a series of camp sites, a large number of immigrant women were flowing into the West. At the height of the Comstock boom and again during the Tonopah-Goldfield expansion, the disparity between the foreign-born male and the foreign-born female population was about three to one. But in both instances, the percentage of foreign-born women to foreign-born men was about the same as among the American born. Indeed, the disparity between immigrant women and im-

migrant men in the mining towns of Nevada apparently was
less than in the mining regions of California, Colorado, or Montana.

Nevada's magnetic attraction for the immigrants was more
fortuitous than planned. The state underwent its most dramatic
economic exploitation between 1860 and 1912, the era of the
great foreign migration into America. The transcontinental rail
line was completed across the state at the beginning of the period
and the state enjoyed easy access from both East and West. The
numerous discoveries of gold and silver changed scores of Nevada
place names into magic words which attracted miners and merchants, opportunists and drifters from around the world.
Nevada's industrial-type mining required the establishment of
complete communities and business centers like Virginia City,
Eureka, and McGill, and the needs of the towns, in turn, drew a
varied and diverse class of immigrants.

After the Civil War there were too few Americans to build
the East and at the same time exploit the West with the speed
demanded by shareholders and local boosters. Therefore, provisioners, promoters, and professional men as well as artisans,
farmers, and laborers had to be supplied, at least in part, from
abroad. By the end of the century, land-hungry Italians, Basques,
and Portuguese found few areas east of the Rocky Mountains
open for settlement. Only the marginal strips of land tucked
away in Nevada's dry valleys seemed readily available for occupancy. Furthermore, the labor needs of the major industries of
Nevada were immigrant oriented from the outset. The building
and maintenance of the railroads, the crushing and refining of
precious ore, the mining and smelting of copper, the breeding
and herding of sheep, the cutting of forests, and the burning of
charcoal called for skills, endurance, and a temperament not
commonly developed by Americans.

Despite Nevada's unusually heavy immigration, few histories have accented the movement; despite the economic, social, and political contributions of the foreign born, few state or local records reflected the influx. The foreign migrants were ignored, in part, because they seemed a natural feature of local life and, in part, because of a provincial myopia which blinded many observers to things non-Western and non-American.

Fortunately the contemporary journalists and a large number of writers and novelists saw the immigrants clearly. They observed the color, conflict, and culture which diverse groups brought to the embryonic society. In addition, the writers rather inadvertently pointed up what the immigrant meant to Nevada and what Nevada meant to the immigrant. They noted the broad and plastic adaptability demanded of the men and women who entered the state, the psychological adjustments which migrants were forced to undergo, and the geographical and social dimensions which new arrivals were forced to overcome. The journalists and novelists reflected the inadequacies, the prejudices, and the crudities of Nevada life and they observed the delicate balance between immigrant success and immigrant failure.

The narrow columns of newspapers were particularly useful in revealing immigrant experiences overlooked by the broad pages of traditional history. Of course, the journalists were not all of a kind. Their works ranged from the hyperbole of Dan De Quille and Mark Twain to the humanism of Henry Mighels and Sam Davis to the histrionics of Joseph Tognini and Lindley Branson. Many newspapers were propaganda sheets and some of the old files became textbooks on boosterism. The campaigns to cut new streets, to secure railways, and to attract immigrants shaped some of the journals into the leading promotional force on the frontier.

Nevertheless, there was a certain echoing concern that seemed to emanate from some of the old papers. Tangible themes were pointed up, themes which readers could take hold of and hang on to—sad, awe-inspiring, reassuring. The better articles did not reflect a literary dilettante who was trying to demonstrate a false compassion or a quick cleverness. Rather they read as though no one was behind the pen. It was not great writing; stylelessness was often the style. The key was the articles' frontal approach. They looked straight at things in order to see things straight. Differing from the novel, the newspapers allowed the immigrant his private existence; they did not try to intrude on his hopes, his fears, or his personal tragedy. The best newspapers were, in the purest sense, documentary; yet Nevada's journalists were not without rhetoric, anxiety, and symbolism in discussing human needs. But above all, the import of an article was transcended by the flavor of the time and place; the fundamental aspects changed little from town to town and from decade to decade. The immigrant image and the various foreign-born themes grew more compelling because they were cumulative.

A large proportion of Nevada's fiction has touched on the immigrant. But too often the stories have tended to be laudatory and obvious rather than iconoclastic and critical. Reminiscences in particular showed a nostalgia for the old ways, and they often implied that the formulas and institutions of the past provided a solution to society's outstanding problems. The deeper conflicts and the harrassments faced by the immigrants either were not recognized or else were inadequately portrayed. The romantic appeal of nineteenth-century individualism and the temporary successes of industrial feudalism became ends in themselves. Too few of the immigrants were cast in the role of the uprooted desperately trying to adapt to an alien environment. Too few were given a moral or a spiritual existence. Too few were seen in the yellow dust of the stamp mill or in the orange glow of the smelter.

Nevertheless, one of the most exciting and unifying features of Nevada literature has been the use made of the foreign born. At least sixteen of the novels discussed in chapter 4 were in some significant way immigrant stories.[1] The eighteen leading immigrant characters found in the sixteen works tended to typify the broad use made of the foreign born. There were three sheepmen, two ranchers, two miners, two spies, one priest, one prostitute, one preacher, one drifter, one bootlegger, one charlatan, one internuncio, one maid, and one traveler. When the foreign born were cast as secondary characters, the diversity of occupations spans the full gamut of human experience—from the confused European peasant detraining at a lonely whistle stop in the Nevada desert to a European count presiding over a salon for the Reno intelligentsia. Nor were the immigrants always seen as a great community asset. Some groups were declared "animals of a fixed color" whose moral sentiments had long since been "starved into extinction" along with their souls.[2] Others were amusing, semieffectual, and subhuman objects of disdain who drifted across the Nevada panorama.[3] There were the Gypsies, the "Bohunks," and the "Bascos," who were the butt of a mild antipathy and of unkind humor. But there were also the beguiling mountebanks,[4] the heartless seducers,[5] and the many victims of circumstance who were reduced to shallow and indecent lives by the forms and pressures of the society.[6]

Many of the more convincing immigrant stories dealt with failures, and at the same time interjected nobility, sublimity, or tragedy into the lives of the characters. Father Lazzaroni of Laxalt's *A Man in the Wheatfield* recognized, when it was too late, his responsibility for the fateful events at Smale Calder's snake pit. Both pity and awe were suggested when Joe Gault

defied his father and married Margarida Irosabal of the hated
Basque family in Drago's *Following the Grass,* and again when
a half-brother and sister, the children of the Basque Bruno
Barratto, were married in Lee's *The Lord's Valley.* Tragedy
was narrowly averted when the English preacher, wrongly convicted for the murder of his wife, was marched to the gallows in
Bailey's *Sage Brush Parson.* The Basque, Justo, in Howles's *No
More Giants,* showed the insufficiency of man and of the Nevada
life, and in so doing, he emerged as a valuable and disturbing
character. Clark's Jacob Briaski in *The City of Trembling
Leaves* and the Mexican in *The Ox-Bow Incident* revealed tragic
examples of human and cultural failure. Both Briaski and the
Mexican were cut off in one manner or another from society, and
both they and society suffered the consequences. Clark's immigrants demonstrated the moral predicament often faced by both
the alien and the native in their relations with each other.

Nevada's ghost towns provided abundant material for a curious type of immigrant failure. Bower's Englishman in *The
Voice of Johnnywater* and Clark's Englishman in "The Indian
Well" never appeared in the narratives, but both left their flimsy
mark of failure in the desert waste. Their unseen and unde-
scribed battles from the past were etched onto an unremitting
present and an uncertain future.

Several authors saw Nevada as a grand paradox where independence and space proved to be barriers rather than avenues.
With all things being possible, nothing was possible. The abra-
sive stimulation of uncertainty sharpened the wits of immigrants,
but dulled their sensibilities. The physical world and the vagaries
of nature loomed particularly large. Entire chapters of Stewart's
Sheep Rock and Wilson's *The Oneness Trail* were devoted to
the landscape and its effect on the immigrant and the frontiersman. Drago, Bower, Howles, Scott, Ross, and other writers

demonstrated not only a solid acquaintance with, but a peculiar fascination for, the geographical areas in which their stories were set. Much of Nevada's immigrant history and the better immigrant literature has been filled with the elemental force of people desperately trying to carve out for themselves a foothold in the desert. The search for human color equal to that of the natural environment and for conflict and struggle that would do credit to the western setting led to an emphasis being given to the foreign born and to the physical geography of Nevada.

In a restless society filled with tensions and dissonance, immigrants sometimes tried to create their own communal islands of peace and solitude. Nevada, unlike Europe, did not build communities for individual men, rather the communities were for all men, for the human masses. Nevada's villages unlike those of Europe, did not shelter or protect their residents, rather they gathered and shuffled them. Furthermore, in Nevada the continuing and often frenzied search for rich ore and sweet water tended to level all men, both native and foreign. Certain immigrants, therefore, drew together because of their common hardships. The febrile activity of Americans, the physical isolation of Nevada, and the traditions and beliefs brought from Europe led some immigrants to desire a closer personal association. They sought a measure of human cohesiveness not often achieved even in the more populous and disciplined foreign-born communities. Drago's Basques and Chinese, Laxalt's Italians, Queen's communitarians, and numerous real-life experimenters enjoyed the strength and comradeship and suffered the tensions and cleavages of people who had chosen to bind themselves together and withdraw from the mainstream of society.

Scores of newspaper articles and a few sensitive novels convincingly demonstrated that certain types of immigrants were physically and temperamentally incapable of living on the frontier. Many people could not undergo the shock of being transplanted to a strange and undisciplined land. Domenico Felesina's murder of his brother, John Murphy's murder of a fellow Scotsman, and the scores of immigrant suicides testified to the instability and recklessness of many Nevada communities. The state attracted large numbers of the misfits, the malcontents, the ambitious, the iconoclasts, and the marginal workers. Many pursued the fortunes of blind chance and relied on myths and rumors in seeking their goals.

Nevada life often unfolded in reverse. The happy ending, which, according to the western legend was the sure reward for trial and error, work and virtue, did not always emerge. The magic of Nevada's wealth was not always adequate, nor were the opportunities sufficient, to quicken the appreciation or provide the happiness demanded by newcomers. Both worthy men and scoundrels failed to achieve a sense of belonging and to acquire a willingness to sacrifice. Many who did sacrifice were faced with momentous and baffling problems in unfamiliar and hostile surroundings. John Booth's account of the death of Madame Pauline Lognoz was a reminder that buried in the lost and isolated graveyards of Nevada are thousands of tragic stories that were never told.

Indeed, the lives of a large body of immigrants were silent records of extraneous incidents, the product of a monotonous and withered existence. Pauline Lognoz of Ophir Canyon, Frances Woon of the Ophir mine, and hundreds of other European women were not disturbed by social injustice or outraged by personal discrimination. They accepted the outward forms of frontier life but succumbed to the anxiety, the loneliness, and the despair which overcame thousands of immigrants of both sexes.

Yet, the ever present examples of immigrant attainment and prosperity and the shibboleths built around self-reliance and hard work led scores of the foreign born to achievement and self-respect. Despite delusion and frustration many immigrants succeeded, and the shibboleths were quickly fashioned into a creed which came to permeate the thinking of most Nevadans. Although often weary and naïve, Drago's Basques showed fortitude and self-reliance, Bower's Irish reflected resilience and independence, and Laxalt's Italians portrayed persistence and egocentrism. An awareness of immigrant goals as well as immigrant problems, and an emphasis on immigrant motivation as well as on immigrant character, highlighted the best fiction.

In any transcription of Nevada society, the awe-inspiring and the prosaic, the symbolic and the plain, the fantastic and the ordinary were indissolubly interlaced. And in interpreting the Nevada immigrant, the absorbed and the repulsed, the accepted and the rejected, the fulfilled and the frustrated all became a part of the state's heritage. Literature has reflected and preserved much of that heritage. It has provided many of the ethnic groups with a dignity, or a distinction, or at least a recognition that they have not enjoyed elsewhere. There have been few more moving images than the rustic simplicity woven by Flannery Lewis around his Irish-American grandmother, and there has seldom been greater fidelity to fact and sentiment than that shown by Robert Laxalt in the portrayal of his Basque father. Through literary use of the foreign born, Nevada fiction has been provided with character and balance, and Nevada history supplied with greater meaning and taste. Finally, the better of the literary works in themselves have become a magnet for excellence, a cultural watering hole in the Nevada desert, and a valuable gauge by which to judge immigrant assimilation in the West.

[1] Chronologically arranged, the sixteen novels are Charles C. Goodwin, *The Wedge of Gold*, 1893; Miriam Michelson, *The Madigans*, 1904; Alice Ward Bailey, *The Sage Brush Parson*, 1906; Sam Davis, *The First Piano in Camp*, 1919; B. M. Bower, *Casey Ryan*, 1921; Bower, *The Trail of the White Mule*, 1922; Henry Sinclair Drago, *Whispering Sage*, 1922; Drago, *Following the Grass*, 1924; Drago, *Secret of the Wastelands*, 1940; James M. Cain, *Past All Dishonor*, 1946; Robert Lloyd Pruett, *Scarf Cloud*, 1947; Anne Burns, *The Wampus Cat*, 1951; Walter C. Wilson, *The Oneness Trail*, 1956; Robert Laxalt, *Sweet Promised Land*, 1957; Virginia Wilson Lee, *The Lord's Valley*, 1963; Laxalt, *A Man in the Wheatfield*, 1964.

[2] Charles C. Goodwin, *The Comstock Club*, p. 196.

[3] Note the many Murbarger short stories dealing with the Chinese.

[4] Note the Englishman in Davis's *The First Piano in Camp*.

[5] Note Justo in Howles's *No More Giants*.

[6] Note the many foreign born in Cain's *Past All Dishonor*.

Bibliography

The one hundred seven literary works and sixty-three newspapers comprising the first part of this bibliography are more the result of a quantitative than a qualitative approach. While no attempt has been made to include all literature touching on the immigrant, the selection of material has been encompassing rather than discriminating. Futhermore, the amount of pertinent literature centered in a small, unevenly populated, and isolated state is not unmanageably large. Newspaper articles, novels, fictionalized history, romanticized memoirs, and dramatized bibliography have provided the chief focus, while plays, short stories, and literary reviews supply a useful supplement. H. G. Wells's quip that literature was only "a copious carelessness in reminiscence," is strangely appropriate to the Nevada setting where many of the literary works could be categorized as fictionalized experiences of the author. Documentary collections and public records like the Alf Doten diaries, the Grant Smith papers, and the Virginia and Truckee Railroad papers, along with the Nevada statutes, the Biennial Homographic Charts, the enumerators' reports of the United States census, and the four general histories are of special value in that they provide a background and a statistical basis for analyzing the society, the literature, and the newspaper stories.

Newspapers

Editors sometimes changed the name of their newspapers with singular casualness; therefore, to avoid confusion, only one title has been used throughout the work. For example, the *Morning Appeal* was variously known as *The Appeal, Carson City Appeal, Daily*

Appeal, Carson City Daily Appeal, Carson Nevada Appeal, and *Carson City Appeal-News.* In typical boom-camp fashion, some of the papers were moved from community to community. The *White Pine Daily News* was founded in Treasure City, but over the following forty years moved to Hamilton, Cherry Creek, Taylor, Ely, and East Ely. Only the more relevant seats of a journal are shown in the bibliography.

The Argus (Lovelock)
The Battle Mountain Herald and Central Nevadan
Battle Mountain Scout
Battle Mountain Weekly Messenger
Beatty Bullfrog Miner
Belmont Courier
Borax Miner (Columbus)
The Bullfrog Miner (Rhyolite)
Caliente Lode-Express
Carrara Obelisk
The Carson City News
The Carson Weekly (Carson City)
Carson Valley News (Genoa)
The Chloride Belt (Candelaria)
Churchill County Eagle (Fallon)
Churchill Standard (Fallon)
Clark County Review (Las Vegas)
Copper Ore (McGill)
Daily Argonaut (Elko)
Daily Free Press (Elko)
The Daily Inland Empire (Hamilton)
The Daily Nevada Tribune (Carson City)

The Daily State Register (Carson City)
The De Lamar Lode (Delamar)
Elko Weekly Post
The Elko Independent
Ely Daily Mining Expositor
The Ely Mining Record
Eureka Daily Leader
Eureka Daily Sentinel
The Gardnerville Record-Courier
Genoa Courier
The Goldfield Daily Sun
Goldfield Daily Tribune
The Goldfield News
The Goldfield Review
Gold Hill Daily News
The Humboldt Register (Unionville & Winnemucca)
The Humboldt Star (Winnemucca)
Las Vegas Age
Lyon County Times (Silver City)
The Mason Valley News (Yerington)
Metropolis Chronicle
Morning Appeal (Carson City)

The Nevada Register (Reno)
Nevada State Journal (Reno)
Pioche Record
Reese River Reveille (Austin)
Reno Evening Gazette
Reno Weekly Gazette and
    Stockman
The Silver State
    (Winnemucca)
Territorial Enterprise (Virginia
    City)
Tonopah Bonanza
Tonopah Daily Sun

Tonopah Miner
Tuscarora Times-Review
Virginia Evening Bulletin
    (Virginia City)
The Wadsworth Dispatch
Weekly Silver Bend Reporter
    (Belmont)
White Pine Daily News
    (Hamilton and Ely)
The Wonder Mining News
The Yerington Rustler
The Yerington Times

Fiction and Semifiction

ARRE, HELEN. The Corpse by the River (New York: Arcadia House, 1953).

ARTHUR, ZUA. Broken Hills (New York: Vantage Press, 1958).

BAILEY, ALICE WARD. The Sage Brush Parson (Boston: Little, Brown and Co., 1906).

BALDWIN, FAITH. Temporary Address: Reno (New York: P. F. Collier and Son Corporation, 1940).

BALLARD, TODHUNTER. Incident at Sun Mountain (Boston: Houghton Mifflin Company, 1952).

BEAUVOIR, SIMONE DE. America Day by Day (New York: Grove Press, 1953).

BOOTHE, CLARE. The Women (New York: Random House, 1937).

BOWER, B. M. The Adam Chasers (Boston: Little, Brown and Co., 1927).

———. The Bellehelen Mine (Boston: Little, Brown and Co., 1924).

———. Black Thunder (New York: Grosset and Dunlap, 1926).

———. Casey Ryan (Boston: Little, Brown and Co., 1921).

———. The Eagle's Wing (Boston: Little, Brown and Co., 1924).

———. The Parowan Bonanza (Boston: Little, Brown and Co., 1923).

———. A Starry Night (Boston: Little, Brown and Co., 1939).

———. *The Trail of the White Mule* (Boston: Little, Brown and Co., 1922).

———. *The Voice at Johnnywater* (New York: Grosset and Dunlap, 1923).

BOWMAN, NORA LINJER. *Only the Mountains Remain* (Caldwell, Idaho: The Caxton Printers, 1958).

BROWN, ZENITH JONES (pseud. Leslie Ford). *Reno Rendezvous* (New York: Farrar and Reinhart Inc., 1939).

BROWNE, J. ROSS. *A Peep at Washoe and Washoe Revisited* (Balboa Island, California: Paisano Press, 1959) ("A Peep at Washoe" first published 1861, and "Washoe Revisited" first published 1865).

BURNS, ANNE. *The Wampus Cat* (Boston: Meador Publishing Company, 1951).

CAIN, JAMES M. *Past All Dishonor* (New York: Alfred A. Knopf, 1946).

CALDWELL, ERSKINE. *Around About America* (New York: Farrar, Strauss and Company, 1963).

CARROLL, WILLIAM L. *From Under Sun Mountain* (New York: Vantage Press, 1961).

CAVE, CLAIR. *Wild Peach* (New York: Gramarcy Publishing Co., 1937).

CHALFANT, W. A. *Gold, Guns, and Ghost Towns* (Stanford: Stanford University Press, 1947).

———. *Tales of the Pioneers* (Stanford: Stanford University Press, 1942).

CLARK, WALTER VAN TILBURG. *The City of Trembling Leaves* (Garden City, New York: The Sun Dial Press, 1946) (first published 1945).

———. *The Ox-Bow Incident* (New York: The Readers Club, 1942) (first published 1940).

———. *The Track of the Cat* (New York: Random House, 1949).

———. *The Watchful Gods and Other Stories* (New York: Signet Books, 1961) (first published 1950).

COHEN, OCTAVUS ROY. *Borrasca* (New York: The Macmillan Company, 1953).

CORLE, EDWIN. *Coarse Gold* (New York: E. P. Dutton and Company, Inc., 1942).

———. *Mojave* (New York: Liveright Publishing Company, 1934).

CRAMPTON, FRANK A. *Deep Enough* (Denver: Sage Books, 1956).

CROFT, HELEN DOWNER. *The Downs, the Rockies, and Desert Gold* (Caldwell, Idaho: The Caxton Printers, 1961).

DAVIS, SAM P. *The First Piano in Camp* (New York: Harper and Brothers Publishers, 1919).

DE QUILLE, DAN (WILLIAM WRIGHT). *Snow-Shoe Thompson* (Los Angeles: L. D. Allen Press, 1954) (first published 1886).

———. *Washoe Rambles* (Los Angeles: Dawson's Book Shop, 1963) (first published 1861).

DRAGO, HARRY SINCLAIR. *Desert Water* (New York: The Macaulay Co., 1933).

———. *Following the Grass* (New York: The Macaulay Co., 1924).

———. *Secret of the Wastelands* (New York: Doubleday Doran and Company Inc., 1940).

———. *Smoke of the .45* (New York: The Macaulay Co., 1923).

———. *Whispering Sage* (New York: A. L. Burt Company, 1922).

DRURY, WELLS. *An Editor on the Comstock Lode* (Palo Alto: Pacific Books, 1936).

FIELD, ISOBEL. *This Life I've Loved* (London: Michael Joseph Ltd., 1937).

FISHER, VARDIS. *City of Illusion* (Caldwell, Idaho: The Caxton Printers Limited, 1941).

GEORGETTA, CLEL. *Wool, Beef, and Gold* (Palo Alto: Pacific Books, 1956).

GLASSCOCK, C. B. *Big Bonanza* (Portland, Oregon: Binfords and Mort, 1931).

GOODWIN, CHARLES C. *As I Remember Them* (Salt Lake City: Salt Lake Commercial Club, 1913).

———. *The Comstock Club* (Salt Lake City: Tribune Job Printing Company, 1891).

———. *The Wedge of Gold* (Salt Lake City: Tribune Job Printing Company, 1893).

GORHAM, HARRY M. *My Memories of the Comstock* (Los Angeles: Sulton House Publishers, 1939).

HAMLIN, JOHN. *Whirlpool of Reno* (New York: Dial Press, 1931).

HART, FRED H. *The Sazerac Lying Club* (San Francisco: Henry Keller and Co., 1878).

HAWKINS, ANNE. *To the Swift* (New York: Harper and Brothers, 1949).

HIGGINS, AILEEN CLEVELAND. *A Little Princess of Tonopah* (Philadelphia: The Penn Publishing Company, 1909).

HOWLES, JOAQUINA BALLARD. *No More Giants* (London: New Authors Limited, 1966).

JANET, LILLIAN (LILLIAN GROOM and JANET CICCHETTI). *City Beyond Devils Gate* (New York: Random House, 1950).

JOHNSON, AXEL P. *Smuggled into Paradise* (Philadelphia: Dorranca and Company, 1958).

JOHNSON, LATIFA. *Sheila Goes to Reno* (New York: Vantage Press Inc., 1952).

LAXALT, ROBERT. *A Man in the Wheatfield* (New York: Harper & Row, Publishers, 1964).

————. *Sweet Promised Land* (New York: Harper & Row, 1957).

LEE, VIRGINIA WILSON. *The Lord's Valley* (New York: Pageant Press Inc., 1963).

LEWIS, FLANNERY. *Suns Go Down* (New York: The Macmillan Company, 1937).

LEWIS, OSCAR. *Sagebrush Casinos* (New York: Doubleday and Company, 1953).

————. *The Town That Died Laughing* (Boston: Little, Brown and Company, 1955).

LYMAN, GEORGE D. *The Saga of the Comstock Lode* (New York: Charles Scribner's Sons, 1934).

MACDONALD, ROSS. *The Galton Case* (New York: Alfred A. Knopf, 1959).

MCELRATH, JEAN. *Aged in Sage* (Private Printing, 1964).

MATHEWS, MARY MCNAIR. *Ten Years in Nevada: Or, Life on the Pacific Coast* (Buffalo: Baker, Jones and Company, 1880).

MICHELSON, MIRIAM. *The Madigans* (New York: The Century Company, 1904).

———. *The Wonderlode of Silver and Gold* (Boston: The Stratford Company, 1934).

MIGHELS, HENRY R. *Sage Brush Leaves* (San Francisco: Edward Bosqui and Company, 1879).

MIGHELS, PHILIP VERRILL. *The Furnace of Gold* (New York: Grosset and Dunlap, 1909).

MILLER, MAX. *Reno* (New York: Dodd, Mead and Company, 1941).

MURBARGER, NELL. *Ghosts of the Glory Trail* (Palm Desert, California: Desert Magazine Press, 1956).

———. *Sovereigns of the Sage* (Palm Desert, California: Desert Magazine Press, 1958).

PAINE, SWIFT. *Eilley Orrum: Queen of the Comstock* (Indianapolis: The Bobbs-Merrill Company, 1958).

PAYNE, HAZEL BELL (pseud. Greer Gay). *The Case of the Well-Dressed Corpse* (New York: Pageant Press, 1953).

Pioneer Nevada, Vol. I (Reno: Harolds Club, 1951).

Pioneer Nevada, Vol. II (Reno: Harolds Club, 1956).

PRUETT, ROBERT LLOYD. *Scarf Cloud* (Minden, Nevada: The Nevada Printing and Publishing Company, 1947).

QUEEN, ELLERY (FREDERIC DANNAY and MANFRED B. LEE). *And on the Eighth Day* (New York: Random House, 1964).

RAINE, WILLIAM MACLEOD. *Bonanza: A Story of the Gold Trail* (New York: Grosset and Dunlap, 1921).

RALLI, PAUL. *Nevada Lawyer* (Culver City, California: Murray and Gee, Inc., 1949).

———. *Viva Vegas* (Hollywood, California: House-Waven, 1953).

RANDALL, JANET. *The Girl From Boothill* (New York: David McKay Company Inc., 1962).

REQUA, MARK L. *Grubstake* (New York: Charles Scribner's Sons, 1933).

ROSS, ZOLA. *Bonanza Queen* (Indianapolis: The Bobbs-Merrill Co., Inc., 1949).

Ross, Zola. *Reno Crescent* (Indianapolis: The Bobbs-Merrill Co., Inc., 1951).

———. *Tonopah Lady* (Indianapolis: The Bobbs-Merrill Co., Inc., 1950).

Ryan, Charles O. *Nine Miles From Dead Horse Wells* (New York: Exposition Press, 1959).

Saroyan, William. *My Name Is Aram* (New York: Harcourt, Brace and Company, 1937).

Schrader, Lary. *Reno Round the Clock* (New York: Exposition Press, 1954).

Scott, Kenneth. *Frozen Grass* (New York: Carlton Press, 1960).

Siebert, Frederick. *George, Wimple, and I* (Oxford, Basil Blackwell, 1929).

Snow, Charles (pseud. Gary Marshall). *Nevada Gold* (London: Wright and Brown, 1937).

Stewart, George R. *Sheep Rock* (New York: Random House, 1951).

Stewart, Ramona. *The Stars Abide* (New York: William Morrow and Co., 1961).

Stoutenburg, Adrien and Baker, Laura Nelson. *Snowshoe Thompson* (New York: Charles Scribner's Sons, 1957).

Stratton, Lilyan. *Reno* (Newark, N.J.: Colyer Printing Company, 1921).

Strobridge, Idah Meacham. *In Miners Mirage-Land* (Los Angeles: Baugarat Publishing Company, 1904).

Swift, John Franklin. *Robert Greathouse* (New York: Carleton Publisher, 1878).

Teal, Evelyn. *Flying Snowshoes* (Caldwell, Idaho: The Caxton Printers Ltd., 1957).

Twain, Mark (Samuel Clemens). *Roughing It* (Hartford, Connecticut: American Publishing Company, 1872).

Vanderbilt, Cornelius Jr. *Reno* (New York: The Macaulay Company, 1929).

Wilson, Walter C. *The Oneness Trail* (New York: Exposition Press, 1956).

254

Selected Secondary Studies

ANDER, O. FRITIOF (EDITOR). *In the Trek of the Immigrants: Essays Presented to Carl Wittke* (Rock Island: Augustana College Library, 1964). See chapter by John T. Flanagan.

ANGEL, MYRON (EDITOR). *History of Nevada* (Oakland: Thompson and West, 1881).

BILLINGTON, RAY ALLEN. *America's Frontier Heritage* (New York: Holt, Rinehart and Winston, 1966).

BRANCH, DOUGLAS. *The Cowboy and His Interpreters* (New York: Cooper Square Publishers, Inc., 1961).

COMMAGER, HENRY STEEL (EDITOR). *Immigration and American History: Essays in Honor of Theodore C. Blegen* (Minneapolis: University of Minnesota Press, 1961). See chapter by John T. Flanagan.

CURTI, MERLE. *The Making of an American Community: A Case Study of Democracy in a Frontier County* (Stanford: Stanford University Press, 1959).

DAVIS, SAM P. *The History of Nevada* (Reno: The Elms Publishing Co., 1913), 2 vols.

DORSON, RICHARD M. *American Folklore* (Chicago: The University of Chicago Press, 1959).

EMIRCH, DUNCAN. *Comstock Bonanza* (New York: The Vanguard Press, Inc., 1950).

FATOUT, PAUL. *Mark Twain in Virginia City* (Bloomington: Indiana University Press, 1944).

GEROULD, KATHERINE FULLERTON. *The Aristocratic West* (New York: Harper and Brothers Publishers, 1925).

GLASS, MARY ELLEN. "The Deutschen of Douglas: The German Foundations of Douglas County, Nevada, 1856–1930," (Thesis, University of Nevada, 1965).

HART, JAMES D. *The Popular Book: A History of America's Literary Taste* (New York: Oxford University Press, 1950).

Historical Statistics of the United States, Colonial Times to 1957 (Washington, D.C.: U.S. Bureau of Census, 1960).

LILLARD, RICHARD G. *Desert Challenge* (New York: Alfred A. Knopf, 1942).

LORD, ELIOT, and others. *The Italians in America* (New York: B. F. Buck and Company, 1905).

MORE, BOYD. *Nevadans and Nevada* (San Francisco: H. S. Crocker Co., 1950).

MUIR, JOHN. *Steep Trails* (Boston: Houghton Mifflin Company, 1918).

MYERS, JOHN. *Print in a Wild Land* (Garden City, New York: Doubleday and Company, Inc., 1967).

PETERSEN, WILLIAM and LIONEL S. LEWIS. *Nevada's Changing Population* (Reno: Bureau of Business and Economic Research, University of Nevada, 1963).

ROWE, JOHN. "Cornish Emigrants in America," *Folk Life. Journal for the Society for Folk Life Studies,* Vol. III, 1965.

SANFORD, CHARLES L. *The Quest for Paradise: Europe and the American Moral Imagination* (Urbana: The University of Illinois Press, 1961).

SCOTT, FRANKLIN D. "Literature in Periodicals of Protest of Swedish-America," *Swedish Pioneer Historical Quarterly,* October, 1965.

SCOTT, FRANKLIN D. (EDITOR). *World Migration in Modern Times.* (Englewood Cliffs, N.J.: Prentice-Hall, Inc., 1968).

SCRUGHAM, JAMES G. (EDITOR). *Nevada: A Narrative of the Conquest of a Frontier Land* (Chicago: The American Historical Society, Inc., 1935), 3 vols.

SHANNON, WILLIAM V. *The American Irish* (New York: The Macmillan Co., 1963).

SMITH, HENRY NASH (EDITOR). *Mark Twain of the Enterprise* (Berkeley: University of California Press, 1957).

———. *Virgin Land: The American West as Symbol and Myth* (New York: Vintage Books, 1957).

———. "The West as an Image of the American Past," *The University of Kansas City Review,* Autumn, 1951.

SMYTH, WILLIAM E. *The Conquest of Arid America* (New York: The Macmillan Company, 1905).

STROUT, CUSHING. *The American Image of the Old World* (New York: Harper and Row, Publishers, 1963).

WALKER, FRANKLIN (EDITOR). *The Washoe Giant in San Francisco* (San Francisco: George Fields, 1938).

WATSON, MARGARET G. *Silver Theater: Amusements of Nevada's Mining Frontier* (Glendale, California: The Arthur H. Clark Company, 1964).

WEISENBURGER, FRANCIS P. *The Fabulous Career of Rollin Mallory Daggett* (Syracuse: Syracuse University Press, 1965).

WESTERGAARD, WALDEMAR. *Denmark and Slesvig* (London: Oxford University Press, 1946).

WITTKE, CARL. *The Irish in America* (Baton Rouge: Louisiana State University Press, 1956).

———. *We Who Built America: The Saga of the Immigrant* (New York: Prentice-Hall, Inc., 1939).

WREN, THOMAS (EDITOR). *A History of the State of Nevada, Its Resources and People* (New York: The Lewis Publishing Company, 1904).

Index

133–135; newspaper stories: distrust and discrimination, 115; rivalry and conflict, 144, 153; *Pioneer Nevada,* 223; *The Sage Brush Parson,* 200–201; Virginia City, 19–20, 22; *The Wampus Cat,* 180–181
Cornish Telegraph, 40
Corriere Di Nevada, 39
Corrigan, Barney: character in *The Comstock Club,* 82
Costentenus, George, 104
Cotter, W. G., 113–114
"The counterfeit Pole of Humboldt." *See* Schollata, Frank
Courrier Français des Etats-Unis, 40
Covered Wagon, The, 164
Cowboy and His Interpreters, The, 164
Cowboys, 163–164
Crampton, Frank: 204; *Deep Enough,* 203
Crawford, O. P., 119
Crèvecoeur, Michel Guillaume Jean de, 163
Crime, 101–107
Croats, 4, 59, 138
Crockett, Davy, 197, 217
Croft, Helen: 204; *The Downs, the Rockies, and Desert Gold,* 202
Curti, Merle, 25
Cyprus, 203, 227

Daily Inland Empire, 41
Daily Nevada Tribune, 39, 84

Dancing instructors, foreign born, 35
Dangberg, H. F., 30, 40
Danish: 15, 16, 41; agricultural colonies, 33; biographical sketches, 231, 233; ethnic and cultural organizations, 17; survey by author, 57–58
Dannay, Frederic. *See* Queen, Ellery
Davidovich, George, 32, 129, 130
Davis, H. L., 161
Davis, Sam: 84, 239; *The First Piano in Camp,* 85–86; *The History of Nevada,* 232–233, 234; *Morning Appeal,* editor of, 85, 232
Dawson, George, 39
Dayton, Nevada: 190; Italians, 7
Deep Enough, 203
Defoe, Daniel, 199
Deidesheimer, Phillip, 113
Del Levis, Parpo, 28
Desch, Dr. Charles, 36
Desert Water, 170
Deutsche Union, 39
Dewey, Nevada, 29
Dice, Johnny: character in *Smoke of the .45,* 169
"Dixie," 177
Dixon, John M., 38
Dooner, Pierton, 160
Doten, Alf, 92
Double Idemnity, 176
Douglas County, Nevada, 17, 142

161; Franco-Prussian War, support of, 102–103, 138–142; *George, Wimple, and I,* 207; Idwal Jones's story, 162; International Hotel, staff of, 27–28; Louisiana, 16; *The Madigans,* 175; Nevada physicians, 35–37; newspaper stories:
color and off-color, 101–102, 103, 106, 107; distrust and discrimination, 115–116; fakery, 94–95; initiative and enterprise, 111, 112; loneliness and despair, 148, 149–150;
Past All Dishonor, 178; *Pioneer Nevada,* 224; religious services in French on the Comstock, 21; "Seventy Years in a Country Store," 221–222; survey by author, 52, 62; *Ten Years in Nevada: Or, Life on the Pacific Coast,* 174; Virginia City, 19, 22, 28

French-Canadians: 13; anti-Chinese, 119; Highland in 1880, 15; Hudson's Bay Co. fiction, 161; newspaper stories, color and off-color, 103, 104; religious services in foreign language on the Comstock, 21; survey by author, 57; *Team Bells Wake Me,* 162; *Well-Dressed Corpse,*

207; woodcutters, 27, 104, 117, 119
French Ranch, 112
Frozen Grass, 210
Fulstone, Robert, 117

Gaerens, Joseph, 115
"Gallant Frenchy," 94
Gambling in Nevada, 205
Garazi, ———, 154
Garland, Hamlin, 161, 187, 188, 199
Garth, Duggary: character in *Scarf Cloud,* 212
"Gathering of the Clans," 22
Gault, David: character in *Following the Grass,* 169
Gault, Joe: character in *Following the Grass,* 169, 241
George, Wimple, and I, 207–208
Georgetta, Clel: "A Pair of Shoes," 219; "They Die in the Spring," 219–220; *Wool, Beef, and Gold,* 219–220, 222, 228
German Jews, 73–75, 142, 175
German Sanitary Fund, 140
Germans: 13, 17, 87–88, 185; *Aged in Sage,* 224; agricultural colony in Elko County, 33; biographical sketches, 230, 231, 232, 235; *Borrasca,* 176; Carson Valley, integration into American life, 607; Columbia River fiction, 161; Eureka, 121; Franco-Prussian War, support of, 102–

newspaper stories:
color and off-color, 104;
distrust and discrimina-
tion, 126–128, 133;
smelters, 27; survey by author, 58, 62; White Pine
County, 4, 127–128, 137–138
Grey, Zane, 183
Grubstake, 178–180
Guisti, John, 28
Gypsies, 219, 241

Hahnlen, J. F., 39
Hamilton, Nevada: 40–41,
141, 152, 153
Hamlin, John: *Whirlpool of
Reno,* 208
Harold's Club, Reno: *Pioneer
Nevada,* 222–224
Harper's Magazine, 71
Harper's Monthly Magazine,
71
Haslam, Robert (English
Bob): character in *To
the Swift,* 202–203
Hausman, Joseph, 123
Hawkins, Anne: *To the Swift,*
202
Hawthorne, Nathaniel, 160
Hay, John, 160
Haycox, Ernest, 161
Hazard, Timothy: character in
*The City of Trembling
Leaves,* 186
Hep, A., 35
Herhily, William (The Emi-
grant), 100–101
Herrick, Hamins, 41

Hibernian Society. *See* Ancient
Order of Hibernians
Higgins, Aileen Cleveland: *A
Little Princess of Tonopah,*
181–182, 192
Highland, Nevada, 15
Hindus, 4, 33, 95–96, 119, 128
Hing, Sam: Chinese character
in *Grubstake,* 180
History of Nevada, The
(Davis), 232–233, 234
*History of Nevada: With Il-
lustrations and Biographical
Sketches of Its Prominent
Men and Pioneers* (Angel),
230–231
History of the Big Bonanza, 73
*History of the Comstock Silver
Lode & Mines, A,* 73
*History of the State of Nevada,
Its Resources and People, A*
(Wren), 231–232, 234
Hogan, Patsy, 20
Hogarth, William, 88
Holm, Beret: character in
Giants in the Earth, 201
Hong Kong Row. *See* Winne-
mucca
Hoover, Herbert, 178
Hop Sing, 24
Horgan, Father T. W., 33
Hough, Emerson: *The Cov-
ered Wagon,* 164; *Fifty-
Four Forty or Fight,* 164
Howles, Joaquina Ballard: 213;
No More Giants, 210, 211,
242
Hudson's Bay Co., 161

Lee, Virginia Wilson: *The Lord's Valley,* 210–211, 213, 242

Lefevre, Dr. ____, 36

Lefevre, "Crazy French," 102

Lemaire, August D.: French character in "Seventy Years in a Country Stores," 221–222

Lewis, Flannery: 204; Irish-American grandmother, portrayal of, 198–199, 245; *Sons Go Down,* 198–199

Lewis, James F., 113

Lewis, Oscar: *The Town That Died Laughing,* 87–88

Linton Wells, Nevada, 29

Little Princess of Tonopah, A, 181–182, 192

Lognoz, August, 149–150

Lognoz, Pauline, 149–150, 244

London, Jack, 162

Lord's Valley, The, 210–211, 242

Lost Horizon, 171

Louisiana, 16

Lovelock District, Nevada, 29–30

Lucca, Duchy of, 4, 53

Luigi: character in *The City of Trembling Leaves,* 187

Lumbering: 3, 238; French-Canadians, 27, 104, 117, 119

Lund, Nevada, 165

Luther, Martin, 195

Lutherans, 21

Lutjen, F. H., 28

Lynch, Philip, 95

Lyon County, Nevada, 17

Lyon County Times, 39

Lyman, George D., 197

McCallum, John, 143–144

McCane, John, 113

McCarthy, D. E., 39

Macdonald, Ross, 206

McDru, Frank, 96

McElrath, Jean: *Aged in Sage,* 224–227, 228; "The Cock Crowed in Basque," 226–227; "Sheep Claim," 224–225

McEwen, Arthur B., 39

McGill, Nevada, 121, 127, 128, 133, 238

McGinnis, "Jolly Irish," 94

McGrath, T. H., 23, 24

McIntyre, John, 151

McKane, John, 113, 114

Mackay, John, 30, 81, 113, 180, 197

McKistry, Ronald: English character in *The Wampus Cat,* 180

Macklay, John: character in *Grubstake,* 179

McLaughlin, Patrick, 113

McMahon Club, 141

McMaster, Dr. Alexander McFirth, 37

Madagascar, 106

Madeiras, Tony: Basque character in *Smoke of the .45,* 169

Madigan, Cecelia: character in *The Madigans,* 175

Madigans, The, 175

Magnini, Joseph, 124

275

"Miller riots," 137

Mines and mining: 27, 32, 110, 238; boom of 1860–1880, immigration in, 5; boom of 1902–1912, immigration in, 5; Eureka, 121; White Pine County, 4

Mississippi River valley: immigration fiction, 161

Missouri River valley: immigration fiction, 161

Mitkiewicz, Count _____, 98

Mix, Tom, 166

Moberg, Velhelm, 161

Molinelli, Lambert, 40, 124

Monaco, Louis, 124–126

Montenegrins, 16, 138

Monteverde, Dominick, 4

Moracci, F., 39

Morina: character in *Past All Dishonor,* 177

Mormons, 2

Morning Appeal, 39, 84, 85, 96–97, 141, 232

Morningstar, Jim: character in *Secret of the Wastelands,* 171–172

Morris, James, 39

Moses, Thomas, 21

Muchado, Roberto: Basque character in *Scarf Cloud,* 212–213

Muir, John, 150–151

Mulcahy, Patrick, 39

Mumford, Lewis, 185

Murbarger, Nell: Chinese, 220, 221, 222; *Ghosts of the Glory Trail,* 200–221, 228; "Man Who Lived in Borax Marsh," 221–222; "Seventy Years in a Country Store," 221–222; "Six-Toed Chinaman of Charleston," 221; *Sovereigns of the Sage,* 221; "Tybo was Allergic to Orientals," 221; "Where Ghosts Wear Pigtails," 221

Murphy, Daniel, 49

Murphy, John, 143–144, 244

Music teachers, foreign-born, 35

My Antonia, 161

"Napoleonic Reserve," 141

Navarre, Frenchy, 102

Negroes, 59, 106, 162

Neroni, Killer, 107

Nevada: "American character," 2; aridity, 2; communal settlements, 195–196; cosmopolitan, 2, 4–5; exploitation by outside governmental, business, and industrial elements, 4, 238; folk heroes, 218; foreign born necessary to existence of, 6; foreign born in state in 1870 and 1880, 13–14; foreign-born states, one of top ten for seventy-five years, 8, 14; Free Silver, a leader in, 2; geographic isolation, 2, 147, 148–151, 237; immigrants' attraction to, 2, 4–5, 7–8, 237–238; immigrants ignored by Nevada histories, 239; individualism, 2; lack of organic structuring of institu-

Vanderbilt, Cornelius, Jr.:
Reno, 208
Van Der Mursch, Dr., 36
Van Hagen, _____: German
character in *The Madigans,*
175
Vanina, Joseph, 123, 124
Varney, Professor, 22
Vaughn, Clement: character in
The Sage Brush Parson, 200–
201, 204
Veaney, Dutch, 111
Venini, Frenchy (Charles), 104
Verdi, Nevada, 204
Veritas. *See* Monaco, Louis
Victoria, Queen, 21, 202
Vigilantes, 103, 115–116, 117
Virginia & Truckee Railroad,
117
Virginia Chronicle, 85
Virginia City, Nevada: 134,
136, 238; *Borrasca,* 176; Bow
Windows, 102–103; Brick
House, 103; celebrations of
Germans, French, Italians,
Cornish, English, Swiss, Chi-
nese, and Irish in 1875, 19–
24; *The City of Illusion,* 197;
The Comstock Club, 82–83;
International Hotel, 22, 27–
28; Irish priests, 37; Japanese
incident, 130; *The Madigans,*
175; *Past All Dishonor,* 176–
177; plays, 76; *Robert Great-
house,* 80–81; shop owners of
North C St., 27–28; *Sons Go
Down,* 198–199; *Ten Years
in Nevada: Or, Life on the*

Pacific Coast, 174–175; Turn-
vereins, 18–20; Von Bokke-
len's Beer Gardens, 20; *The
Wedge of Gold,* 83
Virginia Evening Bulletin, 136
Virginian, The, 164
Viva Vegas, 203
Voice of Johnnywater, The,
166, 242
Von Bokkelen's Beer Gardens.
See Virginia City
Von Huhn, Alexander, 99
Von Richthofen, Ferdinand,
113
Voss, Dutch (the "Daniel
Boone of Nevada Brewing"),
107

Waddell, Frank: English char-
acter in *The Voice of John-
nywater,* 166
Waddell, Richard, 38
Walker River, 33
Waller, Mrs. (the "Pioneer
Mountain Actress,"), 102
Wampus Cat, The, 180–181
Washoe City, Nevada, 25, 26
Washoe County, Nevada:
Basques, 29; Germans, 17;
Italians, 205–206; *Sheep
Rock,* 191
"Washoe Rambles," 73–74
Waugh, Evelyn, 162
Webster, William, 39
Wedge of Gold, The, 83
*Well-Dressed Corpse, The Case
of the,* 206–207